AMERICAN ART SONG and AMERICAN POETRY

Volume III:
The Century Advances

Ruth C. Friedberg

The Scarecrow Press, Inc.
Metuchen, N.J., & London
1987

Music examples 6.15 through 6.26, used by permission of
Composers Library Editions, are acknowledged below each
example. Added to each of these is the following: Sole
Agent, Theodore Presser Co., Presser Place, Bryn Mawr,
PA 19010.

Library of Congress Cataloging-in-Publication Data
(Revised for vol. 3)

Friedberg, Ruth C., 1928–
    American art song and American poetry.

    Includes bibliographies and indexes.
    Contents: v. 1. America comes of age -- v. 2. Voices
of maturity--- v. 3. The century advances.
    1. Songs--United States--History and criticism.
I. Title.
ML2811.F75   784.3'00973   81-9047
ISBN 0-8108-1460-9 (v. 1)
ISBN 0-8108-1682-2 (v. 2)
ISBN 0-8108-1920-1 (v. 3)

To S. J. F.

CONTENTS

FOREWORD

This volume begins where its predecessor ended, with song-writers born in the second decade of this century, and the chapter headings have been arranged chronologically according to the birthdates of the composers treated therein. The single exception to this is Ned Rorem, who will be encountered slightly out of sequence, as his treatment necessitated the dimensions of a full chapter.

It will be readily apparent that this volume is the longest of the three. It covers the greatest time span, includes more composers and poets, and draws on a great deal of material from personal letters, phone conversations, and interviews that has been gathered all over the country since 1975. One or two of the originally projected composers do not appear in these pages. This is due in some cases to scores which remain unpublished and of limited availability to the reader, and in others to the length and shape of the developing manuscript. Subsequent inclusion in a fourth volume is not beyond the realm of possibility, although it is not presently being projected.

Since its beginning ten years ago, the focus of this study has been "the interrelationships between the composer and the poet and the ways in which these have influenced the completed song." The reader is also reminded that, from the outset, these volumes have dealt with "selected examples of important contributions to the performing literature" and have not purported to provide extensive lists of all the American art songs of the period. Where listings exist, however, of complete song catalogs for the individual composers discussed, reference is made to the appropriate source material.

It is the author's hope that others will find the series useful, as she has herself, as a basis for course work, individual research projects, and concert performance material. It is to this end that the three volumes all contain extensive bibliographical suggestions, careful listings of scores and their sources, and descriptions of existent recordings, in the NOTES following each chapter. Several of the recordings mentioned are, in fact, more recently issued than the listings in Carol Oja's excellent discography (see Bibliography, p. 300) which is only current to June, 1980.

Besides this practical academic orientation, the author would also like to believe that her work may suggest a particular approach to the analysis and understanding of text setting in the American song literature. The direction is, indeed, not entirely new. It has been applied in the past to bodies of German and French song literature, but rarely, if ever, to English language settings.

Finally I should like to thank my husband, Samuel Joseph Friedberg, for his unfailing support throughout the decade occupied by this study. My thanks also to Pat Cooper and Peggy Nicholson for their help in preparing the manuscript of Volume III, and to Jan Stark for her invaluable assistance in matters of copyright.

Ruth C. Friedberg

AMERICAN ART SONG AND AMERICAN POETRY

Volume III: The Century Advances

PROLOGUE

All of the songs to be discussed in this volume were written roughly between 1940 and 1980, and the most senior of their creators came to maturity in the middle thirties. By that time, American music had virtually abandoned what Frank Rossiter describes as the "genteel tradition" of the late nineteenth and early twentieth centuries, i.e., a reverence for European Romanticism coupled with disdain for the culture of the American masses.[1]

Breaking free had opened the door to important new influences that manifest in this study. Echoes of the modernist revolt against the German Romantic tradition will be found in the songs of such composers as Hugo Weisgall, Vincent Persichetti, Jack Beeson, and Richard Owen. New sounds and moods from America's mass culture will creep into the folk-like ballads of Paul Bowles, and the Broadway-tinged settings of William Flanagan, Richard Cumming, and Richard Hundley. Even the remaining strains of Romanticism purveyed by Samuel Barber and Norman Dello Joio will strike a different note than that of their German predecessors: a note that will embody the individual's search for a new order in a new world.

*   *   *

An important aspect of the American literary scene in the teens and twenties had been the rise of the "little magazines" (see Introduction to Volume II). By the middle of the third decade a significant musical journal joined their ranks. Modern Music, edited by Minna Lederman, provided a unique and

3

invaluable forum for twentieth-century music, and during the
twenty-two years of its existence (1924-1946) gave rise to the
tradition of the composer-journalist. Pioneers in this new
"criticism by creators" had been Aaron Copland, Roger Ses-
sions, and Virgil Thomson. In the latter years of the maga-
zine, Paul Bowles had become a frequent contributor, and
Israel Citkowitz (teacher of Richard Hundley--see p. 247) had
written an article, crucial to the future of American song, in
which he decried the notion of separating voice from text and
using it "as pure tonal instrument."[2]

By mid-century, the phenomenon of the American com-
poser-journalist was becoming even more firmly established.
Among the composers included in this volume, Weisgall, Dello
Joio, Persichetti, and Flanagan will all be seen as valued con-
tributors to newspapers and/or magazines, and Persichetti will
produce an important book called Twentieth Century Harmony.
Ned Rorem will explode into literature as the author of auto-
biographical diaries and collections of critical articles. And
Paul Bowles will abandon music altogether in deference to his
greater recognition as a novelist.

*   *   *

American poetry, following the enormous vitality of the "poetic
renaissance" (see Volume II, p. 4) had gone into an initial
period of retrenchment. Edwin Seaver, editor of Cross-Section,
a yearly collection of new American writing published from 1945
to 1948, remarked in his introduction to the final publication
that "the literary revolution which began in the second dec-
ade ... and flourished in the twenties and thirties is at an
end." "Today," he continued, "we seem hell-bent for conform-
ity,"[3] and in the years following his assessment, this cultural
trend was to be intensified by the political climate of fifties
McCarthyism. Experiment broke loose once again, however,
as the forces gathered which would produce the sixties' coun-
terculture, and it took the forms of concrete poetry, the
"Beat" influence, and the poetry/jazz movement.

Throughout this period, the "little magazines" had con-
tinued to proliferate. One of the most long lasting, the Part-
isan Review, severed its Marxist ties of the thirties to become
an independent journal dividing its pages between creative
work and the growing emphasis on criticism. William Phillips,
its editor since 1934, made insightful comment on the current

state of literature, writing in 1978 in The Little Magazine in America. "The dominant mood," says Phillips, "is one of confusion. Even though a good deal of serious poetry, fiction, and criticism is being written, an air of uncertainty about our relation to the modernist tradition and to the mass culture hangs over us."[4]

The vicissitudes of literary movements notwithstanding, the American song composers of this period have continued to search for and discover the poetic texts that suit their expressive needs. Many of them will be seen setting the newer poets of the century's middle decades. Among these are Frederic Prokosch, Paul Goodman, Theodore Roethke, Peter Viereck, Kenneth Patchen, and Howard Moss, all of whom were publishing regularly in Poetry, the enduring Grande Dame of "little magazines," as well as in volumes of their own. Other composers will pull back to the slightly earlier generation represented by e.e. cummings and Wallace Stevens, or further into the literary past to set such transitional, pre-"renaissance" figures as Adelaide Crapsey, Sara Teasdale, and the enigmatic Stephen Crane.

Nineteenth-century poets, in the persons of Walt Whitman, Herman Melville, and Emily Dickinson will also continue to speak meaningfully to our twentieth-century composers who set them with unabating enthusiasm. And a whole new category of textual sources will be seen to arise as some composers begin to work extensively in musical theater and to elicit poetic texts from dramatists (Tennessee Williams, Edward Albee, Philip Minor, William Hoffman) whose literary voices they have come to know and trust.

All these, then, are the threads which we will find subsumed into the richly textured tapestry of American song as it continues to be interwoven with its close companion, American poetry. It will be the task of this volume to examine details of its color and design, and to come to a more intimate knowledge of its weavers, as the century advances.

NOTES

1. Frank Rossiter, "The Genteel Tradition in American Music," Journal of American Culture, IV:107-115 (Winter 1981).

2. Israel Citkowitz, "Abstract Methods and the Voice," Modern Music, XX:3 (March-April 1943).

3. Edwin Seaver, ed. Cross-Section, 1948 (Nendeln, Liechtenstein: Kraus Reprint, 1969), p. ix-x.

4. William Phillips, "On Partisan Review," The Little Magazine in America, eds. Elliot Anderson and Mary Kinzie (Yonkers, N.Y.: Pushcart Press, 1978), p. 140.

I. THE SECOND DECADE 1.

Samuel Barber (1910-1981)
James Agee (1909-1955)
Frederic Prokosch (1908-   )

The lyric genius of Samuel Barber was a gift of grace that
occurs only once or twice in a generation. This gift had
the further advantage of being nurtured from early child-
hood by Barber's father, a non-musical but supportive
Westchester physician, and his mother, who came from a
large family of gifted musicians. Indeed, one of Barber's
earliest memories is of being "six [years old] and en-
tranced"[1] at his first Metropolitan opera performance where
his maternal aunt, Louise Homer, was singing Amneris in
Aida. Although his parents did try to encourage other ac-
tivities as well, it soon became apparent that young Sam,
as he wrote in a note to his mother at the age of eight,
"was meant to be a composer."[2] He had started writing
music at seven, composed his first opera at nine, and by
the time he was twelve showed so much promise that his
uncle, Sidney Homer, himself a skilled writer of songs,
began wholeheartedly to encourage the boy's creative goals.

The resources of Westchester, Pennsylvania, a solid
Quaker town with a rich cultural life, proved adequate to
begin the development of the performing skills which Barber
also manifested at an early age. In 1916, he began to study
the piano with William Hatton Green, a Leschetizky pupil,
and six years later was hired as organist by the Westminster
Presbyterian Church. His refusal to allow unmusical distortions

in the hymn-singing resulted in his resignation the following year. By 1924, his growing professionalism was recognized in an audition with Harold Randolph,[3] director of Peabody Conservatory, who advised him to leave school and devote himself to studies in piano and composition.

Following a modified version of this advice, Barber remained in high school but enrolled as one of the first students in the newly opened Curtis Institute of Music in Philadelphia. As president of the Westchester school board, Dr. Barber effected passage of a rule which enabled his son to spend Fridays in Philadelphia attending symphony concerts at the Academy of Music and classes at Curtis. The Institute had been handsomely endowed by Mary Curtis Bok,[4] a daughter of the well-known publishing family, and the finest teachers were available there in all areas of music.[5] Barber absorbed the Romantic tradition in his composition studies with Rosario Scalero, who had worked in Vienna with Eusebius Mandycewski, a close friend of Brahms. Pianistically he flourished under the guidance of Isabelle Vengerova, also a Leschetizky pupil, who had taught at the Petersburg Conservatory. And in his third year of study, he was allowed to begin formal training of his pleasing baritone voice with Emilio de Gogorza, thus becoming the Institute's first triple major.

Barber had a natural flair for languages, and his studies in French, German, and Italian at Curtis strengthened the European influences purveyed by the faculty. At Philadelphia Orchestra concerts, Stokowski's interest in contemporary programming enabled Barber to hear the newest creative products of Europe (and of America as well). It was a stimulating environment for the young composer, and in 1928 his fluency in French caused him to befriend a Curtis student composer newly arrived from Milan who spoke no English. This friendship with Gian Carlo Menotti would become a personal and professional association of many years' duration, and just before the première of Vanessa, Barber would recall with gentle irony how the two, in their student days, had "signed a sort of blood pact never to write an opera."[6]

The year 1928 also brought Columbia University's award of the Bearns prize which supported the first of Barber's many trips to Europe. He visited with Scalero in the Italian

Alps, paid his respects to Mandycewski in the Viennese countryside, and reacted unfavorably to a performance of Parsifal in Munich during which he "choked in a maddening melee of sickly chromaticism."[7] Through inclination and training, Barber's loyalties in the historic Brahms/Wagner controversy had already been clearly established.

Menotti's family in Italy also played host to Samuel Barber on many occasions during these early years, and after graduating from Curtis in 1933, the two young composers wintered in Vienna where Barber studied voice with John Braun, an American teacher. He made his début there singing German lieder and several of his own songs. Another important vocal recital took place in 1934 near Mrs. Bok's estate in Maine where Barber had been invited to spend the summer. The following October, Mary Bok arranged for a private hearing of Barber's compositions with Carl Engel, president of G. Schirmer's, which resulted in the publication of three vocal works written while he was still at Curtis ("The Daisies," "With Rue My Heart Is Laden," and "Dover Beach") plus "Bessie Bobtail,"[8] composed during the previous summer in Maine.

The next decade was one of struggle and eventually of recognition for Samuel Barber. After having been once refused, he received the Prix de Rome in 1935, and was also awarded two traveling Pulitzer fellowships in the mid-thirties. From 1939 to 1942 he taught orchestration and trained the chorus at Curtis, but looked forward to a time when he could give up professional singing and teaching and be totally free to compose. Barber and his music took a sudden leap into world prominence with Toscanini's performance of his Adagio for Strings and Essay for Orchestra in 1938, and by the time he was inducted into Special Services in World War II, his reputation was such that he was encouraged to compose by the armed forces. Mustered out in 1945, he repaired to Capricorn, the comfortable house near Mt. Kisco, New York, which he had purchased with Menotti in 1943. The growing success of his music had brought him the long-coveted time and space for creative work--a way of life which was to last nearly thirty years, until increasing financial problems and waning emotional ties brought about the sale of the property.[9]

By 1981, the year of his death in New York City,

Samuel Barber had published just under forty songs, most of which had been available for several decades in G. Schirmer's familiar gray volumes.[10] It was not a large output for "America's foremost lyricist,"[11] but it was consistently of extremely high quality. The Hermit Songs had become widely recognized, together with Copland's Emily Dickinson settings, as one of the two most important American song cycles of the century, while the James Joyce group[12] and the single settings were firmly ensconced in the teaching and concert repertoires of singers throughout the country. Interestingly, the large preponderance of poetry chosen by Barber for these settings is European in origin, with English, Irish, and French poets (some in translation) holding the clear majority. As suggested above, Barber's mentors at Curtis, his command of foreign languages, and his friendship with Menotti had all contributed to a strongly European orientation in his creative life. One finds, indeed, only a single American in the following list of the composer's favorite authors which was reported by Nathan Broder in 1954: Stendhal, Dante, Goethe, Joyce, Proust, and Melville. Even this one American preference takes on cloudy origins with the realization that Barber's deep attraction to Melville and his never fulfilled desire to base a musical work on his writing began on the occasion of his reading Moby Dick in an Italian translation!

There were, however, two twentieth-century American poets whose texts the composer set in 1938 and 1940 with the fully developed force of his lyrical powers. The first of these was James Agee. By 1938, Barber had been successfully setting poetry for over a decade, and in all these early songs had exhibited the free-flowing Romanticism of the late nineteenth-century tradition to a degree that at once appalled and delighted the avant-garde saturated audiences of the 1930s. Not surprising, then, is the strong artistic affinity which Barber developed for Agee, whose literary style also carried Romantic overtones, and whose life, as well, embodied the passion, conflict, and self-destructiveness of the archetypical Romantic hero.

Agee was born in Knoxville, Tennessee, which is not an immense geographic distance from Westchester, Pennsylvania, but his life experiences were to be psychological light-years apart from those of Samuel Barber. Whereas the composer had a loving, stable childhood and followed a clear, well-disciplined progression toward recognition in his creative career, the writer's youth was torn by grief, and his energies sapped in adulthood by depression, self-doubt, and to some degree a wasteful scattering of his talent.

Agee's father was descended from Matthieu Agee, a Huguenot who had come to Virginia at the beginning of the Colonial period. The family had later migrated west to Tennessee and each generation continued to produce several farmers, such as the writer's grandfather whose farm was at La Follette, near Knoxville. The Tylers, Agee's maternal grandparents, before settling in Tennessee had moved to Michigan from the East Coast, and both had attended the University of Michigan (his grandmother becoming the first woman university graduate in America). It is easy to understand why James Agee saw himself as the product of a two-fold and conflicting heritage, with his mother representing bourgeois refinement, the academic and artistic life, and conventional religion, while his father stood for the rugged, violent, and sensuous world of the proud, isolated "hills people" of the Tennessee mountains.

These opposing strains were not yet a problem in the early childhood of Agee for "the open, celebrative manner of Jay Agee [his father] was complemented by the retiring spirituality of his wife,"[13] and the resulting atmosphere produced a sense of "mysterious happiness"[14] in the boy. It was this pleasant, dreamlike ambiance, underlaid with a growing anxiety, that Agee was to celebrate in Knoxville, Summer of 1915, the haunting fragment of poetic prose which Samuel Barber would set so movingly for soprano and orchestra as his Opus 24.[15] Tragically, the child's anxiety proved only too well-founded. When he was six years old, his father died in an auto accident, and James Agee's life turned upside down, never to be wholly righted again.

From 1919 to 1925, Mrs. Agee, who was a devout Episcopalian, had her son enrolled at St. Andrew's, a school run by the Anglican priests primarily for the nearby Tennessee farmers' sons. Agee flourished here intellectually from his extensive library privileges, free use of the piano for which he was showing considerable talent, and the relationship now beginning with his teacher, Father Flye,[16] who would become a lifelong friend. His personal life, however, held elements of painful loss, for he often stood longingly

11

outside the house of his mother whom he was allowed to visit
only once a week, and who was remarried in 1925 to the
Reverend Erskine Wright, a choice which must have seemed
a cruel rejection of his father's memory.

In the summer of 1925, Father Flye, who had found
Agee an able student of the French language, took him on
what was to be the only European tour of his life. After
his return, the youth's ties to Tennessee were effectively
broken. He spent the next three years at Exeter and the
succeeding four at Harvard, increasingly involved in the
Eastern literary world, while also developing a reputation as
a non-conformist given to nocturnal wanderings, eccentric
dress, and turbulent relationships. During this period he
began to publish his writing and was also demonstrating suf-
ficient fluency and improvisatory skill at the piano to suggest
the possibility of a musical career.[17] He rejected the latter,
sensing that he lacked sufficient self-discipline, but music
remained a strong force in his life, and in the fall of 1930
he decided to become a writer, hoping "eventually to write
works inspired by music--literary symphonies in which ...
the verbal orchestration he was after would enable him to
imitate not only the sonorities of music but also its struc-
ture."[18]

It was a noble aim, and a volume of his poetry called
Permit Me Voyage, published in 1934 by Yale University
Press in their Younger Poets series, seemed to be fulfilling
that promise. But the era was Depression and there were
no family funds to provide a cocoon for creative activity.
Agee was forced to depend on his facile pen which made him
valuable to the Luce publications, Fortune and Time, as a
writer of articles and reviews from 1932 to 1948. This was
a period, too, of increasing dependence on alcohol and of
severe depression, as he admitted in a revealing letter to
the devoted Father Flye. "I realize," said Agee "that I
have an enormously strong drive ... toward self-destruction;
and that I know little if anything about its sources or con-
trol."[19]

Agee's strong dramatic and visual sensibilities proved
further distractions in his attempts at artistic focus. The
medium of film increasingly absorbed him, both as reviewer
and as script-writer, while in 1941 he collaborated with the
photographer Walker Evans on Let Us Now Praise Famous

Men, a stunning portrayal of the lives of Alabama sharecroppers (blood brothers in his mind, no doubt, to the "hills people" of his youth). Beset throughout his life by a strong and possibly, in light of early experience, insatiable need for love, companionship, and continuity, Agee married three times and fathered four children. The first ceremony of marriage (to Via Saunders, the cultivated daughter of a Hamilton College professor) had been performed within the Episcopal church. By the second, to Alma Mailman, a professional violinist, and the third, to Mia Fritsch, a fellow worker for Fortune magazine, his conventional religious ties had been severed. Yet in the deepest sense, his whole life was a spiritual struggle between the consciousness of sin formed in childhood and a maturing mystical experience of oneness in the subjects of his artistic scrutiny.

Superstitiously, Agee prepared for death in 1945, believing that he would die in his thirty-sixth year, as his father had. He did not, but a series of cardiac difficulties began in 1951, brought on by years of overwork, drinking to relieve the stress, and the more recent strain of maintaining the Hollywood pace during his West Coast film assignments. Ironically, Destiny did repeat itself, but ten years later than it had been expected. On May 16, 1955, the anniversary of his father's death, James Agee suffered a fatal heart attack and died as his father had done, in an automobile --in this case a New York taxicab.

As is so often the case, Agee's life and literary career began to receive much attention after his death which "evoked the image of a young genius cruelly brought to an end before his time"[20] and of a talent laid waste by contemporary America's failure to support the creative imagination. As the decade turned over into the sixties, Agee became a legend and model to his generation, and the embodiment of a magnificent dream "of a world from which all sterility would be banished."[21] His film scripts were posthumously published, as was A Death in the Family (see note 14), and in 1968, the Collected Poems and Collected Short Prose appeared with Robert Fitzgerald, a longtime friend, as editor.

The Collected Poems leave no doubt that Agee's poetic muse declined in later years with his pull toward other and longer literary forms, and the consequent investing of his prose with "the poet's eye for detail [and] the poet's ear for phrasing."[22] But the youthful Permit Me Voyage (the only poetry ever published by the writer himself) contains many treasures among its lyrics and sonnets, in which Archibald MacLeish's foreword noted "a mature and in some cases a masterly control of rhythm" and "a vocabulary at once personal to the poet and appropriate to the intention."[23] The riches of this collection, whose title was borrowed from Hart Crane's Voyages and whose style elicited critical comparisons to the English poetic traditions and America's Whitman, created little stir in an era when much of the literary world was experimenting with a breakdown in poetic form. It remained for Samuel Barber, whose own romantic traditionalism was equally out of step with the musical times, to lift one of these lyrics from obscurity. His setting of it became number three in the four songs of Opus 13, that recognized masterpiece of American song literature, "Sure on this shining night."[24]

The world of this poem seems closely related to Agee's world of Knoxville, 1915.[25] Here it is also "high summer" with "hearts all whole," and the poet "weeps for wonder" at the mysterious beauty of the "star-made shadows." The hints of coming dissolution in the phrases "wandering far alone" and "kindness must watch for me" only increase the poignancy of the moment of perfection. The strong appeal of this text to Samuel Barber would have existed on several levels. He was an inveterate walker and lover of nature who had tramped the countryside of America and Europe on many sunny days and "shining nights." The poem (set without change or deletion) offered short lines embodying much compressed emotion which invited musical amplification. And the words themselves exhibited a great deal of sensuous alliteration in their repeated "sh" and "h" sounds,[26] as well as many vocally grateful vowels which could gain artistic reinforcement in a musical setting.

The visual appearance of the poem gives us two verses of four short lines followed by a very long ninth line ("Sure on this shining night I weep for wonder wandering far alone") and a much shorter tenth. Barber's setting in effect creates three equal stanzas, which translate to an exquisitely crafted three-part form. The contrapuntal mastery derived from Rosario Scalero's thorough training in this discipline is apparent as he adapts a two-part canon at the interval of a third to the needs of the text. It begins in quiet description in the first stanza with the piano following the voice by a measure. The second verse begins similarly but at a higher dynamic level. As the vocal contour rises to the joyous affirmation of the long vowels ("All is healed / all is health"), and the emotive climax of the piece is reached, the piano's canonic imitation stops, as though to allow momentary prominence to vocal and verbal values. The voice line having descended to a position of rest on the poetic summation, "Hearts all whole," the piano now takes over the canonic melody in a gorgeous burst of sound which prepares the vocal restatement.

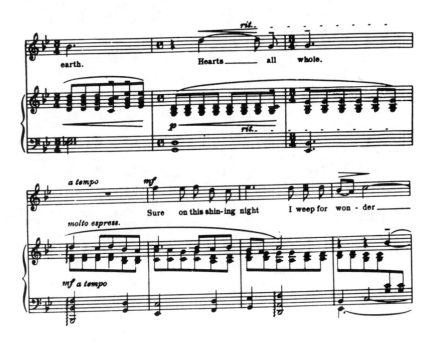

Example 1.1, measures 18-24. Copyright © 1941, G. Schirmer, Inc.; used by permission.

Though the harmonic scheme of this song is in no way unique, it becomes fresh and meaningful in the hands of a youthful master. The opening B flat major pulls to the relative minor through the sub-dominant chord for the somberness of "This side the ground." It affirms D minor through

the authentic cadence which supports the crescendo, then
moves suddenly, with a dynamic drop, back to B flat major--
the hushed realization of a wondrous wholeness, whose spir-
itual origins are subliminally suggested by the plagal cadence
of the pianistic takeover (see Examples 1.2 and 1.1).

Example 1.2, measures 12-17. Copyright © 1941, G. Schir-
mer, Inc.; used by permission.

Although at this stage in his writing Barber is still
using meter signatures, his frequent variants of two- and
four-beat measures from the basic three demonstrate a nat-
ural sensitivity to the prosodic flow, and lend a rhythmic
fluidity to the lyrical outline. Finally, the evidence of a
meticulous craftsman's orientation toward the microcosm of
musical structure is to be found in the accents which the
composer places in the pianistic conclusion over the interval
of a minor third, one of the most prominent components of
the canonic melody (see Example 1.3, p. 17).

James Agee had spent the summer of 1930 working at

16

Example 1.3, measures 30-34. Copyright © 1941, G. Schirmer, Inc.; used by permission.

odd jobs around the country, and his short story "They that Sow in Sorrow Shall Reap," grew out of this experience. The following quotation from the work is a revealing indication of Agee's general concept of music as an analog to life, and seems also to serve in particular as a characterization of the remarkable "Sure on this shining night":

> As a rule, experience is broken upon innumerable
> sharp irrelevancies, [yet at times the mind may be-
> come aware] of a definite form and rhythm and mel-
> ody of existence: ... out of long contrapuntal pas-
> sages of tantalizing ... elements there emerges
> sometimes an enormous clear chord. And at that
> moment ... the whole commonplace of existence is
> transfigured, becomes monstrously powerful, and
> beautiful, and significant.[27]

The second American poet whom Barber chose to set in his Opus 13 songs was Frederic Prokosch. Born in Madison, Wisconsin, in a year variously recorded by biographers as 1906 and 1908, Prokosch is a second-generation American whose ties to Europe have exerted strong influences throughout his life. His Austrian-born father, Eduard, came to the United States in 1898 and attended the National German-American Teachers' Seminary in Milwaukee. Here he met and married the director's daughter, Mathilde Dapprich, a well-known pianist who had been born in Baltimore. After earning a doctorate in linguistics and philology from Leipzig in 1905, Eduard held teaching positions at the University of

17

Wisconsin, and at the University of Texas at Austin. He was dismissed from the latter in 1919 in the wave of anti-German sentiment that followed World War I, but in a year's time resumed an illustrious teaching career that was to last for two more decades and include prestigious appointments at Bryn Mawr College, Yale, and New York University.

As evidenced in his later writing, Frederic Prokosch was to regard the Wisconsin years as a time of innocent childhood, and the Texas experiences (1913-1919) as a period of lost innocence and maturation.[28] A formative year just after the family's move to Austin was spent by young Frederic attending school in Austria and Germany, and on his return to America in 1915, his spoken German was better than his English. As might have been expected, the boy had inherited both his father's scholarly aptitude for languages and literature and his mother's artistic endowment. The creativity started to surface during his high school years at Bryn Mawr where he put on a number of puppet shows, and after entering Haverford College in 1922, he became increasingly committed to the writing of poetry.

Prokosch's first published poem was printed in the Virginia Quarterly Review of July, 1927, alongside a contribution by Allen Tate, one of the earliest participants in the barely emerging Southern literary renaissance. Thereafter, his poems appeared in many American and British magazines and in 1936 he published his first volume of verse which he titled The Assassins. During this same period Prokosch had taken graduate degrees at Haverford, Cambridge, and Yale, and had followed in his father's footsteps with teaching positions at Yale and New York University. There was yet a third side to the colorful personality of this artist-scholar whose sociability had emerged as an undergraduate along with considerable athletic prowess as a tennis and squash player. The Yale instructorship was to produce a reputation for dramatic teaching, as well as for a rather dashing life-style, which included a yellow convertible and a large German shepherd.

By 1937, having published two novels and won the Guggenheim Award and Harper Prize, Prokosch abandoned teaching and began to travel abroad. His second volume of poetry, Carnival, was published in 1938, and a third, Death at Sea, in 1940. Both received a rather cool critical reception, and Prokosch has written little new poetry since that time, the Chosen Poems of 1948 being a selection from the earlier volumes. Concurrently with and subsequently to the poetry, Prokosch has remained active as a novelist, his most recent work in this medium being America, My Wilderness in 1972.

Since the death of his father in 1938, Prokosch, who now lives in Paris, has returned to America only for a brief period in 1942 to work for the Office of War Information, and for a short stay in 1953-54. Living in Lisbon in 1940 after the fall of France, he was surrounded by flocks of political agents and desperate refugees, and much of his writing around this time reflects the growing conflagration that was gradually engulfing Europe and that was on its way to becoming World War II. The poetry of Carnival also shares in this environment of impending war, while it continues to exhibit the two principal characteristics of The Assassins: a strong orientation toward places and journeys, and a richly musical style which suggests the influence of Yeats.

One of Carnival's most striking poems is "Nocturne," whose effortless lyricism receives a tight metric structure in five verses of extremely regular four-stress lines. In adapting the poem for his purposes as number 4 of the Opus 13 songs,[29] Barber first chose to omit the third verse, which begins "Condors of the future rise / Through the stupor overheard." This had the effect of mitigating the looming historical disaster and of concentrating the poem's focus on love, with all its falsehood and frailties, as a refuge from the pain and hopelessness of the human experience. Next the composer decided to impede the flow of trochees with a recurrent vocal rhythmic figure of dotted quarter notes. This allowed time for the development of an agitated pianistic embroidery of broken arpeggios in the right hand and a rocking figure in the left, which suggests a lullaby behind "Close my darling both your eyes" (see Ex. 1.4, p. 20).

The leaping contour of the opening vocal line (see Ex. 1.4, page 20) is maintained and intensified throughout the setting, as the tumult of emotion rises. In a moment of exquisite musical correspondence, Barber then has the singer descend via chordal skips over a distance of an octave and a third in representation of grateful release, which is heightened by the suspended 5/4 meter resolving to the lesser tension of 4/4 (see Ex. 1.5, pp. 20-21).

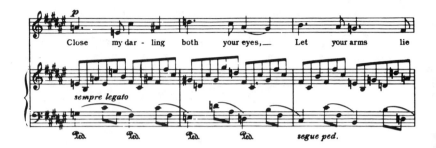

Example 1.4, measures 3-5. Copyright © 1941, G. Schirmer, Inc.; used by permission.

Example 1.5, measures 18-24. Copyright © 1941, G. Schirmer, Inc.; used by permission.

Quiet, two-measure interludes, in which the piano imitates the preceding vocal lines, follow the conclusions of verse one ("And the wind of lust has passed") and verse two (see Ex. 1.5). From this point on, there is no pause in the dynamic and expressive crescendo which Barber derives from such incendiary phrases as "Blaze with such a longing now" and "Northward flames Orion's horn." Propulsive chords become the dominating accompaniment figure for verse three, and the shattering climax of the song is achieved with the addition of portentous dotted note figures in octaves to the returning broken chords, while the voice holds a defiantly ecstatic A flat.

Example 1.6, measures 38-39. Copyright © 1941, G. Schirmer, Inc.; used by permission.

This climax is also impelled harmonically by an enharmonic movement through an altered A sharp chord to one on B flat which introduces the most expansively diatonic phrase of the setting, an island of certainty in the surrounding sea of shifting chromaticism.

Example 1.7, measures 34-37. Copyright © 1941, G. Schirmer, Inc.; used by permission.

Paul Frederic Bowles (1910-   )
Tennessee Williams (1911-1983)

Paul Bowles began his life in a New York City brownstone where the family lived in an apartment above his father's dental office. To all outward appearances, it was a privileged, nurturing environment for a growing child, but the

22

strain of its emotional climate engendered withdrawal mechanisms that Bowles would cultivate out of a healthy instinct for self-preservation.[30] In his autobiography, written after sixty years filled with artistic friends and a long marriage, the composer revealingly concludes that "Relationships with other people are at best nebulous; their presence keeps us from being aware of the problem of giving form to our life."[31]

Restrained by parental veto from a hoped-for career as concert violinist, Bowles' dentist father was a man given to raging outbursts over minor domestic details. Often, they were directed at this son whom he could not forgive for having diverted his wife's attention from himself. The boy's mother gave Paul what support she could in their uneasy household, and from her he learned the useful technique of "making his mind a blank and holding it," a skill he later credited for developing "whatever powers of self-discipline I have now."[32]

Bowles' pleasantest childhood memories were of visits to the maternal grandparents at Happy Hollow Farm in Massachusetts. In strong contrast was the gloomy Elmira home of his father's parents: two somber intellectuals who spent most of their time reading. His paternal grandmother was a theosophist and two of her siblings were also devoted to yoga and other occult sciences. Bowles came naturally, then, to several instances of precognitive dreaming and "out-of-body" experiences during his childhood and adolescence. These predisposed him to a strong interest in exotic mysticism as an adult, and also fostered the sense of detachment from the physical universe which enabled him to psychically survive the definitive skirmish with his father at the age of nineteen. Having on this occasion declared "It's not my fault I'm alive, I didn't ask to be born" and having angrily hurled a meat-knife, Bowles was convinced that he must leave home for the sake of all concerned, while "as usual [reminding himself] that since nothing was real it did not matter too much."[33]

The bizarre aspects of his childhood having made a "loner" of Paul Bowles, he was drawn at an early age to creative expression in the arts of music and literature. At eight he began piano lessons, also studying theory and solfège so that he could record his own musical ideas. A cracked sounding board in the piano caused a cessation in music lessons and Bowles turned to writing, thus laying the

Paul Bowles

foundation for his second creative career. In junior high
school, the piano lessons resumed, using an old Chickering
sent by his grandmother from Elmira. By the time of his
high school graduation, he had served as humor and poetry
editors of the school magazine, become an avid buyer of
books, and was in regular attendance at Carnegie Hall for
the Saturday Philharmonic concerts.

College seemed a logical place to further his training,
but the atmosphere at the University of Virginia proved too
"country club" for his level of hard-won maturity. Bowles

enjoyed tramping the countryside around Charlottesville, and was grateful for the introduction to T.S. Eliot, Gregorian Chant, and Prokofiev. Nevertheless, early in the spring semester he packed his belongings and left for Europe, impelled by what he had come to regard as his "other self," which had, on a previous occasion, functioned independently of his physical body.

During the next decade, Paul Bowles was in and out of Paris, Berlin, America, Morocco, and Mexico, having begun his lifetime pattern as a world traveler. This was also the period of his development as a serious composer, which was strongly influenced by his studies with Aaron Copland and his many contacts with Virgil Thomson. In the early thirties, six of his songs received an excellent reception when presented at the Yaddo summer festival, and he formed his own company called Éditions de la Vipère[34] to publish his songs and piano pieces, as well as works by David Diamond and Satie. Money was always a problem and a succession of odd jobs supported him, together with a small legacy from an aunt, once he had turned twenty-one.

There were two other important influences on Paul Bowles during these formative years. One was Gertrude Stein, who, obviously fond of the young man, declared him more of a "Freddy" than a "Paul," and whose texts he set on several occasions including a personal note which became "Letter to Freddy."[35] The other was his first experiences with Morocco, a country which he found languorous, violent, and totally magical, with an appeal so strong that it would eventually draw him back as a permanent resident. Toward the end of the thirties he traveled to Mexico and met Revueltas, Moncayo, Galindo, and others of the group of young composers who were revitalizing their country's music.

In 1937, just before her twenty-first birthday, Bowles married Jane Auer, a vivacious and talented young woman who would eventually publish a small but notable body of writing. Having gotten his first theatrical commissions two years earlier with the help of Virgil Thomson, the composer now began to be in demand as a writer of scores for Broadway plays, and enjoyed fruitful collaborations with William Saroyan,[36] and with Tennessee Williams, who had introduced himself to Bowles when both were staying in Acapulco in 1939.[37] This period of the composer's life also resulted in

25

the writing of a number of his finest songs, including most
of the Tennessee Williams settings. In 1945, Peggy Glanville-
Hicks, the British composer and critic, stressed the impor-
tance of Bowles' work in this genre. "His contribution to
the modern song repertory," she said, "is one of the most
exceptional in recent years. [The songs] are spontaneous
and fresh, they have a great vitality and a most original
melodic form and colour."38 In the same Music and Letters
article, Glanville-Hicks also commented on Bowles' overall
musical characteristics of a "neatness of execution, contra-
puntal linear outlook, and fastidiousness of expression."39
These she felt to be tendencies of the French school, trans-
mitted to Bowles through Copland and Thomson, who had
both been pupils of Boulanger. Copland himself, writing in
Modern Music in 1936, had called attention to the young com-
poser's work, and three years later had added "a talent as
.fresh as that of Bowles is not often found."40

   Still another aspect of his musical career unfolded for
Bowles when he began to write music criticism for Modern
Music around 1940, and was shortly thereafter persuaded,
again by Virgil Thomson, to join the daily reviewing staff of
the New York Herald Tribune. He stayed at the Tribune
until 1945, at which time he began to have recurrent dreams
of a "magic city." Realizing at last that it was Tangier, he
returned there to live, and to begin a new creative life as a
writer of fiction and of travel pieces based on his perceptive
explorations of Asia and Africa. He continued to produce
some theatrical scores, principally for Tennessee Williams,
but his involvement with serious concert music gradually
ended as critics and performers seemed to have lost interest
in that aspect of his composition. His personal life, too,
encompassed loss. Paul and Jane Bowles had for twenty
years been the "golden couple" of a circle of friends, which
included Bernstein, Barber, Menotti, Gore Vidal, Truman
Capote, and many other composers and writers. In 1957,
Jane suffered a slight stroke which left her with some apha-
sia and visual disturbance. As her husband was later to
write, "the good years were over."41 Her health and pow-
ers continued to decline until her death in 1973, after which
Bowles, always ill-at-ease with the brashness and superfici-
ality of much of American culture, chose to remain cradled
in the reserved mystery of Tangier where "all around in the
night sorcery (was) burrowing its invisible tunnels."42

Over the years Bowles assumed the task of familiariz-
ing the Western world with the riches of Moroccan culture
through his collections of native music, and translations of
Moroccan literature. He also introduced many of his friends
to the beauties of his adopted country and among these was
Tennessee Williams who made several visits there beginning
in 1949. That Williams had indeed become a friend as well
as a professional associate is evidenced by his letters to
Bowles of the late fifties following Jane's stroke, in which
he expresses his concern for both of them and his high re-
gard for Jane's worth as a person and an artist.[43]

Tennessee Williams' forbears had included Sidney La-
nier, several Indian fighters, and a brother of St. Francis
Xavier. It was a fitting ancestry for a man with a poetic
ear and a propensity toward strong drink who was to be-
come the American theater's "laureate of the outcast."[44]
Williams' early childhood was spent in the peaceful, pleas-
ant towns of Mississippi which, after a family move to St.
Louis in 1919,[45] would come to represent the lost Eden of
his mythic Southern birthright. His boisterous, extroverted
father was a traveling salesman who spent most of his time
away from home. As a result, Williams developed a strong
attachment to his mother, fostered by two years of recu-
peration at home from diphtheria. When he was eleven, his
mother bought a typewriter for this son who was too shy to
speak in class, and by the age of fourteen he had already
dedicated his life to writing.

His literary efforts began to be recognized at the Uni-
versity of Missouri, where he enrolled in 1929, only to be
removed by his father for failing ROTC. He returned to
college in 1936 when his grandmother financed a year at
Washington University; here he was not only introduced to
the poetry of Rilke and Hart Crane but also had three plays
produced by Willard Holland's little theater group. Williams'
Bachelor of Arts degree was finally earned at the University
of Iowa in 1937--the same year that his beloved sister Rose
underwent a pre-frontal lobotomy.

The next six years were a time of writing, wandering,
and financial struggle. In 1943, Audrey Woods, Williams'
able agent, arranged a six-month's contract with Metro Gold-
wyn Mayer. Ironically, MGM rejected all the scripts he

produced including The Glass Menagerie which would shortly
establish the author as one of America's major dramatists.
In 1944, between the Chicago and New York productions of
the play, Williams' poetry appeared in a volume called Five
Young American Poets. Most of these poems, some in re-
vised form, would be republished in In the Winter of Cities
(1956), and a few would reappear in his poetry collection of
1977 called Androgyne, Mon Amour.

The Glass Menagerie was presented with a background
musical score by Paul Bowles. Over the next two decades
Bowles, now living abroad, made return trips to New York
to write scores for other of Williams' important plays such
as Summer and Smoke (1948), Sweet Bird of Youth (1959),
and The Milk Train Doesn't Stop Here Anymore (1963).
During the remaining years of his life, Williams suffered
from intermittent depression and "the attrition of dramatic
power that affects most playwrights after the age of 50."[46]
The panic and sense of isolation attendant on this depression
are movingly portrayed in his poem called "Tangier: The
Speechless Summer," which is in the collection Androgyne,
Mon Amour. Both Jane and Paul Bowles appear in this
poem, and it is clear from the following lines that Williams'
pain over his "speechlessness," which may be in part a
symbol of failing creativity, also extends to the difficulty of
communicating his despair to these dearest of friends:

> I love Paul, but once he said to me: "I've never had
> a neurosis."
>
> Jane, I said to you: "Jane, I can't talk anymore."
> and you said to me: "Tennessee, you were
> never much of a talker."

In the title poem of the earlier collection, In the Win-
ter of Cities, Williams had already begun to record his own
haunting fears that the vital, creative years of his life were
over:

> Those who ignore the appropriate time of their going
> are the most valiant explorers,
> going into a country that no one is meant to go into,
> the time coming after that isn't meant to come after.

From the acknowledgement of this bitter insight, in the

mid-fifties, to the end of his life, was a tormented span of nearly thirty years. In 1983, he died, like James Agee, in the same setting as his father had--in this case a lonely hotel room, where he choked on the swallowed cap of a medicine bottle. It was a death-scene which Tennessee Williams himself might have written. The "laureate" had become one with the "outcast."

Williams' poetry then, like his plays, not infrequently bore a close connection to his own experience. As regards its position in his total literary output, critics for the most part are in agreement with Felicia Londré's estimate that "despite the fact that he has written some of the most poetic lines spoken on the American stage ... [Williams'] poetry, as such, is extremely uneven."[47] Some of the most successful verses in the collections are the compact, unpretentious folk-like ballads often written in rhymed couplets, which employ Williams' genius for dramatic portrayal of both comic and tragic figures, and his unfailing ear for idiomatic language. The source of the folk idiom is primarily the writer's memories of the years of his rural, Southern childhood, and the literary world evoked by these ties is full of a healthy and unsophisticated tenderness, even toward its failures, that is a far cry from the violence and emotional excess of so much of his other writing.

The texts of the Bowles-Williams settings to be discussed below are all drawn from this world. Despite his highly cultivated and urbane intellect, Paul Bowles has always been quite at home, musically, in the folk milieu, and the "new simplicity"[48] of his style, praised by the critics of the forties, found a counterpart in this poetry. Bowles describes the selection process, saying "There's not much I can tell you about the text sources for the Tennessee Williams songs. In each case Mr. Williams handed me typed pages with the lyrics, saying that I might find them suitable for setting to music. There were other lyrics, but I chose the ones that appealed to me."[49]

"Blue Mountain" of the Blue Mountain Ballads[50] (1946) is a mythical town in Mississippi which represents Camden and/or Clarksdale where Williams had lived happily with his grandparents as a boy. In a number of Williams' plays set in the south, there are recurring references to towns such as Blue Mountain or Glorious Hill, Mississippi; in the early one-act play <u>At Liberty</u>, for instance, Gloria Greene, a former road show dancer, is back home in Blue Mountain, suffering from a chronic chest ailment. All four texts of the <u>Ballads</u> have four-stress lines with poetic feet of varying meters. All are in rhymed couplets, with the exception of "Lonesome Man" which is in triplets, the third line in each case being a slightly varied echo of the second. Three of the four--"Heavenly Grass," "Sugar in the Cane," and "Lonesome Man"--are dramatic monologues written in the first person, while "Cabin," the fourth, is a narrative, but paints an extremely vivid picture of human character and the events of its creation.

"Cabin" is a morality tale of a seduction, drawn with simple but powerful imagery, in which the sunny, flower-trimmed cabin seems to stand for the woman's innocence, and the winter storm which now sweeps it, for the passion which destroyed them both. Bowles' opening tempo suggestion is "Like a ballad," and the introduction establishes this ambiance with the warmth of its flowing, diatonic thirds in the right hand, and the suggestion of a plucked folk instrument in the spacing of the left hand's broken chords.

Example 1.8, measures 1-4. Copyright © 1946, G. Schirmer, Inc.; used by permission.

The body of the song has an ABA form and harmonic scheme, with the A sections in F sharp minor. The B section, which incorporates the line "where they kissed and sinned," moves to the modal form of A, which forms a somber contrast to the bright expectations promised by the A major of the introduction. The contour of the vocal line is folk-song-like in its emphasis on chordal leaps and stepwise

motion but the dissonant ninths in the accompanying chords
add both a suggestion of menace, and a contemporary per-
spective on a timeless tragedy.

Example 1.9, measures 5-7. Copyright © 1946, G. Schirmer,
Inc.; used by permission.

Notice that by lengthening the second and fourth poetic
foot in each line (Ex. 1.9), Bowles creates a flexible and re-
sponsive rhythmic scheme of 6/8 combined with 9/8 measures,
and adds a sense of spaciousness to the telling of the tale.

In "Heavenly Grass" we encounter one of the first-
person monologues, in this case spoken by a simple, devout
individual whose plain speech is transformed by Williams into
intensely poetic imagery. One is reminded of Agee's view of
"the mountain people" as drawing both poetry and spiritual-
ity from their closeness to the earth, as the protagonist
likens the journey of the soul to a walk from "heavenly

Example 1.10, measures 1-3. Copyright © 1946, G. Schirmer,
Inc.; used by permission.

grass" to earthly terrain, and back again. Bowles first
provides a lightly textured, poignant piano introduction in
which twanging major ninths underly the melodic motif of a
minor third plus a second. This motif takes on a "question
and answer" quality, as each statement is followed by its in-
version, and the minor third (a favorite interval of Bowles')
is also prominent in the contour of the vocal line (see Ex.
1.11).

As the voice enters, the composer continues to employ
musical device in a perfect correspondence to the artful sim-
plicity of the poetry. The overall form is a recurring AB
pattern in which the first line of each couplet is given a
modal setting and a faster-moving 5/4 meter, while the sec-
ond line takes on a slower, wandering 4/4 meter and the
contrastingly ecstatic brightness of the G major key.

Example 1.11, measures 4-9. Copyright © 1946, G. Schirmer,
Inc.; used by permission.

The only exception to this scheme is the setting of the third couplet, which incorporates the birth experience. This is clothed in the faster tempo plus the urgency of a 3/4 meter, and the voice line descends with the weight of human pain, and the sorrow of heavenly loss.

Example 1.12, measures 13-18. Copyright © 1946, G. Schirmer, Inc.; used by permission.

Glanville-Hicks had observed that "a peculiarity [Bowles'] music has in common with certain folksong material, and even with modal harmonization of folk tunes, is that a point of rest or complete finality can be arrived at on all manner of tonal degrees other than a tonic."[51] In the magical conclusion of "Heavenly Grass," Bowles repeats the final line ("But they still got an itch for heavenly grass") and changes the last note to end on the sixth degree of the scale, in a reverie of suspended longing (see Example 1.13, page 34).

Example 1.13, measures 25-27. Copyright © 1946, G. Schirmer, Inc.; used by permission.

"Sugar in the Cane" is a very different portrait. Here Tennessee Williams uses his considerable comic talents to bring before us a nubile young woman whose metaphorical allegations of innocence ("I'm potatoes not yet mashed," etc.) appear to be somewhat exaggerated. In the collection In the Winter of Cities, Williams had published two poems called "Kitchen Door Blues" and "Gold Tooth Blues" which clearly had the "feel" of song lyrics, particularly the second, whose structure included a refrain. "Sugar in the Cane" falls into the same category, and is a fine idiomatic imitation of the rhythm, language, and sexual innuendo of the typical "blues" lyric.

Bowles' style in the setting is a precisely perfect blend of elements taken from the appropriate areas of American popular music. He employs the tied-over syncopations and pianistic octaves of early ragtime:

Example 1.14, measures 1-5. Copyright © 1946, G. Schirmer, Inc.; used by permission.

together with the ornamental "smears" and flatted thirds derived from the vocabulary of "blue notes."

Example 1.15, measures 12-14. Copyright © 1946, G. Schirmer, Inc.; used by permission.

Stylistic quotation is, of course, in an art song framework, and therefore not slavishly derivative. Bowles uses a ten-measure vocal strain rather than the usual twelve measures of "the blues," and replaces the typical sub-dominant harmonic contrast with a secondary dominant to the V chord. The ending of both verses of the strophic form is also interesting in that it is idiosyncratic to the composer. Once again, as in "Heavenly Grass," Bowles selects the sixth degree of the scale as his final note, and also sets the concluding word with his "trademark" falling third.

Example 1.16, measures 24-26. Copyright © 1946, G. Schirmer, Inc.; used by permission.

Though the key (G major) and scalar relationship of the sixth is the same as the ending of "Heavenly Grass," the effect is a far cry from "heavenly," and indeed, in this context of low range, insistent rhythmic accent, and strident cluster harmonies, becomes insinuatingly provocative.

"Lonesome Man," the last of the Blue Mountain Ballads, is a swift, brilliant characterization of one of Williams' "outcasts" from society. The speaker in this case knows he is too old to win love for himself, refuses to pay for it, and at the same time mocks the suffering brought down by his pride on "an old fool's head." The poem itself has a rueful quality which Bowles turns to humor with his spirited use once again of ragtime syncopations in the accompaniment. This figure clearly derives from the opening line of text ("My chair rock-rocks by the door all day") and the recurring interpolations of 7/16 in the overall 4/8 meter suggest that an agitated state of mind is causing an occasional acceleration in the chair's regular rocking.

Example 1.17, measures 5-10. Copyright © 1946, G. Schirmer, Inc.; used by permission.

In another instance of the composer's sensitivity to the dramatic action, two recitative-like passages over held piano chords set the poignant phrases "I don't want love from the mercantile store" and "While the moon grins down at an ole fool's head." The culturally but not musically incongruous comparison that springs to mind is Schubert's "Gretchen am Spinnrade." Like the young girl's spinning wheel, the old man's rocking chair has momentarily stopped, as he muses over the joy and sorrow of love.

Example 1.18, measures 35-37. Copyright © 1946, G. Schirmer, Inc.; used by permission.

"Three"[52] is a Bowles-Williams song published in 1947, slightly later than the Blue Mountain Ballads. It is a short, two-page setting of a simple but powerful poem about three loves. Again the text is in the first person, and the lover's sorrowful realization is that the one who died ("is sheltered under frost") is also the one who "stayed in [his] heart forever." Stylistically, the setting is somewhat reminiscent of "Heavenly Grass" with its modal constructions and unelaborate but convincing vocal contour. The piano interlude before the last stanza exhibits a meltingly effective use of pianissimo chords in parallel fifths and octaves. As the text returns, this figure is hauntingly continued in the accompaniment.

Example 1.19, measures 14-19. Copyright 1947, Hargail Music Press; used by permission.

A Tennessee Williams text called "Her Head on the Pillow"[53] was set by Paul Bowles in Tangier in 1961, and is now being published for the first time. Like "Cabin," this is a story centered on passion's destructive force, this time told by the man, who is filled with remorse as "her head on the pillow" reminds him of "Holy Mary's Crown." The poem is in three six-line stanzas, and in the fashion of many examples of folk-poetry and folk-song lyrics, lines five and six of each stanza are a subtle variant of three and four. This affords Bowles the opportunity for musical amplification and emotive intensification at the end of each verse setting, which occur in the form of more arching vocal lines, and fuller pianistic figurations. Dramatic contrast is skillfully achieved by the composer through a change of meter and tempo in the middle section of a three-part form. The outer sections, embodying the protagonist's repentant adoration, are in a slower reflective 4/4, while his painful memories ("when I took the lady by storm") are mirrored in an agitated, whirling 3/8.

Not surprisingly, Paul Bowles has also set his own texts on a number of occasions. One of the most successful of these, "Once a lady was here,"[54] has been anthologized,[55] and appears frequently on recital programs.[56] Indeed, it was not only included in the recorded selections of the Rockefeller project's New World Records, but even provided the disc's title--But Yesterday Is Not Today--which is the last line of the poem.[57] This song and "In the Woods"[58] (also to a Bowles text) are both from the middle forties, the same period as most of the Williams settings, but Bowles setting Bowles produces a more emotionally complex, sophisticated product than the simple, direct expression of Blue Mountain's inhabitants. In these Bowles texts, he is the narrator/observer, who comments on the passing scene with a kind of detached compassion. It is as though the lady who once "sat in this garden and ... thought of love" and the girl who "hears a bird ... in the woods" are seen from a veiled distance, as microcosms in the universal scheme, rather than as possibilities for human involvement. The quality is the same as that which Glanville-Hicks describes in Paul Bowles' music as "an emotional-mystical quality ... at once personal and remote."[59]

"Once a lady was here" has a musical-theater flavor, drawn from the composer's extensive experience in the style. The chordal constructions, dotted note patterns, and "off" notes are all out of ragtime and blues through Broadway and are elements which become increasingly common in American art song as the twentieth century progresses. (See Ex. 1.20, page 40.) Bowles' considerable skill at handling subtle, asymmetric rhythmic patterns is evident in his undulating metric scheme of 4/8 5/8, and his most uncommon melodic gift is once again revealed in the seemingly inevitable contours of the vocal line.

Example 1.20, measures 1-8. Copyright © 1946, G. Schirmer, Inc.; used by permission.

"In the Woods" has a shifting, chromatic accompaniment of soft parallel tone clusters which seems to shed an Impressionistic haze over the scene.

Example 1.21, measures 1-4. Copyright 1945, Associated
Music Publishers, Inc.; used by permission.

A striking contrast to the pianistic color is provided by the
composer's request that the repeated descending fourth (see
last two notes of Ex. 1.21) be whistled, in direct imitation
of the bird's "music-making." Interestingly, in this context
the whistle does not emerge as a cheerful sound. Rather,
it becomes wistfully hypnotic in its repeated downward leaps,
and emphasizes the aloneness of the girl with her "tears that
careless thoughts can sometimes bring."

Hugo Weisgall (1912-)
Adelaide Crapsey (1878-1914)
e.e. cummings (1894-1962)
Herman Melville (1819-1891)

Hugo Weisgall was born in Ivancice, Czechoslovakia, and in
1920 his family emigrated to America from a Europe suffering
the chaotic aftermath of World War I and the Russian Revolu-
tion. Like Sergius Kagen and other European-born artists
of his generation, Weisgall became a rich contributor to the
creative life of this country. He also became an ardent ad-
vocate of American music, and, in a 1965 article, roundly
castigated The Musical Quarterly for devoting its fiftieth an-
niversary issue to a survey of European rather than Ameri-
can music.[60]

Weisgall's mother came from a highly cultured family,

Hugo Weisgall

and his father was a professional opera singer and cantor.
From an early age, the boy developed his vocal and instru-
mental skills as he sang in synagogue choirs and played
piano accompaniments while his father performed lieder and
operatic arias. In 1921 the family settled in Baltimore, and
except for the period of World War II and the travel demands

of a busy career, Weisgall remained a Baltimore resident until 1960. Peabody Conservatory, then, was a natural place to start his professional musical training. He won a scholarship there and studied from 1927 to 1930, at the same time beginning an overlapping course of study in Germanic literature at Johns Hopkins University which would eventually result in a doctorate (1940).

During these early years, Weisgall was performing professionally as a singer, an actor, and a conductor of choirs and amateur orchestras. In 1936 he accepted a conducting scholarship at Curtis with Fritz Reiner and for the next three years also worked in composition with Rosario Scalero. The latter's conservatism, however, had less influence on Weisgall's developing style than did his intermittent studies (1933-1941) with Roger Sessions. As he had done with Finney and Naginski (see Volume II, Chapter 4),[61] Sessions opened the young composer's mind to the musical innovations of Stravinsky and Schoenberg as well as of contemporary Americans such as himself.

Having enlisted as a private in 1942, Weisgall soon found himself assigned on diplomatic missions to England and the continent, after U.S. military intelligence discovered his command of languages and European background. In 1946-47, he remained as American cultural attaché in Prague, during which time he took advantage of frequent "guest conductorships" to perform many contemporary American scores throughout Europe. On his return to the United States, Weisgall developed an impressive teaching career which included appointments at Juilliard, Peabody, and Queens College, and at the same time emerged as one of America's leading composers of opera. His numerous contributions to the synagogue liturgy, and wide experience in the performance of Jewish music, also brought him an appointment in 1952 to the chairmanship of the Faculty of the Cantors' Institute of the Jewish Theological Seminary. He currently lives in Great Neck, New York, where he continues to teach and compose.

As Bruce Saylor has pointed out, "the vocal impulse is primary" in Hugo Weisgall's music,[62] and the composer himself has said "If I can't sing it, I don't write it."[63] In 1931, he had won Columbia University's Bearns prize with a set of songs called Four Impressions, and in 1933 he composed Five Night Songs. Both of these works remain in manuscript, and the only American poet whose texts appear therein is Amy Lowell in the Four Impressions. However, in 1934 Weisgall set another American poet, this time so successfully that the Four Songs to Adelaide Crapsey's poetry became, as Opus 1, his first published work.

In a letter to the author dated September 7, 1983, Hugo Weisgall comments on the poets that have attracted him in this and subsequent periods of his composition. "Specifically concerning Crapsey," he says, "I discovered her poetry way back in the late twenties or early thirties while I was still an undergraduate. I had always written songs from early childhood and among my early unpublished work there are settings of Amy Lowell. Somehow or other I seemed to have set a large number of women poets. I don't know why that is. I have known and do know," he concludes, "a great many American poets, some of them quite well, and at present I am working on a large cycle of texts by John Hollander."

Adelaide Crapsey's life has been treated at some length in Volume II, Chapter 2 of this series. It was a tragic life in which a brilliant, creative woman who had been elected to Phi Beta Kappa at Vassar, taught poetics at Smith College, and invented a compressed and elegant five-line verse structure called the "cinquain," was doomed to an early death from tubercular meningitis. Her health waned during the last decade of her life, and after a complete collapse in 1913 she was taken to Dr. Trudeau's widely recognized nursing home at Saranac Lake, New York. Here she spent the year before her death looking out the window at the graveyard she called "Trudeau's Garden" and using her poetic gift to record her muffled anguish over the approaching end.

Except for the Oriental influences that had prompted the "cinquains" of 1911-1913, Crapsey's verse shows little evidence of the experimentalism in poetic form and language of her contemporaries. But study of the Japanese hokku models had contributed a Dickinson-like brevity and directness to the author's expression, and her "courageous refusal to soften ... despair with vague appeals to the immortality of the soul"[64] was a direct precursor of the growing twentieth-century tide of Existentialism.[65] Weisgall's Four Songs[66] use an apparent minimum of musical device so as not to lessen the stark poignancy of the textual message, and the result is a devastatingly powerful example of a musical "soft sell."

Each of the four takes its title directly from the poem. In number one, which is only one page long, the "Old Love" of the title seems fittingly interpreted as the dimly remembered face of Death, a "ghost" whose "eyes most strangely glow." Weisgall makes of the six verse lines a small three-part form in which the two A sections, and the piano introduction, employ a circular, chant-like figure hovering around three adjacent scale degrees. This figure suggests the terrible hypnotic power of the phantom's gaze, while the variously changing 3/4 2/4 meter and continuous small waves of dynamic rise and fall add the ambivalent victim's attraction and revulsion.

Example 1.22, measures 1-11. Copyright 1940, Theodore Presser Co.; used by permission of the publisher.

45

Number two, called simply "Song," uses an all treble register, tinkling piano part and regular, flowing vocal rhythms to create the semblance of a springtime ballad. But the opening E minor key and softly clashing dissonances provide the clue to the chilling deception soon revealed by the text ("I make my shroud, but no one knows").

Example 1.23, measures 1-10. Copyright 1940, Theodore Presser Co.; used by permission of the publisher.

In the most telling, eerie moment of the setting, Weisgall moves to G major for a seemingly innocent, light-hearted melisma on "a little wand'ring air" over a folkish, drone-like bass in the accompaniment (see Ex. 1.24, page 47). The poetic contrast between the visual and aural images of life and the secret knowledge of Death is perfectly captured in this setting by its use of the myriad available contradictions of musical language.

In number two, Weisgall had repeated Crapsey's final line ("So shimmering fine it is and fair") in order to form a coda for his mock folk-ballad structure. For his third setting, "Oh, Lady, Let the Sad Tears Fall," the composer uses

Example 1.24, measures 22-33.   Copyright 1940, Theodore
Presser Co.; used by permission of the publisher.

text repetition three times in a litany of sorrow whose lyric
contours, long sustained tones, and pauses in the vocal line
suggest a struggle with overwhelming emotion.   The familiar
Baroque "affection" of chromaticism in the context of anguish
is expanded to a moving bi-tonal climax in the accompaniment
following the word "pain" (see Ex. 1.25).   In two other skill-
ful instances of "word painting," Weisgall writes a brief vocal
rest before the word, "sigh," and applies a descending line
in the lowest tessitura of the cycle to "where / Pale roses
die" (see Ex. 1.26, page 48).

Example 1.25, measures 6-14. Copyright 1940, Theodore Presser Co.; used by permission of the publisher.

Example 1.26, measures 28-33. Copyright 1940, Theodore Presser Co.; used by permission of the publisher.

The fourth and final setting is of a poem called "Dirge"[67] which is a polite, understated description of Death as an approaching absence of sensation, particularly the sense of hearing. The music has the restraint of the text (this setting, too, is one page long) with only subtly altered chords attesting to the sharpness of the coming loss.

Example 1.27, measures 7-14. Copyright 1940, Theodore
Presser Co.; used by permission of the publisher.

In the foregoing example, the apparently simple rhythmic
repetition in the vocal line which clothes "Tap at thy window-
sill" becomes an inspired closing of the cycle, as it suggests
both a lively, feathered visitor, and the bony finger of Death
itself.

Hugo Weisgall's next song cycle was <u>Soldier Songs</u>,[68]
written a decade later (1944-46) as a direct result of his
war-time service. Deeply moved by the futility and horror
of war, the composer chose for setting nine poems by British
and American authors which had been written as a result of
the poets' personal experiences. To these he added his own
experience, and recalls writing one of the set in an air-raid
shelter of the Brussels Radio Station; another after returning
from a "tour" of a German concentration camp. The work was
premiered in New York in 1954 by Grant Garnell, baritone,
and Stanton Carter, pianist. In 1966 the orchestral version
received its first performance with Robert Trehy, baritone,
and the Baltimore Symphony conducted by Peter Herman Ad-
ler.

Two of the <u>Soldier Songs</u>, which are settings of Ameri-
can texts, demonstrate the wide variety of poetic mood and
musical treatment found in the cycle. Number four sets "my
sweet old etcetera," written by e.e. cummings, whose initial
treatment in this series occurs in Volume II, Chapter 3.
Basically, cummings was a pacifist, but had felt impelled
toward some type of humanitarian service as World War I
decimated a generation of European youth. In April of 1917,
having only recently moved to New York and begun to work

49

for Collier's, he enlisted with the Norton Harjes ambulance group which was based in France. The entire enterprise was to prove ill-fated, after a bad beginning in which cummings failed to find his unit and located it only after a week's delay in Paris. Then a misinterpretation by French censors of apparently pro-German comments in cummings' letters resulted in his internment in a kind of concentration camp at La Ferté-Macé. He was eventually released through intervention by the American government, but it was a bitter experience which became the basis of The Enormous Room, his first long prose work, published in 1922.

Back in the United States, he was drafted and sent to Camp Devens, forty miles west of Cambridge. This proved physically beneficial, but psychologically difficult for cummings, and his wartime experiences left him with a value system that included a deep need for personal freedom from social structures, as well as the recognition of human vulnerability to chance and the forces of nature.[69] In 1926, the continuing bitterness surfaced again in his writing, with a group of anti-war poems that were included in is 5. This volume had been contracted by Horace Liveright following the promising appearance of Tulips and Chimneys, cummings' first collection of verse, three years earlier. This time the publisher requested an introduction that would help people understand the poet's style, but the one which cummings supplied did little to accomplish this purpose. The poems of is 5 show much of the same visual experimentation and word-play of his first volume, but there is a marked increase in satire: in the war poems, in those commenting on contemporary American life, and in lyrics such as "my sweet old etcetera" which combine both elements.

The picture presented here is of a useless flurry of homefront activity ("my sister isabel created hundreds of socks") and of the empty talk by elderly relatives about the meaning of the war and the "privilege" of participating. As a final ironic touch, cummings, whose sexual initiation had occurred during his week in Paris in 1917, ends the poem with himself, lying "quietly in the deep mud," dreaming, not of the glories of combat, but of "Your smile/eyes knees and of your Etcetera." The poem has the poet's typical visual distortions of word groupings, but parts of speech are all used conventionally except for "Etcetera" which after previous heavy employment in its usual function, becomes a noun in the final line quoted above.

In Weisgall's setting, the distorted word groupings disappear, and connected verbal ideas become musical phrases. Thus lines such as

> what everybody was fighting
> for
> my sister
> isabel created hundreds

are rejoined into the following:

Example 1.28, measures 8-17. Copyright 1953, Merrymount Music Press; used by permission of the publisher.

The composer demonstrates, in this song, his tendency to

underline strong emotion by musical repetition not in the poetic original. Suggesting the poet's suppressed rage at his father's facile and fatuous statements, Weisgall incorporates one repetition each of "my father" and of "if only he could," while "a privilege" receives four repetitions, a series of sharp staccato leaps, and a hysterical crescendo of sound.

Example 1.29, measures 30-34. Copyright 1953, Merrymount Music Press; used by permission of the publisher.

As can be seen in the above examples, Weisgall's style remains basically tonal in these pieces, but incorporates a more dissonant, disjunct vocal line, and considerably more chromaticism in the harmony than the Four Songs of 1934. The change was discernible throughout his works of the forties and is certainly appropriate to the grim and often tragic texts of the Soldier Songs. A unifying element in the cycle is the interval of a major sixth (which opens the cummings setting) and the minor third, its inversion (which closes it).

Example 1.30a, measures 1-3. Copyright 1953, Merrymount Music Press; used by permission of the publisher.

Example 1.30b, measures 47-49. Copyright 1953, Merrymount Music Press; used by permission of the publisher.

Finally, one of the most striking features of the song is Weisgall's use of popular dance rhythms, such as the dotted-note patterns of ragtime in Example 1.29, measures 30-31, and the syncopated "beguine" accompaniment of Example 1.30a, which pervades much of the setting. This device characterizes with a dramatic stroke the poet's vision of wartime America's selfishness and merely superficial concern for her soldiers.

The last song of the set is "Shiloh," a musical treatment of a poem from the collection titled Battle-Pieces and written by Herman Melville, whose life will be discussed at some length in Chapter 2 of this volume. Melville had dedicated Battle-Pieces "to the memory of the three hundred thousand who in the war for the maintenance of the union fell devotedly under the flag of their fathers."70 Although largely ignored at its publication in 1866, the volume is now ranked with Walt Whitman's Drum Taps (see Volume II, Chapter 4) as among the best of the Civil War poetry.

"Shiloh's" subtitle is "A Requiem (April, 1862)" which date refers to the terrible "Sunday fight / Around the church of Shiloh" in southern Tennessee which resulted in the slaughter of nearly 25,000 Union and Confederate troops. The moving poem contrasts the peaceful present as swallows skim the field, with the remembered scene of desolation, filled with groans of the dying, who had been "Foemen at morn, but friends at eve."

Weisgall's setting is in the key of E minor, established at the outset by the lowest voice of the accompaniment which outlines the tonic triad in steady quarter note motion. On top of this, the rest of the accompaniment and the voice line participate in the creation of dissonant seconds and sevenths,

Example 1.31, measures 1-7. Copyright 1953, Merrymount Music Press; used by permission of the publisher.

whose pianissimo dynamic context suggests a shimmering veil
of lingering horror over the peaceful surface. (Although
the dramatic mood is quite different, the technique is remi-
niscent of "Song," discussed above in the Crapsey settings.)

The song has a basically three-part structure with a
shortened return to A. The middle section, which describes
the battle itself, has an agitated leaping vocal contour (see
Ex. 1.32) while the two outer sections present a more lyric
and stepwise line. Two startlingly dramatic portamentos, one
of an octave and the other of a tenth, occur in a crescendo
context (piano to a sudden forte) and are totally shocking,
like the bloody events of the day (see Ex. 1.32). Two brief
but powerful instances of musical pictorialization further
heighten the drama. One is a measure in which the soft,
staccato pulse of the pianist's left hand recalls the menacing
march with its accompanying drum-beat (see Ex. 1.31, meas-
ure 6) and the other is the sharply accented, bitonal, for-
tissimo chords which suggest the deadly impact of a bullet
(see Ex. 1.32).

Example 1.32, measures 31-33. Copyright 1953, Merrymount
Music Press; used by permission of the publisher.

The poem's refrain-like fourth line ("The forest-field
of Shiloh") and final line ("And all is hushed at Shiloh")
receive similar melodic and harmonic treatment which serves
to unify the individual setting, while the minor third conclud-
ing the vocal line ties this song to the rest of the cycle (see
Ex. 1.33, page 56). The sense of ancient ceremony which
Weisgall achieves at the end of "Shiloh" is largely due to the
last two accompanying chords. The first chord uses a lowered

second step (found in the Phrygian ecclesiastical mode) and the second is an empty, open fifth sonority in the medieval and Renaissance tradition.

Example 1.33, measures 38-42. Copyright 1953, Merrymount Music Press; used by permission of the publisher.

NOTES

1. Samuel Barber, "On Waiting for a Libretto" Opera News, vol. 22, no. 13 (Jan. 27, 1958), p. 4.

2. Nathan Broder, Samuel Barber (New York: G. Schirmer, 1954), p. 9.

3. Harold Randolph also taught John Duke, as discussed in Volume II, Chapter 2, of this series.

4. Mary Curtis Bok was the mother-in-law of Nellie Lee Bok, a next generation patron of the arts, and friend of the composer Paul Nordoff (see Volume II, Chapter 4).

5. Marcella Sembrich, later at Juilliard, was on the voice faculty of Curtis at its opening. (For her connections with the composer Sergius Kagen, see Volume II, Chapter 4.)

6. Barber, "On Waiting for a Libretto," p. 5.

7. Broder, p. 19.

8. "Dover Beach" (G. Schirmer) is scored for baritone and string quartet, and was recorded with Barber himself singing the voice part. The other three songs all appear in the

Collected Songs of Samuel Barber (New York: G. Schirmer, 1971), which are available for high and medium voice.

9. See Irvin Kolodin, "Farewell to Capricorn," Saturday Review/World, I (June 1, 1974), pp. 44-45.

10. All songs by Samuel Barber written and published up to 1969 are in the Schirmer collection (see note #8).   Three Songs written in 1972 are published separately by Schirmer.

11. Nicolas Slonimsky, comp., Baker's Biographical Dictionary of Musicians (New York: G. Schirmer, 1978), p. 97.

12. The James Joyce settings include "Rain Has Fallen," "Sleep Now," and "I Hear an Army."

13. Mark A. Doty, Tell Me Who I Am (Baton Rouge: Louisiana State University Press, 1981), p. 3.

14. Genevieve Moreau, The Restless Journey of James Agee (New York: William Morrow, 1977), p. 29.

15. Samuel Barber, Knoxville, Summer of 1915 (New York: G. Schirmer, 1949).   Actually, Barber sets only excerpts from this work, begun by Agee in the middle thirties, and republished posthumously as a preface to his autobiographical novel, Death in the Family.

16. See Letters of James Agee to Father Flye (Boston: Houghton Mifflin, 1971).

17. For a graphic description of James Agee's piano playing, see the introductory "Memoir" in Robert Fitzgerald, editor, The Collected Short Prose of James Agee (Boston: Houghton Mifflin, 1958), p. 42.

18. Moreau, p. 94.

19. Letters to Father Flye, New York City, September 21, 1941.

20. Peter H. Ohlin, Agee (New York: Ivan Obolensky, 1966), p. 3.

21. Moreau, p. 276.

22. Dwight MacDonald, "Death of a Poet," New Yorker, XXXIII:38 (Nov. 16, 1957), p. 226.

23. James Agee, Permit Me Voyage (New Haven: Yale University Press, 1934).

24. This song appears in the 1971 collection, and an or-chestration is available from the publisher. Recorded per-formances are to be found in: a) John K. Hanks and Ruth C. Friedberg, Art Song in America, vol. 1 (Durham, N.C.: Duke University Press, 1966); b) Bethany Beardslee and Robert Helps, But Yesterday is Not Today (New York: New World Records, 1977).

25. Compare the following quotation from Knoxville, Summer of 1915 with the text of "Sure on this Shining Night": "Now is the night one blue dew ... The stars are wide and alive, they seem like a smile of great sweetness, and they seem very near."

26. See Volume I, pp. 13-14, of this series.

27. This quotation from the Collected Prose (ed. Fitzgerald) is given by Moreau on p. 93.

28. Radcliffe Squires, Frederic Prokosch (New York: Twayne Publishers, 1964).

29. This song is also published in the 1971 collection, and recorded by Hanks and Friedberg in Vol. I of their anthology (see note 24).

30. See Peter Garland, "Paul Bowles and the Baptism of Solitude" in Americas: Essays on American Music and Cul-ture, 1973-80 (Santa Fe: Soundings Press, 1982).

31. Paul Bowles, Without Stopping (New York: Putnam, 1972), p. 69. See also: a) Millicent Dillon, A Little Original Sin--The Life and Work of Jane Bowles (New York: Holt, Rinehart and Winston, 1981); b) Millicent Dillon, ed. Se-lected Letters of Jane Bowles (Santa Barbara, CA: Black Sparrow Press, 1985).

32. Ibid., p. 43.

33. Ibid., p. 103.

34. Only 100 copies of each composition were printed by this company, and most are long gone. A few are held in the Humanities Research Center of the University of Texas in Austin, which has a number of Paul Bowles items.

35. Paul Bowles, "Letter to Freddy" (New York: G. Schirmer, 1946). Medium voice.

36. Bowles composed three songs for Saroyan's play Love's Old Sweet Song (1940). One of these, "A Little Closer Please (The Pitchman's Song)" is included in Paul Bowles, Selected Songs (Santa Fe: Soundings Press, 1984).

37. Bowles, Without Stopping, p. 229.

38. Peggy Glanville-Hicks, "Paul Bowles--American Composer," Music and Letters, XXVI:2 (April 1945), p. 94.

39. Ibid., p. 88.

40. Quoted in Garland, p. 216.

41. Bowles, Without Stopping, p. 336.

42. Ibid., p. 369.

43. These letters are held by the Humanities Research Center (see note 34).

44. T.E. Kalem, "The Laureate of the Outcast," Time (March 7, 1983), p. 88.

45. Ironically, Dakin Williams had his brother buried in St. Louis (a city which Tennessee had always disliked) because he felt it was centrally located for the many people who would be wanting to visit the grave.

46. Kalem, p. 88.

47. Felicia Hardison Londré, Tennessee Williams (New York: Frederick Ungar, 1979), p. 23.

48. Glanville-Hicks, p. 94.

49. Letter from Paul Bowles to the author, April 26, 1983.

50. Paul Bowles, <u>Blue Mountain Ballads</u> (New York: G. Schirmer, 1979). Medium voice. "Lonesome Man" and "Sugar in the Cane" are also included in the Soundings Press Collection.

    All four songs were recorded by Donald Gramm in <u>Songs by American Composers</u> (Desto, 6411/6412). Hanks-Friedberg (note 24) include "Cabin" and "Heavenly Grass" in Vol. 1 of their recording.

51. Glanville-Hicks, p. 93.

52. Paul Bowles, "Three," Soundings Press collection. Medium voice.

53. Paul Bowles, "Her Head on the Pillow," Soundings Press collection. Medium voice. The collection also contains a number of other Bowles songs being published for the first time. Among these are settings of poetry by Paul Bowles, Jane Bowles, and other Tennessee Williams texts, as well as four poems in Spanish by García Lorca.

54. Paul Bowles, "Once a Lady Was Here," Soundings Press collection. Medium voice.

55. This song is included in: Bernard Taylor (comp.), <u>Songs by 22 Americans</u> (New York: G. Schirmer, 1960).

56. At the First International Art Song Festival in Petit Jean, Arkansas (May, 1983), this song was performed in a Paul Bowles group presented as part of Paul Sperry's American art song recital.

57. New World Records (see note 24).

58. Paul Bowles, "In the Woods," Soundings Press collection. High voice.

59. Glanville-Hicks, p. 94.

60. Hugo Weisgall, "The 201st Quarterly," <u>Perspectives of New Music</u>, III:2 (1965), pp. 133-136.

61. Another notable Sessions student was David Diamond, whose life and training are discussed in Chapter 2 of this volume.

62. Bruce Saylor, "The Music of Hugo Weisgall," Musical Quarterly, LIX:2 (1973), p. 241.

63. Ibid.

64. Edward Butscher, Adelaide Crapsey (Boston: Twayne Publishers, 1979), p. 16.

65. "Existentialism" is a philosophical system which postulates Man as alone in an unfriendly universe, doomed to an existence which can be given meaning only by his own courage.

66. Hugo Weisgall, Four Songs (Bryn Mawr, PA: Theodore Presser, 1940). High or medium voice.

67. John Duke has also set this poem in a song which is included in: Songs by John Duke, Volume 2 (San Antonio: Southern Music Co., 1985). See Volume II, Chapter 2, for a discussion of Duke's song "Rapunzel," which is another Crapsey setting.

68. Hugo Weisgall, Soldier Songs (New York: Merrymount Music Press, 1953). Baritone.

69. The foregoing sentence is based on material in Richard S. Kennedy, Dreams in the Mirror (New York: Liveright, 1980), pp. 172-188.

70. Herman Melville, Works-Vol. 16, Poems (New York: Russell and Russell, 1963).

II. THE SECOND DECADE 2.

Norman Dello Joio (1913-   )
Stark Young (1881-1963)

Music was always a natural element to Norman Dello Joio, and the lyricism that dominates his vocal and instrumental works was seeded by heredity and nourished through environment. His father, Casimir Dello Joio, was an Italian organist and composer who emigrated to the United States and settled in New York City. He married an American, and assumed the post of organist at the Church of Our Lady of Mt. Carmel. Norman's earliest memories were of creeping out of bed to listen to his father's musician friends, all ardent fans of Italian opera, performing Verdi arias far into the night.

The boy soon demonstrated his native talent by beginning to pick out the major arias on the piano. Casimir then undertook his formal instruction in piano and organ and at the age of fourteen Norman Dello Joio was given the first of several subsequent positions as organist and choir director in a church of his own. During his teens, he composed music for recreation, and in his remaining leisure hours became so proficient at baseball, that he is probably the only American composer ever to have been offered a place on a professional ball team.

Having chosen to sacrifice immediate glory for the longer lasting satisfaction of an artistic career, Dello Joio undertook his advanced musical training at City College and

Norman Dello Joio

the Institute of Musical Art, after which he won a fellowship in composition under Bernard Wagenaar[1] at the Juilliard Graduate School. One of the teachers who influenced him the most was Paul Hindemith, with whom he studied in the opening session of the Berkshire Music School. This program had been established by Serge Koussevitzky as part of the summer festival at Tanglewood, and Dello Joio's classmates in that exciting 1940 season included Leonard Bernstein, Harold Shapero, and Lukas Foss. Dello Joio continued to study with Hindemith during the next winter at Yale University, and returned to Tanglewood with him the following summer. By the end of this time, the young composer had been encouraged by the older master to follow his own creative instincts, and the clarification and development of the Dello Joio style were well under way.[2]

During the past four decades, Norman Dello Joio has been not only one of America's most established and prolific composers, but has also been a major force in the philosophy and practice of music education in this country at many levels. He taught composition for a number of years, first at Sarah Lawrence College from 1945 to 1950, and subsequently at Mannes College of Music from 1956 to 1972. He then continued his university career at the administrative level, as dean of the School for the Arts at Boston University (1972-78). He also became involved, in the late fifties, with a Ford Foundation project, which placed young composers in the public schools to write for their performing groups. As an outgrowth of this, Dello Joio served as chairman of the Contemporary Music Project for Creativity in Music Education, under the joint sponsorship of the Music Educators' National Conference and the Ford Foundation.

In his comments which were part of a long retrospective article published in 1968 on the work of the Project, the composer dated his personal concern with the teaching of musicianship from his Sarah Lawrence appointment. Here he had come to realize that students who wanted to be musically creative through their "intuition" were hampered by their lack of musical knowledge and discipline. Having then committed his energies to the introduction of this discipline at the public school level, and as a result of his work for the Ford Foundation, he began asking himself a series of such fundamental questions as: "Is an academic degree a guarantee of professional competence?" and "Are our teacher training programs and curricula adequate?"[3]

These questions were particularly relevant in the sixties, that vanished decade of seemingly unlimited university funding which appeared to promise a haven of support for all types of artistic activity. In "The Composer and the American Scene," Dello Joio warned that the proliferating fine arts centers would be no better than the level of activity taking place inside them, and that teachers' colleges must beware of spending "more time on methods of teaching than on music itself."[4] At the same time, he emphasized the importance of the creative artist's mission in a world dominated by the destructive potential of nuclear warfare. "The fruit of his labor," said Dello Joio, "is an expression of humanity's will to survive," and added "The artist is also in a sense today's penitent, for he atones for much of modern man's abandonment of his own soul."[5]

In the course of his career, Norman Dello Joio has composed several operas, and a number of choral works. Among these choral pieces are settings of texts by the American poets Stephen Vincent Benét and Walt Whitman. Concerning the latter, the composer states "I have written extensively to the poetry of Walt Whitman because his thought was so all embracing and ... lent itself to epic musical expression."[6] Another American setting of sweeping proportions is Dello Joio's Songs of Remembrance[7] for baritone and orchestra, written to the poetry of John Hall Wheelock, "a neighbor and close friend in my town of East Hampton, New York. Unfortunately," adds the composer, "he did not live to hear the première of the work with the Philadelphia Symphony."[8]

It is clear then, that Norman Dello Joio has been drawn to set the work of American poets on a number of occasions. What has not appeared to attract him strongly is the intimate medium of the art song with piano, although the Six Love Songs of 1949,[9] his major effort in this genre, remain a valuable addition to the literature. Only one of the six, "The Dying Nightingale,"[10] is to an American text, and the composer has this to say of its origins:

> Stark Young wrote the poem for me. It was to be an aria in a projected plan I had for a short opera based on Oscar Wilde's fairy tale, "The Nightingale and the Rose." The opera was never completed.[11]

Stark Young was an extremely versatile man of letters

who never forgot his birthplace and his early influences in the town of Como, Mississippi. His father was a respected family doctor and his mother a beautiful, dark-haired, blue-eyed young woman who died when Stark was only eight, leaving him unable to speak of his profound loss for many years. The society which surrounded his childhood was still suffering the painful after-effects of the Civil War and Reconstruction, but Young perceived this environment as gentle and loving, and recounted the colorful reminiscences of his youth in an autobiography called The Pavilion published in 1951.[12]

Young's father and other relatives supported Stark through his university education with great determination, despite limited family resources. He took his undergraduate degree at the University of Mississippi, and while in the city of Oxford, came to know William Faulkner, who was then a young man beginning to write verse. After earning an M.A. in English at Columbia University, Young began a teaching career which lasted from 1904 to 1921, and included positions on the faculties of English literature at the University of Mississippi, University of Texas, and Amherst College. In 1921, he abandoned teaching for journalism and joined the editorial staff of the New Republic and Theatre Arts Monthly. After a two year stint (1924-25) as drama critic of the New York Times, he returned to the New Republic and stayed on as drama editor until his retirement in 1947.

Stark Young's criticism was greatly prized by his literary contemporaries, and his pivotal position in the theatrical world during his working years is clear from that portion of his correspondence now held by the University of Texas.[13] In this collection are letters from and to such playwrights as Sherwood Anderson and Eugene O'Neill, and actors and actresses of the stature of Alfred Lunt, Katharine Cornell, and Eleonora Duse. Composers are also represented, with a Christmas card from Igor Stravinsky and thank you notes to Gian Carlo Menotti and Norman Dello Joio.

Besides his high-level criticism, Stark Young also wrote a number of his own plays, as well as several novels. He was identified as a writer with the so-called "Southern Renaissance" that emerged in the middle decades of the twentieth century, and he had indeed contributed an essay in 1930 to a collection called I'll Take My Stand which was a

manifesto of American Southern agrarianism. Young's attach-
ment to Southern soil had been strengthened by a number of
months spent living in the North Carolina mountains, both
before and after his graduate year at Columbia. In time, he
also began to perceive meaning in the social patterns of the
South, which growth in perception he described in these
terms:

> The affability and grace of Southern manners ...
> made the surface of things easier and pleasanter;
> but I felt that it was merely the surface. It was
> only much later that I came to understand the value
> of forms and ritual and symbols [and to] understand
> that to think within a tradition of forms and words
> may be to think within what is solid and human.[14]

Like many creative individuals, Stark Young was gifted
in more than one art form. Although his father denied his
request for painting lessons at the age of eleven, the writer
eventually became a painter as well and exhibited in the New
York galleries in the years following his retirement. His
earliest creative medium, however, was poetry, and in 1906
he had published a collection of poems called The Blind Man
at the Window and a verse play entitled Guinevere. It is
easy to see why his years of experience with dramatic and
poetic forms made him desirable to Norman Dello Joio as the
librettist for his projected opera, The Nightingale and the
Rose.

The Oscar Wilde tale, which was to have been the ba-
sis of the work, is taken from his Complete Fairy Stories,
and like so many of this genre, is almost too painful for
adult contemplation. In it, a young student is desperate
for lack of a red rose to give to the lady of his choice, and
a nightingale who loves him, sings all night pressing her
breast against a thorn, so that her dying heart's blood may
color the flower. Stark Young's text for "The Dying Night-
ingale" represents the dramatic climax of the story: the
final moments during which the bird invokes Death to "Come
with thy sweet darkness," as she willingly enters a night in
which she will "sing forever." The lines are unrhymed,
mostly containing four stresses in varying poetic meters,
and the phrase "Come, sweet Death" occurs at the beginning
of the outer sections of a three-part form. The middle sec-
tion is an inspired transfer into the first person of Wilde's

passage describing the effect of the nightingale's last faint notes on the listening natural world. "Does the white moon hear me?" she asks. "Do the river reeds carry my voice to the sea?"

Dello Joio has set this poignant text in a freely moving, arioso style in which the rhythmic pulse holds to the quarter note throughout, but variously contains three, four, five, or six beats per measure. The free flow of rhythm is counterbalanced by several tightly controlled formal elements, even as the bird's movement is constrained by the terms of her sacrifice. The first of these is the motivic germ of a perfect fourth, expressed in the rhythmic pattern of a dotted quarter and eighth note which is announced in the piano introduction and restated in inversion as the voice enters.

Example 2.1, measures 1-7. Copyright 1954, Carl Fischer, Inc.; used by permission.

The second is a pandiatonic harmonic scheme which opens in D major and proceeds to vary this tonality with passages in other aspects of D (i.e., D flat major, C sharp minor, and the Dorian mode). This aspect of the writing comes together with the third element, a three-part musical structure that coincides with the poetic one indicated above. Thus, section three entering with "Come, sweet Death" repeats its original Dorian context (see Ex. 2.1) in D flat major, with the motif transposed up to a passionate statement beginning on the chordal seventh.

Example 2.2, measures 23-24. Copyright 1954, Carl Fischer, Inc.; used by permission.

Finally, the harmony ends its restless wandering with a quiet return to the opening piano material in the original key, as the text portrays the end of the nightingale's pain in peaceful death.

Example 2.3, measures 32-37.   Copyright 1954, Carl Fischer, Inc.; used by permission.

The motivic fourth in a dotted note pattern which recurs in Example 2.3 suggests an actual component of birdsong, and the topmost line in the opening three measures state this basic interval followed by two variants thereof (see Ex. 2.1). Also reminiscent of the nightingale's cadence are the many instances of syllabic vocal setting on rapidly moving sixteenth notes, which are suggestive of gentle, bird-like twittering.

Example 2.4, measures 19-21.   Copyright 1954, Carl Fischer, Inc.; used by permission.

David Diamond (1915-)
Herman Melville (1819-1891)

David Diamond was born in Rochester, New York, a city
that has been a focal point in his life, and which he chose,
in 1964, to again make his home after many years' absence.
Diamond's parents were Austrian-Jewish immigrants, his
father a carpenter by profession, and his mother a former
dressmaker with a deeply-rooted love of music and theater.
Young David early began to exhibit his mother's musical
propensities. By the age of seven he had taught himself
to play the violin on a borrowed instrument, and had begun
to write down original melodies in an ingenious notation of
his own devising.

Unfortunately, there were no family funds to assure
the growth of this precocious talent, and David Diamond's
musical training was to be gained in years of struggle dur-
ing which his studies were supported entirely by scholar-
ship. In 1925, his family was forced to leave Rochester for
financial reasons and go to live with relatives in Cleveland.
Here he attracted the attention of a Swiss musician named
André de Ribaupierre, and was enabled to attend the Cleve-
land Institute of Music from 1927 to 1929. When the family
returned to Rochester in 1930, Diamond became a scholarship
student at the Eastman School and remained there for four
years, studying composition with Bernard Rogers, and play-
ing second violin in the conservatory orchestra.

His next mentor in composition was Roger Sessions,
with whom he studied at the New Music School and Dalcroze
Institute in New York. Once again there was scholarship
aid, but living was now a problem as well, and Diamond held
a series of menial jobs to earn expense money. In 1935, his
work began to be recognized, and he won the $2500 Paul
Whiteman award for his Sinfonietta, based on a Carl Sand-
burg poem. The same summer, he received a fellowship to
the MacDowell Colony in Peterborough, New Hampshire, and
in 1936 was elated when e.e. cummings accepted him as the
composer of music for his ballet Tom.

The commission proved important not only for itself
(the ballet was never actually produced) but because its fi-
nancial backers sent Diamond to Paris to collaborate with
Leonid Massine, the choreographer. Having been already

David Diamond
(Photo: J. Petticrew)

attracted to contemporary French musical influences, the young composer was now excited to find himself in their midst, and returned to France a second and third summer to study at Fontainebleau with Nadia Boulanger. Germany's declaration of war against France brought an end to this fruitful and pleasant period. Back in the United States, the struggle for acceptance began again, and again the forces were mustered by which America supported her promising composers in mid-century. Diamond was given successively a residence at the Yaddo estate in Saratoga, a renewal of his 1938 Guggenheim fellowship, the cash prize of the Prix de Rome (war preventing residence in Italy), and finally the National Academy of Arts and Letters grant.

The citation that accompanied the National Academy's 1944 grant mentioned "the high quality of [Diamond's] achievement as demonstrated in orchestral works, chamber music, and songs."[15] Although this was relatively early in his career, solo song did indeed prove to be a major genre in Diamond's prolific catalog, and he published forty settings between 1940 and the early fifties. This same period also saw him engaged in composing music for theatrical productions, which included three film scores and incidental music to Shakespeare's Tempest and Romeo and Juliet as well as Tennessee Williams' The Rose Tattoo.

At the age of thirty-five, David Diamond began a series of sporadic teaching appointments in Europe and the United States with a year spent at the Metropolitan School of Music in New York City. In 1951, he went to Europe as a Fulbright professor, eventually settling in Florence where he remained until 1965 except for brief appointments at the University of Buffalo in 1961 and 1963. He chaired the composition department at the Manhattan School of Music from 1965 to 1967, was visiting professor at the University of Colorado in Boulder in 1970, and a faculty member at Juilliard in 1973. Between the last two positions, he returned to Italy as composer-in-residence at the American Academy which had awarded him the Prix de Rome thirty years earlier.

As Slee professor of music at the University of Buffalo in 1961, Diamond delivered a series of three lectures entitled "Integrity and Integration in Contemporary Music," "The Babel of Twentieth Century Music," and "Beethoven and the Twentieth Century." In the first of these, discussing contemporary aspects of the American scene, he remarked that "nowhere else in the Western World have so many disparate cultural influences worked advantageously and productively,"[16] and described the merging of contributions from Europe, Africa, China, Japan, and Latin America with folk, jazz, and popular theater music in the melting pot of our national style. Three years later, the articulate composer aired his views in the Music Journal on the future of a contemporary music which seemed to many, in 1964, to be floundering for direction. "It is my strong feeling," he said, "that a romantically inspired contemporary music, tempered by reinvigorated classical technical formulas, is the way out of the present period of creative chaos in music.... A composer's greatness," he added, "is gauged by how he enlarges and extends spiritual communication between himself and humanity."[17]

One of the areas of David Diamond's most successful communication with humanity has certainly been that of the art song. Hans Nathan observed in A History of Song that Diamond "has cultivated the art song more consistently than any other American composer of his standing" and that "among the variety of forms that he commands, his songs represent his finest achievements."[18] His ability to set a wide variety of literary styles is most striking, as William Flanagan, a song composer himself, remarked in 1952: "Diamond's choice of textual material knows practically no limit in diversity."[19] About half the writers set by David Diamond were American, and he has this to say of the selection process:

> My friendship with the poet e.e. cummings ... produced a full flowering of my taste in choosing texts for settings; also my friendship with Carson McCullers and Katherine Anne Porter, miraculous women, alas, gone forever. My love of Melville stems from my adolescent years reading his poetry--then Moby Dick and Billy Budd and eventually everything else between 1939-1951. Melville to me is like reading Job or Isaiah. But he is also a kind of Great Father, Great Lover, Great Prophet, Great Martyr. He nourishes me when I am most depressed.[20]

It is easy to understand why David Diamond, who had known years of physical and psychological struggle toward recognition as an artist, would identify with and draw strength from Herman Melville, whose rightful place in American literature was denied him until twenty years after his death. Melville was born in New York City, to parents whose families had old roots in America. His mother's ancestors, the Gansevoorts, were linked to the greatest Dutch patroon families who had settled New York, and his father had traced his line even farther back to Scottish Renaissance courtiers and a Queen of Hungary. Melville's early childhood was spent in luxury, but his father's business reverses and subsequent death in 1832 made "poor relations" of his whole family, who moved to Albany and became dependent on the care of the Gansevoorts. Herman left school at twelve, holding various jobs (including a year of teaching) until 1839, when he began the five years at sea which would form the basis of much of his writing and life experience.

In 1846, with two successful novels, Typee and Omoo, behind him, he married Elizabeth Shaw, daughter of the Chief Justice of Massachusetts, and bought a house in New York City, to which he brought not only his bride, but his mother, four sisters, and his younger brother Allan and wife as well. Success, however, was to prove short-lived. Subsequent novels gained only intermittent approval of critics and the public, and in 1850 he moved his family to a farm at Pittsfield, Massachusetts, where he continued work on Moby Dick despite his publisher's refusal to advance him money. Melville's responsibilities were growing (by 1855 he had two sons and two daughters), and he now began a new career as short-story writer for Harper's and Putnam's, the Putnam's stories being published eventually as The Piazza Tales.

In 1856, Melville was forced to sell part of his farm and, close to a nervous collapse, was sent by his father-in-law on an extensive trip to Europe and the Levant. These travels, during which he kept a journal, also nourished his later work, although on his return, he did not write for several years.

The decade of the 1860s proved to be the most difficult of all for Herman Melville and his family. Devastated by the collapse of his literary career and the repeated failures of his attempts to find a government job in Washington, Melville's behavior suffered to the extent that his wife began to fear for his sanity. A turning point was reached in 1866 when the writer obtained a political job as deputy customs inspector in New York City, and after the suicide of their son, Malcolm, in 1867, Melville and his wife drew closer together. He remained in his position as customs inspector for the next twenty years, when a series of legacies finally enabled him to retire and spend all his time writing.

During the last thirty years of Melville's life, he produced a considerable body of poetry, most of which attracted very little attention at the time. Battle-Pieces (see Chapter I, p. 53) was published in 1866 by Harper's and by 1868 had sold only 486 copies. "Clarel," a long, philosophical poem which has been characterized as one of America's most thoughtful contributions to the conflict between religious faith and Darwinian skepticism,[21] was published with funds designated in a specific bequest from his dying uncle Peter Gansevoort. The majority of the poems written after "Clarel" were collected into two volumes and printed privately by Melville through the Caxton Press shortly before his death in 1891. At about this same time, something like a Herman Melville "revival" was beginning to get underway, particularly in England, but it ended with his death. The works remained in relative obscurity until the centennial of his birth in 1919, which occasioned a wave of new scholarship and a reevaluation of his many long-neglected masterpieces.

Although largely self-educated, Herman Melville possessed an unusually reflective and philosophical mind, and spent a lifetime trying to construct a moral and metaphysical system which would account for the inequities and ambiguities of human experience. His preoccupations with the ultimate problems of life, death, and the vagaries of Destiny pervade his poetry as well as his prose works, and find a perfect musical counterpart in David Diamond's settings. Reflecting the fact that Diamond's performing instrument was the violin, these settings have accompaniments which are for the most part contrapuntally conceived and show little exploitation of pianistic figuration. This affords prominence to the "great and tender texts"[22] (the phrase is the composer's) and to the vocal line which carries them in a highly sensitive prosodic rendering that clings to the original poetic accents.

"Epitaph,"[23] composed in 1945, sets another of Melville's Battle-Pieces, this one included in a group designated as "Verses Inscriptive and Memorial." Its original title, printed by Diamond as a subtitle, was "On the Grave of a Young Cavalry Officer Killed in the Valley of Virginia," and the mood of the poem forms a peaceful contrast to the bloody memories of "Shiloh" (see p. 54). In five skillfully concentrated lines, a swift portrait is painted of a young man gifted in his "beauty ... manners ... and friends," and who

possessed "gold--yet a mind not unenriched." The final
line which describes "his happier fortune in this mound" is
surprising in the face of Melville's avowed and uncomfortable
agnosticism, and of his many Battle-Pieces which deplored
war's waste of youthful promise. The line, therefore, may
represent a mellowing toward hope that is observable in some
of the poetry of the later years or it may also be seen as an
almost intolerably ironic view of "heroic" death in battle.

Diamond chooses to interpret the "inscription" positive-
ly and creates an atmosphere of serenity not unlike that of
Hugo Wolf's "Anakreon's Grab" in which another noble life
and well-deserved rest in death are commemorated. A cor-
responding quality of musical "tenderness" is achieved
through the quiet simplicity of a transparent texture, steady
rhythmic flow in quarter notes (predominantly 3/4), and an
unassuming but poignant melodic motif stated in the opening
piano phrase.

Example 2.5, measures 1-4. Copyright 1946, Associated Mu-
sic Publishers, Inc.; used by permission.

This motif is carried into the vocal contour to set "with
manners sweet," and also functions structurally in the ac-
companiment during the singer's rests. (See Ex. 2.6,
page 78.)

The effect of these carefully calculated vocal pauses
in this and other Diamond settings is twofold: they at once
afford added emphasis to the words thus highlighted in tem-
poral space, and at the same time suggest an imaginatively
inflected verbal reading of the text. Also notice in Exam-
ple 2.6 the many chordal sonorities containing open fifths

with man-ners sweet,   and friends-

Example 2.6, measures 5-9. Copyright 1956, Associated Music Publishers, Inc.; used by permission.

and fourths which tend to emphasize the lightness of texture and its analogy to the undeveloped life cut off before its flowering.

"Monody" comes from Melville's Timoleon, one of the poetry collections he had printed in 1891, in an edition limited to twenty-five copies. The book was dedicated to Elihu Vedder, an American artist whom Melville admired but had never met, and the poem "Monody" is widely believed to refer to another creative artist admired by Melville: the writer Nathaniel Hawthorne. Melville and Hawthorne had begun a friendship around 1850 when Melville had reviewed Hawthorne's Mosses From an Old Manse for Literary World in most favorable terms. "Monody" is a lament for a beloved friend from whom the protagonist has become "estranged in life," and literary historians point out that no estrangement occurred in this case except that of distance and intervening events in the writers' lives. It is also true, however, that by the time of the Melville "revival," many valuable biographical materials had been lost, including Hawthorne's letters, which had been burned by Melville himself. An undocumented estrangement therefore remains a possibility.

Though the genesis of the poem is in doubt, its artistry is not, and it falls into that category of "elegiac subjects" which, as Hans Nathan points out, are particularly suited to Diamond's idiom: those subjects, that is, that "speak of a valuable person or a moral quality that has disappeared but is remembered with sad affection."[24] "Monody"[25] was also composed in 1945 and together with "Epitaph" seems to have captured the particular devotion of the American public. In speaking of his Melville songs, Diamond says "I am always being written to about them, especially 'Epitaph' and 'Monody.'"[26]

"Monody" shows the same contrapuntal interweaving of voices, pauses between poetic phrases, and meticulous attention to prosodic detail as "Epitaph," and adds an arching lyrical voice line whose convincing contours follow the rise and fall of passionate grief and wintry resignation. The harmonic language is tonal but highly colored with Diamond's frequent chords of the seventh and ninth, and a brief excursion into chromatic alterations occurs for the setting of the crucially painful line "And now for death to set his seal." Neither "Monody" nor "Epitaph" exhibits much use of "word-painting" or descriptive musical device. The composer concentrates rather on the overall mood of the text and with a broad palette enlists all stylistic elements in its service.

"A Portrait,"[27] set by Diamond in 1946, is rather different. This setting is of another poem from Timoleon, originally titled "The Marchioness of Brinvilliers," and describes a painting viewed during Melville's travels in the late 1850s. The lady in question, though obviously beautiful, was also ruthless and amoral, and the painter's task, according to the custom of the time, seems to have been to record the surface while merely suggesting what lay beneath. The poet, describing the painter's art, reflects this in such ambiguous verbal constructions as "Light and shade did weave," "mystery starred in open skies," and "her fathomless mild eyes"--all of which recalls the lethal sweetness of the Gioconda smile.

Irony is a state of mind difficult to depict in musical terms, and if he recognized it, David Diamond chose to ignore it in favor of a more straightforward interpretation of the text. The result is a lively piano figuration inspired by the opening line ("He toned the sprightly beam of morning"), which pervades the entire song, while a lyric vocal line in longer note values represents the gentler aspects of the lady's nature. (See Ex. 2.7, page 80.) The many metric alterations between 5/8 and 6/8 also give a sense of "light and shade," i.e., the fluctuations of her personality, and the move from B flat major up to D major for the melodic outline of "Brightness" seems a direct response to the verbal

With twi - light   meek   of ten-der   eve,

Example 2.7, measures 4-9. Copyright 1947, Elkan-Vogel
Co.; used by permission of the publisher.

call for an increase in musical brilliance, through the addi-
tion of upper overtones. (See Ex. 2.8 below and page 81.)

Diamond's versatility as a musical dramatist is evident
in the juxtaposition of the graceful, ornamental, and some-
what artificial style of "A Portrait" with the rugged, folk-
ballad milieu of his "Billy in the Darbies."[28] This song,
written in 1944, was the earliest of his Melville settings,
and like all the others is faithful in every syllable to the
original poetic text. The poem is from the middle 1880s,

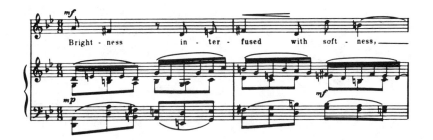

Example 2.8, measures 10-14. Copyright 1947, Elkan-Vogel Co.; used by permission of the publisher.

and is based on the hanging of an American seaman in 1842, which Melville transposed to a British warship in 1797. An expanded and re-expanded head-note to the poem eventually became Billy Budd, Sailor, a story left almost finished at his death, in which Melville examined for the last time the conflicting claims of authority and individuality.

"Billy in the Darbies" shows the young sailor, condemned to die for an act of violence against his nature, awaiting his imminent death, and imagining the events and aftermath of the hanging. The pervading folk atmosphere of the setting is established immediately by the drone-bass of the accompaniment figure's tonic-dominant emphasis, by the modal (Dorian from G) scale, and by the meter and accent pattern drawn from the British sailor's "hornpipe."

Example 2.9, measures 1-6. Copyright 1946, Elkan-Vogel
Co.; used by permission of the publisher.

As the ballad progresses, the vocal line becomes in-
creasingly agitated with accented syncopations and a rising
tessitura. A pianistic drum roll depicts the call to grog
that a dead Billy will not hear (cf. "Dirge," p. 48) and a
pair of octave leaps is his last outcry before resigning him-
self to sleep, and dreams of "oozy weeds."

Example 2.10, measures 86-91. Copyright 1946, Elkan-Vogel
Co.; used by permission of the publisher.

Example 2.10 climaxes one of the song's most vivid passages (in the contrasting mixolydian mode transposed to F) and the reader is referred to Hans Nathan's article for an extended quotation and treatment of this section.[29]

Vincent Persichetti (1915-)
Wallace Stevens (1872-1955)
Emily Dickinson (1830-1886)

Vincent Persichetti's contributions to the musical life of twentieth century America are of staggering proportions. As well as the composer of a large catalog of works in almost all media, Persichetti has also been a virtuoso performer, a teacher, administrator, governmental advisor, editor, reviewer, and writer of important musical texts. Still living in Philadelphia, which was his birthplace and the center of much of his activity, the composer continues to function in many of these capacities.

Like many of the most creative musical talents, Persichetti was a child prodigy. At five, he began to study piano and organ, and soon added double bass, tuba, theory, and composition. His early musical education was materially aided by a fantastic sight-reading ability at the keyboard which enabled him to play at the piano all the scores heard at weekly concerts of the Philadelphia Orchestra. In later years, this ability, coupled with an insatiable musical curiosity, would lead him to play through the vast majority of the twentieth century vocal and chamber music repertoire.

In 1935, he earned a Bachelor of Music degree at Combs College, and immediately thereafter was appointed to head its theory department, while simultaneously studying conducting under Fritz Reiner at the Curtis Institute, piano with Olga Samaroff at the Philadelphia Conservatory, and composition with a number of mentors including Paul Nordoff (see Volume II, Chapter 4). Six years later, he became head of the Philadelphia Conservatory's theory and composition department, and also married a pianist and teacher named Dorothea Flanagan. The composer recalls that "when Dorothea and I were married in 1941, we absolutely had no money,

Vincent Persichetti
(Photo: William Thompson; courtesy of Elkan-Vogel, Inc.)

but ... for my birthday, she came in with this big package
for me [of] the Sandburg Lincoln books--all of the volumes.
That cost ... a fortune for us in those days and I still don't
know how she did it," he adds, in appreciative admiration.[30]

A daughter and son were born to the Persichettis in
1944 and 1946, respectively. In 1947, the composer joined
the faculty of the Juilliard School of Music, becoming chair-
man of the Composition Department in 1963. He still holds
this position, as well as that of Director of Publications for
Elkan-Vogel, Inc. (a division of Theodore Presser Co.),

which he assumed in 1952. The author had the privilege of observing Vincent Perischetti both in the role of an exciting teacher/performer during his visit to the Duke University campus in the middle sixties, and as a discerning, articulate music editor during an interview in his high-ceilinged, manuscript-laden office in Bryn Mawr, Pennsylvania, in 1975. In all situations, his is an impressive musical presence which has drawn the accolades of such colleagues as William Schumann ("Persichetti is a teacher with remarkable insights")[31] and Virgil Thomson ("Persichetti is a marvelous pianist and his piano writing is suited to the instrument better than almost anything written in America today").[32]

The composer's writings on musical subjects have indeed constituted almost a mini-career of their own and have kept him at the vital center of the contemporary American musical scene. In the forties, he reported and commented on performances of twentieth-century works in his city of Philadelphia for the League of Composers' journal Modern Music and for the "Current Chronicle" section of the Musical Quarterly. Through the fifties, he wrote book and record reviews for Musical Quarterly, and during the same period, contributed occasional reviews of new music publications to Notes, the journal of the Music Library Association. All of these articles, which are of varying lengths, are written in a uniquely attractive style and are full of cogent observations clearly stemming from a highly-trained, objective, compassionate, and creative musical mind. These same characteristics were brought to bear on essays concerning twentieth-century choral and orchestral music in two books edited by Robert Hines,[33] and in a biography of William Schumann of which Persichetti was co-author.[34] But the crowning literary achievement of all has certainly been his Twentieth Century Harmony, Creative Aspects and Practice, which was published in 1961. Herein the composer brilliantly accomplished his announced objective of "defining the harmonic practice of the first half of the twentieth century and making it available to the student and young composer."[35] He did so in a work that is far from standard textbook fare and which William Schumann has characterized as containing "penetrating insights into the materials of music" in writing which has "an élan--a dash that even includes--shades of e.e. cummings--the invention of words."[36]

Persichetti was uniquely qualified to define the param-

eters of twentieth-century harmonic practice, given his life-
long approach to his own composition. He sees himself as
an "amalgamator"[37]--one who has drawn from many diverse
elements of contemporary musical practice, yet without aban-
doning what was useful and meaningful in traditional tech-
niques. Persichetti's opus 1 (a serenade for wind instru-
ments) was written in 1929, but it was not until sixteen
years later that he made his first essay into vocal music,
with his e.e. cummings songs. The composer explains that
although he had always read poetry and had great love and
respect for the medium, he hesitated to set it to music, feel-
ing that a good poem was already complete in itself. Finally,
he realized that "poetry is, in reality a distilled concept full
of implications that you can interpret many ways [and] my
composition is a statement of one of the implications of the
poem."[38]

Of Persichetti's eleven opus numbers devoted to solo
songs, six are settings of American poets, and of these only
the Wallace Stevens and Emily Dickinson settings have been
published. The e.e. cummings, Sara Teasdale, Carl Sand-
burg, and Robert Frost songs remain in manuscript, and
Persichetti has not pursued their publication because of the
commonly encountered problem of clearing copyrights on the
poetry. There is some feeling on the part of the composer
that his songs have not been afforded the same public ac-
ceptance as his instrumental music ("People think they've
heard my songs when they haven't").[39] He also is of the
opinion that "voice teachers pay lip service to American
songs but teach few, maybe because they're afraid of the
medium."[40]

Persichetti's major solo vocal work in size and scope is
the song cycle Harmonium (1951) based on poetry by Wallace
Stevens, whose writing embodied the composer's own qualities
of sensuous elegance, and deep feeling held under classical
restraint. Stevens, too, was from Pennsylvania, having been
born in Reading, which was both an industrial and a provin-
cial city, being surrounded by woods and farmland. It was,
however, a city not without culture, and its traditions, ex-
tending back to William Penn, included a love of music and
pageantry. Stevens' father was a lawyer by profession who
contributed poetry to the Reading Times and who was inter-
ested in both the intellectual and aesthetic development of
his son. Wallace Stevens' own literary talents began to surface

in high school where he won prizes for oration and essay writing. Entering Harvard in 1897, he began to publish both prose and poetry in the Harvard Advocate during his sophomore year, and had become its president before leaving in 1900. Witter Bynner and Arthur Davison Ficke (see Volume II, Chapter 2), who would also become notable poets, were friends of Stevens' undergraduate years. It was a period of general sterility in English and American poetry, which would soon be revitalized by the growing influence of the French Symbolists, and the rediscovery of Whitman and Dickinson (see Introduction to Volume II).

Stevens spent the year after graduation as a reporter for the New York Herald Tribune. Having by then decided against the life of a professional writer, he attended New York University Law School and adopted the parental pattern of legal vocation/poetic avocation. He married in 1909, and in 1916 moved with his wife to Hartford, Connecticut, where he entered the legal department of the Hartford Accident and Indemnity Company. The Stevens' only child, Holly, was born in 1924, and ten years later the poet followed in Charles Ives' footsteps by becoming the vice-president of the insurance company, a position he held until the end of his life. It was not an unconflicted combination of professions, and there were a number of "dry" years during which Stevens wrote little or not at all. In retrospect, these emerged as periods of gestation which preceded changes in the direction of his poetic thought, and his life as a whole yielded a substantial body of work.

The first public recognition of Wallace Stevens' writing came from Harriet Monroe's publication of Phases (four poems) in the November, 1914, edition of Poetry magazine.[41] This was a "war" issue which had been about to go to press, but which was torn apart to make room for the talented unknown. In late 1915, Poetry also awarded Stevens a prize of one hundred dollars for his one-act play in free verse, Three Travellers Watch a Sunrise. This play was produced five years later at the Provincetown Theater in New York City, and another one-act play, Carlos Among the Candles, received productions in both Milwaukee and New York. The writer had, however, been in no hurry to publish a book of poetry which, in his frequently quoted phrase, he held to be "a damned serious affair." The first such volume, therefore, which was Harmonium, did not appear until 1923, in the writer's forty-fourth year (a second edition following eight years later).

In fact, Stevens had waited none too long, for neither the public nor the critics were as yet totally prepared for the form or the content of Harmonium. Early criticism characterized him as an "intellectual poet," as a "poet's poet," and the final pejorative, as a "critic's poet," who had never sought, and was unlikely to gain, a popular audience. The passage of time, however, has brought a wider acceptance and a clearer perspective on Stevens' work. Robert Buttel, among others, has come to see him as "a direct descendant of the Romantic poets in his unceasing exploration of the relationships between the inner, subjective, human point of view and outer, objective nature--or as he so often stated it himself, between 'imagination and reality.'"[42] Yet, despite this philosophical preoccupation, Stevens' poetic world is full of light, color, and sound, and Babette Deutsch holds that "none of Stevens' juniors has celebrated being with a like sensual precision, sparkle, and energy."[43]

The contemporary reader, struck by Stevens' "bold, bizarre, and immaculate phrasing, imagistic concreteness, (and) incisive prosody,"[44] can also identify with the poet's emphasis on the "process of seeing the world, (and his) exercises in creative perception,"[45] particularly in the light of suggestions by mid-twentieth century quantum physicists concerning the possible influence of the observer on observed systems. The strong appeal of Wallace Stevens' thought and poetic language to Vincent Persichetti is evidenced by the composer's statement in 1973: "I guess I really got into working for the voice through Wallace Stevens. My song cycle Harmonium is based on a book of poetry of his by the same title. I wrote him for permission to use his poetry, and he replied that his permission was not needed-- for me to go ahead."[46]

Although the affinity of a composer for a poet cannot be successfully predicted before the event, ex post facto examination reveals several interesting parallels between Stevens and Persichetti. One thinks, for example, of the poet's debt to the philosophy and techniques of the French Symbolists and compares it to Persichetti's finding influences in his own work from Honegger and Stravinsky,[47] both purveyors of the French musical traditions. Equally striking

are the similarities between two quotations which describe
the eclectic orientations of these two creative artists. Ste-
vens, says Joseph Riddel, is "a traditional poet, yet experi-
mental; an imagist, but also a symbolist; a romantic, but
disconcertingly impersonal."[48] Robert Evett counters with
"Persichetti enjoys the almost unique distinction of never
having belonged to the Right or the Left, or for that mat-
ter, the Middle of the Road."[49] Not surprisingly, Stevens,
whose musical preoccupations speak clearly in the very title
of Harmonium, liked Persichetti's settings very much. The
two men had, indeed, planned to collaborate on an opera
based on Three Travellers Watch a Sunrise, but to Persi-
chetti's great sorrow, Stevens' death put an end to the
project. "I was very angry at him," the composer admitted
to this writer, and added ruefully, "I had lunch with his
daughter, but it wasn't the same thing."[50]

Persichetti's monumental cycle[51] sets twenty poems se-
lected from Stevens' Harmonium. There are no narrative
connections between them, but a number of recurring themes
lend cohesiveness to the set, in the manner of Copland's
Twelve Poems of Emily Dickinson. Number one, "Valley Can-
dle," can be seen as a succinct statement of Stevens' contin-
ual speculation on the relationship between the individual
consciousness (the candle and remembered image thereof) and
its environment (the valley, the night, and the wind).
Persichetti's angular, leaping vocal line serves a word-
painting function for the phrases "immense valley" and "huge
night." Interestingly, his leaps enlarge in the second poetic
triplet, where the candle's image is seen instead of the thing
itself, thus suggesting the limitless capabilities of the imagi-
nation.

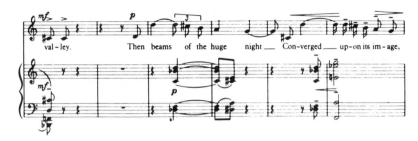

Example 2.11, measures 21-31. Copyright 1959, Elkan-Vogel Co., Inc.; used by permission of the publisher.

Besides the alternation of scale passages and large interval leaps in the voice line, another musical style characteristic which will pervade the cycle appears in "Valley Candle." This, as seen in the introductory measures for piano, is the polytonal implication of much of the harmony, an appropriate musical symbol for the conflict between "imagination and reality" which much of the poetry delineates.

Example 2.12, measures 1-5. Copyright 1959, Elkan-Vogel Co., Inc.; used by permission of the publisher.

The second song sets "The Place of the Solitaires," which the poet indicates should be "a place of perpetual undulation." There are several different definitions of the word "solitaires," both in English and in French, a language with which Stevens felt very much at home and to which he often alludes in his poetry. All of them point toward a poetic meaning based on the primacy of movement ("motion," "noise," "thought") in the constitution of our universe, a movement which is incomplete without the lone consciousness that perceives, and that is perhaps, in some mysterious way, the source of the "manifold continuation." Since the second poem is clearly tied to the theme of "Valley Candle," Persichetti chooses to relate the musical material also, and brings back both the angular intervallic leaps and the unisons that often precede them, now expanded in chant-like repetition. A new device, that of a "perpetual motion" figure in the accompaniment, is also introduced, which at once grows out of the textual emphasis on movement, and also prefigures the texture of "The Snow Man," a focal point of the cycle.

Example 2.13, measures 1-6. Copyright 1959, Elkan-Vogel Co.; used by permission of the publisher.

In number three, "Theory," the poet presents the notion that human personality is tied to its physical surroundings ("One is not Duchess / A hundred yards from a carriage.") Persichetti's vocal contour now becomes more rounded, with an opening vocal phrase in consecutive fourths that will expand into the full-blown lyricism of number nineteen ("Of the Surface of Things"). The quiet, slowly moving syncopations and "white-key" chordal dissonances of the piano opening introduce an "American" sound that is frequently associated with Copland (see Ex. 2.14, page 92).

Example 2.14, measures 1-11. Copyright 1959, Elkan-Vogel
Co.; used by permission of the publisher.

The song ends in quite a different mood, however, as the
dynamic profile of the last line adds an intensity in the mu-
sical setting which is lacking in the poem.

Example 2.15, measures 37-47. Copyright 1959, Elkan-Vogel
Co.; used by permission of the publisher.

Number four sets "Lunar Paraphrase," one of three poems in Harmonium that were based on the Lettres d'un Soldat of Eugène Emmanuel Lemercier. He was a young painter who had been lost in action on the Western Front in 1915, and these records of war, as seen through an artist's eye, took on considerable importance to Stevens. Nine poems of this series had originally appeared in Poetry magazine in 1918, on which occasion fragments of the original letters were published as epigraphs. The fragment which preceded "Lunar Paraphrase" described a night march in late November when the moonlight fell tenderly on bare branches, ruined houses, and suffering soldiers ("le pathé-tique de calvaires"). Stevens takes over most of this scene into the poem, but uses Jesus as a universal symbol for suf-fering, thus making this a "war" poem only by association with its origins.

The restrained compassion of these powerful lines is well-matched by Persichetti's setting, a twentieth-century recitative with a strong emotive contour. The composer chooses to repeat the poem's first line, in a narrow-range hypnotic chant which is organized by softly insistent rhyth-mic impulses from the piano.

Example 2.16, measures 1-5. Copyright 1959, Elkan-Vogel Co.; used by permission of the publisher.

93

With the establishment of an ominous C sharp minor, the scale passages which describe the figures of Jesus and Mary begin an episode of growing intensity, culminating in the desperate reiteration of the major sixth interval.

Example 2.17, measures 11-16. Copyright 1959, Elkan-Vogel Co.; used by permission of the publisher.

The song ends as it begins, with a chant-like repetition of the dominant phrase ("The moon is the mother of pathos and pity"). This time it deserts the unison to conclude with a descending diminished fifth, whose coldness gives the lie to the moonlight's illusory comfort.

94

The fifth setting, "Death of a Soldier," is also based on the Lemercier Lettres, and the poem is generally conceded to be one of the strongest in the Harmonium. The epigraph (translated) had read "The death of a soldier is close to natural things." Stevens equates this occurrence with the expected passing of life forms in autumn, the season of death, and contrasts the unmarked fall of the soldier with the ceremonial passage of a "three days personage" who "imposes his separation." The poem's structure is carefully chiseled into four diminishing tercets in which, as one critic has graphically suggested, "each end-stopped stanza is like a tombstone."[52]

Persichetti's setting is as strong and economical as Stevens' verses. For the most part, it alternates lines of text sung over sustained chords, with incisive comments from the piano, whose dotted figures and accents carry an ironic reference to martial rhythms.

Example 2.18, measures 1-4. Copyright 1959, Elkan-Vogel Co.; used by permission of the publisher.

Two instances of word-painting are absorbed into the starkness, as "the soldier falls" takes a descending arpeggio to

95

the lowest note of the song, and "calling for pomp" is given a pseudo trumpet-call figure in a brilliant upper register.

Example 2.19, measures 11-12. Copyright 1959, Elkan-Vogel Co.; used by permission of the publisher.

Unifying devices in the song are the melodic interval of the perfect fourth, which is seminal to the whole cycle, and a chordal figure of two minor triads in the second inversion, usually presented as a sixteenth followed by a dotted eighth note, with an accent over the first (see Examples 2.18 and 2.19). At the end of the song, after the text has philosophically concluded that life goes on ("The clouds go, nevertheless, / In their direction"), the sudden, brutal reiteration of this chordal figure carries a reminder of individual loss.

Example 2.20, measures 23-24. Copyright 1959, Elkan-Vogel Co.; used by permission of the publisher.

In number six, "The Wind Shifts," Stevens has once again used a favorite symbol, the wind, to stand for the consciousness of human beings who, in this instance, are the old, the disillusioned, and the defeated. Persichetti employs stepwise, largely chromatic triplets to portray the subtle movements and gradations of thought.

Example 2.21, measures 4-11. Copyright 1959, Elkan-Vogel Co.; used by permission of the publisher.

He also brings in some of his most expansive piano writing in instrumental interludes which suggest the successive emotions of tenderness, passion, and desperation implied by the text. All of this contracts at the end to a single, repeated vocal note over sparse piano figures, signifying the depressed silence of a "human ... who does not care."

Example 2.22, measures 74-82. Copyright 1959, Elkan-Vogel
Co.; used by permission of the publisher.

Stevens' small gem of a poem called "Tea" appears as
number ten of the cycle, and reminds us of the poet's abil-
ity to celebrate the visual. As he contrasts the colorless-
ness of the outside world ("Shrivelled in frost") with the
indoor warmth and exoticism of "shining pillows" in "sea-
shades and sky-shades," the poet conjures the Orientalized-
French atmosphere of a Matisse painting. He also reminds
us, as Deutsch has pointed out, that blue is a color which
predominates in his scenery, and is often "associated ...
with the adventures of the mind."53

Persichetti's appealing setting of "Tea" creates a mu-
sically analogous atmosphere of cozy intimacy with its trans-
parent texture and low dynamic level. The opening vocal
line and accompaniment figures carry an echo of the amuse-
ment "park," remembered from crowded summer days, while
the "jazzy" added sixths and seconds of the piano's right-
hand chords lend a sophisticated, urban flavor.

Example 2.23, measures 1-12. Copyright 1959, Elkan-Vogel
Co.; used by permission of the publisher.

For the setting of the last line, "Like umbrellas in
Java," Persichetti moves to a melisma in the exotic (in this
context) key of C sharp major. In the piano postlude,
reality, in the form of C major, gradually regains the upper
hand, although the penultimate measure includes a single C
sharp as a remaining trace of the fantasy.

Example 2.24, measures 62-73. Copyright 1959, Elkan-Vogel
Co.; used by permission of the publisher.

"The Snow Man" of number eleven is a prime example
of Stevens' many "mind of winter" poems in which his other

preoccupation (with summer and the South) gives way to the frozen bleakness of the North. These verses are also cast in the typically simple diction and flexible, unrhymed tercets characteristic of much of the poet's work, and all five stanzas constitute a single, complex sentence. Although on the surface the wintry scene seems equivalent to a climate of negation, many critics see the figure of the "Snow Man" as an affirmation of the role of the poet, who must summon the courage to confront primary, unadorned reality and to see "nothing that is not there and the nothing that is."

The composer's setting uses a filigree of crystalline, unpedalled pianistic scales to create most successfully an aural context of icy cold.

Example 2.25, measures 1-5. Copyright 1959, Elkan-Vogel Co.; used by permission of the publisher.

The vocal line frequently imitates these scale passages at a slower rhythm (see measures 4-5, Ex. 2.25), but also incorporates some jagged, accented leaps in a high tessitura to suggest the rough outlines of the ice-laden trees. (See Ex. 2.26, page 101.) The scales stop for a few phrases as the "listener ... listens in the snow" to the wind "That is blowing in the same bare place." They resume in the piano postlude, which takes on a circular, never-ending aspect

100

Example 2.26, measures 12-17. Copyright 1959, Elkan-Vogel Co.; used by permission of the publisher.

from the direction of the figures, and from the unresolved, polytonal overlap of the final measure.

Example 2.27, measures 45-50. Copyright 1959, Elkan-Vogel Co.; used by permission of the publisher.

One of the most haunting moments of the cycle is the setting of "Infanta Marina," number fourteen, which Persichetti transcribed for viola and piano in 1960 as his opus 83.[54] This poem is a prime example of a Stevens tropical land-and-seascape, complete with sand, sails, and palm trees, as well as a mysterious, fascinating creature (the "Infanta") who has dominion over the magical kingdom. The rich visual images of the text are well matched by Persichetti's rapidly shifting harmonic color, and the reader is recommended to Robert Evett's analysis of the piano introduction and its implications of an E tonality.[55] The last phrase of the song, in fact, fulfills all the originally suggested pandiatonic elements of E, with the repeated F and final vocal interval on "sound" deriving from the Phrygian mode, while the accompaniment G sharps establish the overlapping claims of E major. Notice also the added sixth (C sharp) of the last chord, which contributes still another shade of warmth to an already lush harmonic palette.

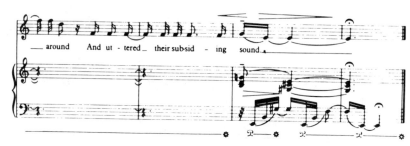

Example 2.28, measures 31-34. Copyright 1959, Elkan-Vogel Co.; used by permission of the publisher.

"Of the Surface of Things," number nineteen, sets a poem in which seemingly Romantic images clothe the contemporary concept that the poet's true reality can be drawn only from the evidence of his own perceptions. Therefore, "the gold tree is blue" (with blue once again standing for the processes of the mind) and the moon's true existence is in "the folds of the [singer's] cloak," that is, in his own individual picture of his environment. Persichetti skillfully captures the duality of mood between the thought and language of this poem. In a flowing, sustained 6/4 meter, he lets the previously mentioned germ phrase of number three flower into a lyrical line of melting contours, then structures this line as a tightly controlled canon at the unison between the right-hand of the accompaniment, and the voice, which follows it one and a half measures later.

Example 2.29, measures 1-6. Copyright 1959, Elkan-Vogel Co.; used by permission of the publisher.

"Thirteen Ways of Looking at a Blackbird" completes the cycle and is like an apotheosis of the settings that have preceded it. "In this poem," says Persichetti, "I found that all of the previous nineteen poems were related in one way or another and so I did this with all the music. I wrote Stevens about this," adds the composer, "and he replied that he had not realized this connection."[56] "Thirteen Ways" therefore includes a number of musical quotations from the rest of the cycle, particularly in the piano writing. These appear where the textual content is reminiscent of an earlier song or where it serves the musical structure. The last "way of looking" is introduced by the masterful stroke of a quotation from "Infanta Marina," which recalls a far different "evening" and a colorfully dramatic contrast to the stark black and white of the bird as it is seen for the last time on the snowy cedar limbs.

103

Example 2.30, measures 275-284. Copyright 1959, Elkan-Vogel Co.; used by permission of the publisher.

Persichetti extends the text for this lyrical conclusion with two repetitions of "the blackbird" which arch up to an expressive climax, and then fall back to a thoughtful, mid-range retreat. This final phrase might well be seen as a representation of the dichotomy between the artist's passionate perceptions, and his need to subject them to the linear processes of technical structuring.

The black - bird sat___ In the ce - dar - limbs.. The black___

bird. The black - bird.___

Example 2.31, measures 285-290. Copyright 1959, Elkan-Vogel Co.; used by permission of the publisher.

*   *   *

The poetry of Emily Dickinson has been treated earlier in this series in connection with the settings of Bacon and Copland (Volume I, Chapter 4) and John Duke (Volume II, Chapter 3). Vincent Persichetti's opus 77,[57] written six years after Harmonium, (i.e., in 1957), also sets four poems by Dickinson, one of the writers to whom he feels strongly connected, by virtue of her poetic "message."[58] The rediscovery of Walt Whitman and Emily Dickinson during the teens and twenties of this century had of course led to new publications of their poetry, and Persichetti's settings follow the Dickinson poems as they appear in the 1937 edition put out by Martha Dickinson Bianchi and Alfred Leete Hampson. The definitive Thomas H. Johnson edition, published by Harvard University Press, did not appear until 1958, the same year in which the Persichetti songs came into print, but there are only a few discrepancies in these texts from the poetic originals, and for the most part, they do not involve major changes of meaning where they occur.

The style of Persichetti's Dickinson settings is marked-
ly different from his Harmonium. In general, these songs
have a thinner texture, less complex rhythmic treatment,
and a more diatonic harmonic orientation. The piano writing
is more transparent, and the vocal lines more stepwise and
lyrical in contrast to the frequently angular and declamatory
lines of the earlier work. It is as though the composer were
attempting to capture both the childlike innocent wonder of
Dickinson's original perceptions of the world, and the bare-
bones simplicity that is another hallmark of her greatness.
The attempt was successful, and these songs have attracted
considerable attention from performers and teachers.

The four poems of this set were all written between
1859 and 1863, an exciting yet disturbing period in Emily
Dickinson's life (see Volume II, Chapter 3 for a more de-
tailed discussion). These selections, however, are mostly
sunny, affirmative poems, celebrating nature and human af-
fection, with only occasional undertones of her growing sense
of alienation from the "normal" patterns of society. Number
one, "Out of the Morning," asks "where the place called
morning lies" and "could I see it from the mountains": re-
fusing to take for granted the daily miracle by which dark-
ness is ended. Persichetti sets his vocal lines, which most-
ly descend in a questioningly doubtful inflection, against an
arpeggio figure spread widely over the keyboard, like the
verbal suggestion of a stretch to see the sunrise.

Example 2.32, measures 1-15. Copyright 1958, Elkan-Vogel, Inc.; used by permission of the publisher.

The poetic rhythm has here been quietly assimilated by the increased note values of the phrase endings ("morning," "day," etc.) and this device also serves to lend a note of wide-eyed pathos to the conclusion of each question (see Ex. 2.32).

In the second poem of the group, "I'm nobody! Who are you?", Dickinson's disdain of notoriety is couched in the images of her playful wit ("How dreary to be somebody! / How public, like a frog"). The fact is, of course, that Emily Dickinson was already "somebody" by birth and association. Her father had been one of the founders of Amherst College; her brother became a respected lawyer; and she herself "was not ... a rural poetess or spinster, but a princess."59 Nevertheless, by 1861, when the poem was written, it was already clear to Emily, now entering her thirties, that she was doomed to find little understanding among friends or members of the literary Establishment, and her gradual withdrawal from society dates from about this time.

The Johnson version of this poem differs only in the last word of the penultimate line which is "June," instead of the more euphonious but less original "day" of the 1937 edition. Rhythm is one of the most important elements that Persichetti uses to establish the mockingly humorous mood of the setting. The piano introduction seems like a cross between American folk derived and syncopated jazz figures, and this instrumental material returns between vocal phrases like a teasing refrain. (See Ex. 2.33, page 108.) The vocal line throughout most of the song shares in the syncopated patterns which suggest the darting, secretive movements of a pair of conspiratorial children (see Ex. 2.34, page 108),

Example 2.33, measures 1-10. Copyright 1958, Elkan-Vogel, Inc.; used by permission of the publisher.

Example 2.34, measures 20-24. Copyright 1958, Elkan-Vogel, Inc.; used by permission of the publisher.

but achieves telling contrast at the end with a string of accented quarter notes that describe the horrifying picture of fame (see Ex. 2.35, page 109).

"When the Hills Do" is a statement of devotion to an unknown person whom the 1937 version identifies as "O friend" (end of line seven), whereas the Johnson edition reinstates the more revealing "Sir." The latter echoes the

Example 2.35, measures 39-48. Copyright 1958, Elkan-Vogel Co.; used by permission of the publisher.

tone of the "Master" letters, which were written by Dickinson between 1858 and 1862, in deep affection and respect, but whose source of inspiration is still shrouded in mystery and conjecture.[60] Whoever the object might have been, the poem, written in 1863, is a compressed and elegant statement of unending love, for which Persichetti finds a remarkably appropriate musical framework. He writes a series of legato and expressive harmonic sequences for the piano, then has the voice join with the upper chord tone at the end of each, like a coming together in gentle embrace.

Example 2.36, measures 1-6. Copyright 1958, Elkan-Vogel Co.; used by permission of the publisher.

This method of embedding the text within the musical phrase has the effect of preserving some of the original poetic meter, whose square simplicity carries much of the strength of these verses.

"The Grass" is the fourth and longest poem, and also incorporates an interesting deviation from the original. The lines which Persichetti sets as "As lowly spices gone to sleep / Or amulets of pine" appear in the Johnson edition as "Like lowly spices, lain to sleep / Or spikenards perishing." This is yet another instance of Dickinson's courageous and exciting use of language being smoothed over by her "helpful" editors, and it is challenging to speculate on how differently Persichetti would have set the original lines had he had them available. The composer himself appears to have changed "a" hay to "the" hay in the last line of the song, but this seems likely to be a printing error in view of his usually unremitting faithfulness to the poetic text.

The poem personifies the grass, and envies the sights and sounds with which it is surrounded: butterflies, bees, sunshine, breezes, and all the accoutrements of the outdoors in a New England summer, of which the writer was so fond. Once again, in this setting, rhythmic factors are of prime importance. Persichetti uses a recurring accompanying figure of an eighth note and dotted quarter which dovetails with the opposite vocal figure to set up a peacefully rocking pattern, suggestive of a child moving aimlessly and happily through a meadow.

110

Example 2.37, measures 1-3. Copyright 1958, Elkan-Vogel
Co.; used by permission of the publisher.

Persichetti sets the first two stanzas without a break
in the vocal line, changing his 4/4 meter to 3/4 just before
the piano interlude takes over the melodic material. Again
the dramatic reference is to the world of childhood, and to
an enthusiastic story-teller who runs on and on in excite-
ment, and as suddenly stops.

Example 2.38, measures 10-15. Copyright 1958, Elkan-Vogel
Co.; used by permission of the publisher.

111

In the last verse, the composer repeats the phrase "and dream the days away," setting the repetition with a contrapuntal interweaving of voice and piano, like the texture of a mind woven through with fantasy.

Example 2.39, measures 33-38. Copyright 1958, Elkan-Vogel Co.; used by permission of the publisher.

Persichetti also adds a repetition to the last poetic line ("I wish, I wish I were the hay") and has his concluding statement of the melodic theme turn wistfully downward in the piano postlude, as though the wish were destined to denial.

Example 2.40, measures 39-44. Copyright 1958, Elkan-Vogel Co.; used by permission of the publisher.

Finally, it should be noted that Vincent Persichetti is currently in the process of finishing a one-act opera based on his setting of "The Grass" which he is calling Chicken Little. The libretto is his own, and at this writing he "has been scoring 15 hours a day [with] 300 plus pages of full score" thus far completed.[61]

NOTES

1. Bernard Wagenaar was also an important teacher of John Duke (see Volume II, Chapter 2).

2. For further discussion of the connections between Norman Dello Joio and Paul Hindemith, see a) Madeleine Goss, Modern Music-Makers (New York: Dutton, 1952), p. 437; b) Edward Downes, "The Music of Norman Dello Joio," The Musical Quarterly, XLVIII:2 (April 1962), p. 151.

3. The foregoing paragraph is based on the following article: Norman Dello Joio in "The Contemporary Music Project for Creativity in Music Education," Music Educators' Journal, LIV (March 1968), pp. 4-72.

4. Norman Dello Joio, "The Composer and the American Scene," Music Journal, XXII (March 1964), p. 100.

5. Ibid., p. 31.

6. Letter from Norman Dello Joio to the author, February 9, 1983.

7. Norman Dello Joio, Songs of Remembrance (New York: Associated Music Publishers, 1979). Baritone.
    The keyboard reduction of this orchestral work was reviewed by the author in the March/April 1980 issue of the Bulletin of the National Association of Teachers of Singing.

8. Letter of February 9, 1983.

9. The other five are "Eyebright," "Why so Pale and Wan, Fond Lover?", "Meeting at Night," "All Things Leave Me," and "How Do I Love Thee?"
    Two of these, "Meeting at Night" and "Eyebright" are recorded in the Hanks-Friedberg anthology, Vol. I (see note 24, Chapter I).

10. Norman Dello Joio, "The Dying Nightingale" (New York: Carl Fischer, 1954). High voice.

11. Letter of February 9, 1983.

12. Stark Young, The Pavilion (New York: Scribner, 1951).

13. Humanities Research Center, Austin, Texas.

14. Young, The Pavilion, p. 164.

15. Goss, p. 453.

16. David Diamond, "Integrity and Integration in Contemporary Music," The Alice and Frederick Slee Lectures (University of Buffalo, Spring, 1961).

17. David Diamond, "From the Notebook of David Diamond," Music Journal, XXII (April 1964), p. 25.

18. Hans Nathan, "The Modern Period--United States of America," A History of Song, ed. Denis Stevens (New York: Norton, 1960), p. 444.

19. William Flanagan, "American Songs: A Thin Crop," Musical America, LXXII (February 1952), p. 23.

20. Letter from David Diamond to the author, February 7, 1983.

21. Frances Murphy and Hershel Parker, eds. The Norton
Anthology of American Literature, Volume I (New York:
Norton, 1979), p. 2043.

22. Goss, p. 454.

23. David Diamond, "Epitaph" (New York: Associated Mu-
sic Publishers, 1946). Medium high voice. This song is
out-of-print but available from the publisher in an Archive
edition.

24. Nathan, p. 444.

25. David Diamond, "Monody" (Philadelphia: Elkan-Vogel,
1947). Medium voice.

26. Letter of February 7, 1983.

27. David Diamond, "A Portrait" (Philadelphia: Elkan-Vogel,
1947). Medium high voice.

28. David Diamond, "Billy in the Darbies" (Philadelphia:
Elkan-Vogel, 1946). Medium high voice.

29. Nathan, pp. 446-447.

30. Robert Page, "In Quest of Answers--An Interview with
Vincent Persichetti," Choral Journal, XIV:3 (November 1973),
p. 6.

31. William Schuman, "The Compleat Musician: Vincent
Persichetti and Twentieth Century Harmony," The Musical
Quarterly, XLVII:3 (July 1961), p. 380.

32. Virgil Thomson in the Colorado Springs Gazette Tele-
graph.

33. University of Oklahoma Press, 1963 and 1970.

34. G. Schirmer, 1954.

35. Vincent Persichetti, Twentieth Century Harmony, Crea-
tive Aspects and Practice (New York: Norton, 1961), pp.
9-10.

36. Schuman, p. 381.

37. Page interview, p. 6.

38. Ibid., p. 5.

39. Vincent Persichetti, in an interview with the author at Theodore Presser Co., Bryn Mawr, Pennsylvania, February 3, 1975.

40. Ibid.

41. See index of Volume II for further references to Harriet Monroe and Poetry magazine.

42. Robert Buttel, Wallace Stevens, The Making of Harmonium (Princeton, N.J.: Princeton University Press, 1967), p. x.

43. Babette Deutsch, Poetry in Our Time (Garden City, N.Y.: Doubleday, 1963), p. 285.

44. Buttel, p. x.

45. Joseph N. Riddel, The Clairvoyant Eye (Baton Rouge: Louisiana State University Press, 1965), p. 65.

46. Page interview, p. 5.

47. Interview with the author, February 3, 1975.

48. Riddel, p. 11.

49. Robert Evett, "The Music of Vincent Persichetti," The Juilliard Review, II:2 (Spring 1955), p. 16.

50. Interview with the author, February 3, 1975.

51. Vincent Persichetti, Harmonium (Philadelphia: Elkan-Vogel, 1959). Soprano.
        Recorded performances:
        a) Hanks and Friedberg, Art Song in America, Vol. 2. Contains "The Death of a Soldier," "The Snow Man," and "Of the Surface of Things."
        b) Songs of American Composers, "Sonatina to Hans Christian," sung by Mildred Miller.

52. A. Walton Litz, Introspective Voyager (New York: Oxford University Press, 1972), p. 76.

53. Deutsch, p. 271.

54. The author had the pleasure of performing this work with Julia Mueller, violist, during Vincent Persichetti's previously mentioned visit to the Duke University campus in the mid-sixties.

55. Evett, pp. 22-23.

56. Page interview, p. 5.

57. These four songs are published separately:
   a) Vincent Persichetti, "Out of the Morning" (Philadelphia: Elkan-Vogel, 1958). Medium voice.
   b) Vincent Persichetti, "I'm Nobody" (Bryn Mawr, Pa.: Elkan-Vogel, 1958). Medium voice.
   c) Vincent Persichetti, "When the Hills Do" (Philadelphia: Elkan-Vogel, 1958). Medium voice.
   d) Vincent Persichetti, "The Grass" (Bryn Mawr, PA: Elkan-Vogel, 1958). Medium voice. This song is recorded in vol. 2 of the Hanks-Friedberg anthology.

58. Interview with the author, February 3, 1975. In a letter to the author dated "Early August, 1983," the composer added "Stevens and Dickinson ... both say more about less, rather than less about more, and that is for me."

59. Austin Warren, "Emily Dickinson," A Collection of Critical Essays, ed. Richard B. Sewall (Englewood Cliffs, N.J.: Prentice-Hall, 1963), p. 111.

60. Richard B. Sewall, Life of Emily Dickinson, Volume 2 (New York: Farrar, Straus and Giroux, 1974), chapter 22 (pp. 512-531).

61. Letter of "Early August, 1983."

III. THE THIRD DECADE 1.

Jack Beeson (1921-)
Edgar Allan Poe (1809-1849)
Abraham Lincoln (1809-1865)
Peter Viereck (1916-)

The life and career of Jack Beeson represent a triumph of the human spirit operating through one of its principal manifestations--the impulse toward artistic creativity. Beeson was born with a serious metabolic disorder, and was given just a few months to live when he was six years old. The following year, instead of dying, he began to study the piano at his own request, and to nurture an inner compulsion toward music-making which could have received but little stimulation within the family circle or in his hometown of Muncie, Indiana.[1]

The medium of radio, and the Saturday afternoon broadcasts from the Metropolitan, enabled the boy to identify and begin to cultivate a life-long passion for opera. Buying piano scores of operatic works with his savings, he would play along with the performances, and in his teens made three abortive attempts to write music and libretti for operas of his own. In 1936, his first piano teacher, Luella Weimer, turned him over to Percival Owen, who had come from Canada to join the music faculty of Ball State College, and who, like many of the first-rank piano instructors of that era, had trained under Leschetizsky. With Owen's assistant, Beeson began to study theory and music history, and at the same time was learning to play the clarinet and xylophone.

Jack Beeson
(Photo: Pach Bros., N.Y.)

In similar fashion to Westchester's creating special dis-
pensations for Samuel Barber, the Central Senior High School

of Muncie rewarded sophomore Jack Beeson's A student status with permission to attend classes only in the morning, in order to have afternoons free for practicing and composing. When he was seventeen he followed Percival Owen's advice and began studies at the Royal Conservatory in Toronto, where he earned certificates in piano and theory. Following his high school graduation, Beeson was awarded a fellowship to the Eastman School in Rochester, where he studied composition with Bernard Rogers, Burrill Phillips, and Howard Hanson, and enrolled in the many liberal arts courses prompted by the broadening scope of his interests.

By 1944, he had received bachelor's and master's degrees from Eastman and was working toward a doctorate in music, when his father's death and a resulting legacy conferred temporary financial independence. Beeson interrupted his doctoral studies to spend a privileged year studying composition with Béla Bartók, who had recently fled the Nazi takeover of Hungary, and was suffering the lean years of neglect which became the retrospective shame of the American musical community. Having already begun to compose songs at Eastman (in the absence of opportunities for opera, his first love), Beeson showed Bartók his settings of W.B. Yeats, and was told by the master composer that he couldn't attempt to judge poetic settings in a language not his own. He added that he himself had written few songs because there was so little lyric poetry in Hungarian, and, as he put it, "I have too much respect for one's native language to set another language's poetry."[2]

During the period of his graduate studies at Eastman (1942-44), Beeson had commuted to New York City and a teaching fellowship in theory at Columbia University. After his year with Bartók, he returned to the University to study conducting and musicology, and to begin a long series of faculty appointments culminating in his selection as MacDowell Professor of Music in 1967, and the conferral of Columbia's Great Teachers' Award in 1979. In addition to the fostering of his teaching career, the University also provided the long-sought opportunity for Beeson's development in the art and craft of opera. He served as coach and conductor of both the Columbia Opera Workshop (1945-1950) and Columbia Opera Theater Associates (1945-1952), and in a natural flowering of events, had his own first operatic production (Hello Out There--a one-act work with libretto adapted from a William Saroyan play) presented at the University in 1954.

Jack Beeson still occupies a large office, filled with books and scores, on the fourth floor of Columbia's venerable Dodge Hall at 116th Street and Broadway. Beeson himself is a slight, intense, graying but youthfully active man who handles a schedule that involves the split second juggling of his academic and creative lives. During the hour of the author's interview, sandwiched between the composer's classroom commitments, Beeson fielded student needs and telephone calls from "the media" with equal aplomb, evidencing years of practice. Columbia University, one senses, has been a kind of anchor point to Beeson's career, and he has also served it in a number of administrative capacities: As chairman of the Music Department, member of the Senate, head of new music publications for Columbia University Press, and officer in charge of the Alice M. Ditson Fund.

In 1947, Beeson married Nora Sigerist, and they had a daughter and a son, the latter being fated to die in a tragic auto accident at the age of twenty-five. The years 1948-1950 saw the Beesons in Rome, supported by the Prix de Rome and a Fulbright Fellowship, and it was here that the composer completed his first opera. Called <u>Jonah</u>, it used Beeson's own libretto, adapted from a play by Paul Goodman (see Chapter 5 of this volume) and although it won special mention in a La Scala competition, remains unproduced to this day. Another American artist in Rome on a Guggenheim Fellowship during this time was Peter Viereck and the Beesons got on very well with him. "He was tone-deaf," says the composer, "but he kept showing me his poetry, and at the time I didn't feel it was appropriate for musical setting."[3]

Back in the United States, Beeson proceeded to make a name for himself as an opera composer, following <u>Hello Out There</u> (mentioned above) with a production of <u>The Sweet Bye and Bye</u> (libretto by Kenward Elmslie) at the Juilliard Opera Theater in 1957. In an article in the <u>Opera News</u> of January 5, 1963, entitled "Grand and Not So Grand," he predicted that the future of American opera did not lie with Broadway, nor in the old established houses, nor in the University opera workshops. Rather, he felt, it would emerge from the newly developing metropolitan and regional opera companies around the country and from new developments in the artistic use of the media. His prophecies were proven accurate by his own subsequent productions. It was

121

the innovative New York City Opera who commissioned his
Lizzie Borden in 1965; the growing medium of National Edu-
cational Television which produced My Heart's in the High-
lands in 1970 (again, a Saroyan adaptation, with Beeson as
a walk-on bit player); and an excellent regional company,
the Kansas City Lyric Theater, which in 1975 presented
Captain Jinks of the Horse Marines, under a bi-centennial
commission from the National Endowment for the Arts.

Other journal articles by Beeson have recorded his
appreciation of and sense of indebtedness to his elder col-
leagues in the composing world. His memorial to Douglas
Moore[4] (see Volume I, Chapter 4) who had been an es-
teemed fellow faculty member at Columbia for over twenty
years, traces the geographical and historical roots of Moore's
musical "Americanism," and lauds his expressive and dra-
matic gifts as an opera composer. In a 1977 article on Vir-
gil Thomson,[5] published in the literary magazine Parnassus,
Beeson discusses the older composer's important contributions
to our contemporary understanding of English language word
setting. Beeson, on interview, had indicated to the author
his own constant awareness in his vocal writing of the faster
pace of English vowels ("People set it as though it were Ger-
man"),[6] the necessity for fixed accents, and for the verbal
syncopations which have inevitable musical consequences. In
the Parnassus article, he acknowledges Thomson's scattered
writings on declamation and his widely given lecture "Words
and Music" as the partial stimulus for his own thinking, while
taking mild exception to Thomson's overstated claim in 1976
that "Nobody else was doing anything about (setting English
properly)."[7]

After his initial encounter with song-writing in East-
man days, Beeson has returned frequently to this form
throughout his composing career, and feels that his songs
"are different from the songs that others write. The texts
chosen," he says "are different from others' choices, and
are often not conventional lyrics. Often they are inherently
dramatic, which, of course, makes the songs tend to be
more dramatic."[8] It might be noted here that Jack Beeson
has himself written a fair amount of poetry, including 100
lines of the challenging "terza rima" form. He also reads
much poetry, and within two lines knows whether or not a
poem appeals to him as a possible song text.

Beeson's first setting of an American text was Edgar Allan Poe's "Eldorado." Written in 1951 and revised in 1967 and 1977, this song was published for the first time in a 1982 Galaxy collection[9] of twenty previously unprinted American songs. Poe, who is treated initially in Volume I, Chapter 2 of this series, had published his fourth volume of poetry, The Raven and Other Poems, in 1845. During the four agonizing years which remained to him, years that encompassed the death of his wife and his own physical and emotional deterioration, a dozen of his poems appeared in various periodicals and "Eldorado" is one of them. Although a seemingly straightforward tale of a "gallant knight" who spends his life in a vain search for the mythical city of gold, it has proved enigmatic to its interpreters, some of whom see it as embodying "the pursuit of the ideal"[10] while others find it an "ironic" and "worldly wise"[11] mockery of such a quest. Historical perspective is helpful here, for it must be remembered that 1849 was the year of a major American epidemic of "gold-fever." Poe had responded to this phenomenon with satirical essays decrying his countrymen's materialism, and with the last of his fictional hoaxes--"Von Kempelen and His Discovery"--which purported to be a scientific method for turning lead into gold.

Given this background, it seems most likely that the knight's journey is an ironical representation of the national madness: a frenzied search for wealth that could carry a man "Down the Valley of the Shadow" to the very gates of Death. This poem of four six-line stanzas has Poe's typically tight control of rhyme and rhythmic elements, and a resultant musical flow which tends to obscure the deeper level of metaphysical speculation which has a parallel if not primary function. Besides the creation of nightmare visions and detective stories which our century has chosen to consider his most important legacy to us, Poe's gifts included a curiously contemporary mystical sensibility which saw the material world as an emanation of divine consciousness ("The Universe is a plot of God") in which each man must recognize his own existence "as that of Jehovah."[12] In this writer's opinion, Poe's world view, although never his poetic style, has strong ties to that of Stephen Crane, another unique literary figure who defies categorization, and who raised a despairing cry against the compassionless God of common acceptance. The reader is invited to compare Poe's gold-crazed knight whose courage sustained his misguided quest, with Crane's "man pursuing the horizon" (to be treated in the following section) and his endless, Existential journey.

Although Poe was preeminently a lyric poet, "Eldorado" does possess the dramatic elements which Beeson indicates are a prime consideration in his settings. The figure of the knight and his changing patterns of movement are clearly delineated by manipulation of tempo, rhythm, and phrasing. The opening indication for the "gaily bedight" figure is "Swinging," but already the asymmetrical effect of cross-accents between vocal and instrumental phrases introduce a suggestion of the jerky, uncontrolled trotting of a stumbling, Don Quixote-like nag.

Example 3.1, measures 1-8. Copyright © 1982, Galaxy Music Corp. New York, N.Y.; used by permission.

The beginning tempo is almost hysterically fast but slows to nearly half "as his strength (fails) him" in verse three. Harmonic factors parallel this change, and the opening sharps of the pandiatonic B major/minor context (see Ex. 3.1) give way to the more somber B flat elements. (See Ex. 3.2, page 125.) As the misleading "shade" spurs the rider on in his fruitless travels, the deceptively hopeful

124

Example 3.2, measures 33-39. Copyright © 1982, Galaxy Music Corp., New York, N.Y.; used by permission.

original tempo and sharp dominated harmony return. This time the contour of the vocal line rises to its highest point as the phantom mocks the other's desperate obsession.[13] (See Ex. 3.3, below and page 126.)

In contrast to "Eldorado's" agitated vignette of the wanderings of an anti-hero, "Indiana Homecoming,"[14] written in 1957, is a gentle landscape in which a sensitive observer's view of the present is overlaid by the hazy scrim of memory. The text is adapted from a rare poem of Abraham Lincoln's

Example 3.3, measures 57-65. Copyright © 1982, Galaxy
Music Corp., New York, N.Y.; used by permission.

which was included in his letter of April 18th, 1846, to
John D. Johnston, his stepbrother.[15] Lincoln's family, it
will be remembered, had moved in 1816, when he was eight,
from Kentucky to Indiana, partly over the slavery issue, and
partly because of the difficulty of land titles in Kentucky.
The family endured hard times 'til the land was cleared and
a cabin built, and the boy's mother died in 1818. The fol-
lowing year his father married Mrs. Sally Johnston, a widow
with three children, who proved to be a kind stepmother to
young Abe. In 1830, all the Lincolns, including Mrs. John-
ston's two daughters and sons-in-law came in ox-drawn wag-
ons to settle in Illinois on the Sangamon River, and Abe be-
gan a series of jobs which eventually led to law, politics,
and the historical role for which Destiny had prepared him.

    The year 1844 had found Lincoln practicing law in
Springfield as part of the Lincoln and Herndon partnership,
recently rejected as a delegate to the Whig convention, and
two years away from the Congressional nomination he would
receive in 1846 after General Hardin's withdrawal from the
race. In the aforementioned letter, he describes the circum-
stances of his Indiana visit, and its attendant poetic genesis
in these terms:

        In the fall of 1844, thinking I might aid some to
        carry the State of Indiana for Mr. Clay, I went
        into the neighborhood in that state in which I was
        raised, where my mother and only sister were bur-
        ied, and from which I had been absent about fifteen

years. That part of the country is, within itself, as unpoetical as any spot of the earth; but still, seeing it and its objects and inhabitants, aroused feelings in me which were certainly poetry; though whether my expression of those feelings is poetry is quite another question.

Lincoln indicates that the ten stanzas he now quotes constitute one of a projected four cantos,[16] not an easily manageable length for an amateur poet. Although the lines are couched in the typically flowery mid-nineteenth century "literary" language, their author's skill at versification amazes us as much as the strength of his prose writings, coming from a man whose formal schooling totalled approximately one year. Jack Beeson, whose "Bear Hunt" for male chorus (1961) sets another of the cantos, has a very personal identification with "Indiana Homecoming." The song title is his own (the poem being untitled) and he now views it as a "nostalgia piece" reflecting his own Indiana origins, and the fact that he has not been back there since 1958.[17]

The song indicates that the text has been "adapted" and Beeson's changes are of two types: word alteration and stanza omission. He substitutes the word "between" for "twixt" in line six, "seen" for "seem" in line eight (possibly a printer's error) and makes the last two lines of the song read

Where memory will hallow all
We've known, and know no more.

instead of Lincoln's original

But seeing them, to mind again
The lost and absent brings.

The latter change destroys the rhyme scheme, but Beeson's purpose is clear. In the desire to have a text of more workable length, he has cut stanzas 4-5 and the last three. The omission of these final ones, in which Lincoln dwells at melancholy length on the death of many former friends and loved ones, also changes the mood of the song text, removing the air of heavy sorrow, and conferring the peace of "hallowed memory" on what is "known no more."

Despite its lyrical flow, "Indiana Homecoming" has

dramatic possibilities as well, and could easily be seen as a major aria in an opera on the life of Lincoln, with the protagonist alone on stage, surrounded in remembrance. The melodic lines, mostly in chordal skips and stepwise motion, are broadly arching, and a particularly felicitous contour outlined by an octave leap is repeated twice at other pitch levels, always at the low dynamic level of suppressed emotion.

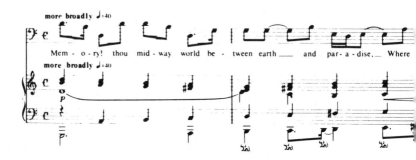

Example 3.4, measures 5-6. Copyright 1973, Boosey and Hawkes, Inc.; used by permission.

The song exhibits mostly diatonic language with flexible movement between tonal structures. Occasional polytonal elements are imaginatively tied to the text as in the following measures where memory rises, "pure and bright" toward a vocal cadence in F major (supported by the piano's right hand) having been "freed from all that's earthly vile," as symbolized by clashing chords and scale passages.

Example 3.5, measures 9-10. Copyright 1973, Boosey and Hawkes, Inc.; used by permission.

In 1951, the year of "Eldorado," Jack Beeson recanted on his earlier rejection of Peter Viereck's poetry, and composed the first of three settings based on his texts. Viereck had been born in New York City, and was the son of George Sylvester Viereck, a free-lance writer who attracted considerable notoriety during both World Wars for his pro-German views. These were emphatically not shared by his son, who, after his academically illustrious years of preparation at Harvard and Oxford began a long career as teacher and writer on historical subjects, which enabled him to express his opposing points of view. Ironically, his brother, George Sylvester Viereck, Jr., had been killed fighting with the Allied forces at Anzio, and Peter Viereck had served in Africa and Italy with the Psychological Warfare Branch in 1943-1944. The following year brought two life-changing events: Viereck met and married Anya de Markov, the daughter of Russian emigrés, and served as history instructor at the U.S. Army University in Florence. It was the latter experience which turned him away from free-lance writing and toward teaching. On his return to America, he taught briefly at Harvard and at Smith College, and since 1948, except for periodic appointments to visiting professorships in the United States and Europe, has been firmly ensconced on the history faculty of Mount Holyoke.

Besides his numerous published works on history and social philosophy, Viereck also wrote four volumes of poetry during the nineteen forties and fifties, and a collection of New and Selected Poems in 1967. He felt that he had an advantage as a professor of history, claiming that a poet who teaches English "becomes self-conscious," and further that "academic poets tend to be critics and analysts rather than [to] feel the joy of spontaneity."[18] Conservative in both politics and literature, he found much modern poetry to be "too critical, too intellectual, too dry, and too lacking in music,"[19] and sought a "return to romantic wildness ... and lyrical passion."[20]

Other strong strains in Viereck's poetry, particularly the early verse, are a kind of "classicism of the industrial age,"[21] and an acceptance and reconciliation of the uncouth aspects of life in New York and in the rest of the country. All three of Beeson's poetic choices fall into this category. "Big Crash Out West" (1951), originally printed in Strike Through the Mask and included in the "Wars" section of New and Selected Poems, chronicled a senseless auto accident

Peter Viereck

encouraged by the invitingly open spaces and smoldering
boredom of western America. The setting, now out of print, [22]
is in the lyrical/dramatic, largely diatonic, melodically expan-
sive style of "Indiana Homecoming." The other two, composed
twenty years later, use poems which Viereck grouped under

"Grotesques" in 1967. They present contrasting Midwest farmland, and eastern big-city themes, and each affords Beeson the opportunity to employ his impressive command of musical characterization in a lighter, quasi-humorous vein.

"To a Sinister Potato" had initially appeared in Terror and Decorum, Viereck's first poetry collection, published in 1948. Its strong element of satire is typical of many of these early poems, as is its personification of an inanimate object in order to make "a witty comment on human existence."[23] In a rapid verbal rhythm accelerated by the refrain "In Indiana or in Idaho," the potatoes "bide their hour" underground, "puffed up by secret paranoia" and envious of the stars moving unconfined through the vastness of space. Jack Beeson's setting, written in 1970,[24] shortens the text by omitting the poem's fourth stanza, which describes the bland potatoes on Kiwanis Club plates deceiving Indiana as to their actual sinister intent. Otherwise, Beeson follows the process that he describes as being "quite literal in his settings, with word repetition as the only change."[25] In fact, only the word "silent" is repeated in this song, and that because it is followed by a melisma, a not infrequent device of the composer's to insure comprehension of a word before its decoration.

Example 3.6, measures 14-15. Copyright 1973, Boosey and Hawkes, Inc.; used by permission.

The dramatic effect of this upward curving melisma is to suggest the softly gathering menace of the "watchers" (see Ex. 3.6), and it forms an interesting contrast to the predominantly fast-moving, syllabic setting with which Beeson matches Viereck's verbal rhythm.

Example 3.7, measures 7-10. Copyright 1973, Boosey and
Hawkes, Inc.; used by permission.

Other dramatic moments are the opening, reiterated, forte
low D in the piano part which establishes the "vastness" of
this "earth-apple" together with the dimensions of its threat,

Example 3.8, measures 1-2. Copyright 1973, Boosey and
Hawkes, Inc.; used by permission.

and the crescendo of doom created in the final measures by
cluster chords, undamped strings, and a leaping vocal

contour which forms an unsettling augmented fourth with
the last piano note.

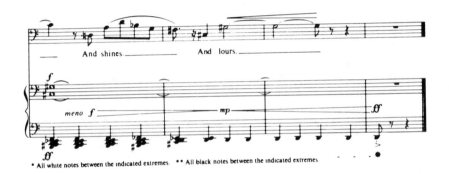

* All white notes between the indicated extremes. ** All black notes between the indicated extremes

Example 3.9, measures 29-34. Copyright 1973, Boosey and
Hawkes, Inc.; used by permission.

As befits the agitated mental state of the power-mad
potato, the vocal line of this song is considerably more jag-
ged than the Lincoln setting, and its harmonic structure
shows the typical Beeson procedures of a suggested tonal
center at the beginning and/or end of the song (D in this
case) with freely ranging cadences in other tonal areas (C,
F sharp, A flat, etc.). An infrequent but effective instance
of word-painting is the treatment of "coiled-up springs," set
with a long piano trill and tremolo that finally "uncoil" in an
arpeggiated release. (See Ex. 3.10, page 134.)

Beeson's third Viereck setting, called "The You Should
of Done It Blues"[26] uses a 1965 poem whose original title was

Example 3.10, measure 11. Copyright 1973, Boosey and
Hawkes, Inc.; used by permission.

"The Lyricism of the Weak." Another poem in the "Gro-
tesques" section of Viereck's 1967 collection, called "The
New Cultural Blues," had been performed to music at Har-
vard's Loeb Theater in 1961, and one wonders if these fac-
tors might have influenced Beeson's view of the poem he
chose to set as a musical blues lament. Interestingly, the
song emerges on a note of ironic, "gallows-humor" self-
deprecation, with an objectivity contributed by the formal
"blues" setting, whereas the poem, lacking that formalized
structure, seems to emphasize the victimization and deep,
though ungrammatical, grief of the protagonist.

Beeson, despite his commitment to "literal" settings,
makes two small changes in this text. One is the omission
of the second "it" in the tenth line: "You should of done it
(which it is no crime)"; and the second is the addition of
the word "be" to line eight: "She is they say, 'no better
than she ought to'." Both of these alterations appear to serve
the purpose of convincing rhythmic patterning in the vocal
line, which displays throughout the syncopated accents,
tempo, melodic shapes, and "off" notes of the "blues" idiom.
(See Ex. 3.11, page 135.)

The original poem, in an unrhymed iambic pentameter
with the opening line repeated at the end, has an interesting
structure of four three line stanzas. As Beeson sets this
affecting monologue according to its expressive content, the
corresponding musical "verses" occupy six, four, six, and
eight measures respectively. The prosodic reasons for this

134

Example 3.11, measures 1-3. Copyright 1973, Boosey and Hawkes, Inc.; used by permission.

discrepancy can be seen as he builds to the emotive climax, with a rapid, syllabic sequence ("It figures who I heard there," etc.) followed by drawn out melismas in the "blues" manner. (See Ex. 3.12, below and page 136.) The clearly defined E flat tonal center of the opening and closing verses seems appropriate to the derivation of the musical style, but the rich coloration of the chromatic overlay carries it far from its "popular" origins. In another device for unification, Beeson applies the original melodic shape to Viereck's repetition of line one as the final line of the song except for a

Example 3.12, measures 8-13. Copyright 1973, Boosey and
Hawkes, Inc.; used by permission.

rhythmic augmentation, inversion, and substitute of seventh
for tonic, in the last two notes (compare with Ex. 3.11).

Example 3.13, measures 20-24. Copyright 1973, Boosey and
Hawkes, Inc.; used by permission.

Richard Owen (1922-)
Stephen Crane (1871-1900)
Robert Frost (1874-1963)
Amy Lowell (1874-1925)

"I believe in my double life," says Richard Owen, and adds
"The scales of music and the scales of justice lend a balance
to each other."[27] This composer, like the poet Wallace
Stevens (see Chapter 2), has spent a lifetime juggling a
notable career as a lawyer with the demands of the creative
avocation to which he is devoted. Owen's father, also a
New York City lawyer, was a great lover of opera, and
Richard attended many Metropolitan performances with his
parents during his boyhood. Having dropped the piano
after a few months of study at the age of six, Owen eagerly
resumed his lessons at twenty-nine, and a year later began
studying composition privately and at the New York College
of Music.

    After serving as a navigator in the Army Air Corps
during World War II, Owen had completed his undergraduate
degree at Dartmouth in 1947. Three years later, in 1950, he
finished Harvard Law School, passed the New York State bar,
and began twenty-four years of practice (in government ser-
vice, in various partnerships, and by himself) in the city of
New York. In 1956, while working as a Senior Trial Attorney
with the Anti-Trust Division of the Justice Department, Owen
had his initial public recognition as a composer, with the per-
formance of his first opera at the local Bar Association. It

Richard Owen

was a one-act opera about a lawyer and his client, and the
singers included a young Juilliard soprano named Lynn Ras-
mussen whom Owen married in 1960. Now there was a new
partner in the family juggling act, as Mrs. Owen divided her

time between an operatic career which included performances at the Hamburg and Zurich operas, and a home life which grew to encompass city and country residences and the birth of three sons.28

During his busy years of law practice, Richard Owen composed two more operas. The first, on commission from the After Dinner Opera Company, was a one-act called A Moment of War, given in concert form in 1958, and subsequently in a number of staged Spanish translation performances in Buenos Aires. The second, a religious work titled A Fisherman Called Peter, was premièred in 1965 in a New York production under the supervision of Dorothy Maynor. For the past ten years, Owen has been United States District Judge of the Southern District of New York, with offices in the Foley Square Courthouse where the author was invited to meet with him. Since that appointment he has written Mary Dyer (1976), based on the life of the Quaker martyr, and his last opera to date, The Death of the Virgin, in 1980.

In the sixties and early seventies, Richard Owen wrote a number of songs, in which settings of American poetry predominated. Among these were two poems by Stephen Crane, an enormously interesting writer whose works had, til then, attracted very little attention from composers. Crane was born in Newark, N.J., a city which one of his ancestors helped to establish. Descended from a line of Methodist ministers, he had a grandfather who was a bishop and founder of Syracuse University. Stephen's father, the mild, unworldly Reverend Jonathan Townley Crane, died when the boy was eight, while holding a Methodist pastorate at Port Jervis, N.Y. His mother, a forceful religious journalist who doted on this last of her fourteen children, then took him to live in Asbury Park, where at seventeen he began to work summers on his brother Townley's Press Bureau.

Crane's university education was spotty and brief. He failed in his first semester as an engineering student at Lafayette College, then spent a single semester (spring, 1891) at Syracuse where he attended but few classes, played on the varsity baseball team, and probably started Maggie: A Girl of the Streets, the landmark naturalistic novel which was to profoundly shock his contemporaries. The next few years brought a series of intermittent jobs as a newspaper

reporter, alternating with periods of extreme poverty, ro-
mantic attachments to unattainable objects, and a constant,
passionate concern over the moral and social ills of society.
A chance meeting with the writer Hamlin Garland led to an
introduction to William Dean Howells, and both men became
interested in the developing talent of the younger man.
Howells, in fact, invited Crane to tea and read Emily Dick-
inson's poetry to him, and it is a commonly accepted belief
that the brevity and power of her verses inspired Crane's
major collection of poems, The Black Riders and Other Lines,
to be written soon after.

The Black Riders was published in 1895, the same
year in which the publication of The Red Badge of Courage,
Crane's famous Civil War novel, brought international renown.
During the last four years of his life he traveled as a war
correspondent to the most dangerous sectors of the Greco-
Turkish, Cuban, and Spanish-American conflicts, returning
to interludes of relatively peaceful living in England with
Cora Taylor. In her, he had finally found a woman who
could match his unconventional, free-spirited approach to
life, and appreciate his artistic goals and sensibilities. She
was, however, dedicated to surrounding her celebrated
author with an overly lavish life-style, which necessitated
his writing furiously against a growing mountain of debt.
In 1900, after a considerable period of failing health, he
succumbed to tuberculosis at the age of twenty-nine, ending
a short lifetime that had been crowded with adventure, in-
tensity, and literary accomplishment.

It is widely believed that Stephen Crane's title of The
Black Riders for his poetry collection, refers to a childhood
dream of his at Ocean Grove, New Jersey, in which black
riders on black horses were charging at him from the surf.[29]
The poems themselves proved more confusing to contemporary
critics who were put off by the angular, short-line, free-
verse structures and the troublesome themes of man's aliena-
tion in an uncaring universe dominated by a vengeful God.
British criticism managed a truer perspective from a greater
geographical distance, and H.G. Wells wrote, shortly after
Crane's death, that "he is the first expression of the open-
ing mind of a new period ... beginning ... with the record
of impressions ... of a vigor and intensity beyond all prece-
dent."[30] Two decades later, Carl Van Doren pointed out
that during the American "poetic twilight" of the 1890's,

only Crane had challenged the conventions of poetic form and diction of late Victorian verse: a challenge curiously similar to that of French Symbolism, despite Crane's ignorance of Symbolist verse and philosophy.[31] Following the appearance of Crane's Collected Works in 1926, his poetry became more widely available, and it was now clear that he had indeed been a forerunner of many of the movements of the "poetic renaissance." By 1950, John Berryman was able to proclaim him as "the important American poet between Walt Whitman and Emily Dickinson on one side, and his tardy-developing contemporaries Edwin Arlington Robinson and Robert Frost and Ezra Pound on the other."[32]

Two characteristics of Crane's style in The Black Riders set him apart as unique despite twentieth-century literature's belated attempts to draw him in: one is his extreme brevity and concentration which relates only to the isolated attempts by Crapsey, Lowell, and Pound to adapt Japanese haiku forms; the other is his narrative emphasis, which has spawned few followers in an era dominated by lyric and dramatic expression.[33] These two characteristics prove to be energizing points of correspondence in Richard Owen's settings, for his declamatory vocal style is appropriate to the "story-telling" verbal mode of the narratives, while the brevity of the verses permits musical amplification through both temporal and expressive elements.

"There were many who went in huddled procession" contrasts "mass-man" with a single, courageous soul "who sought a new road ... and ultimately died alone ... (in) direful thickets." It perfectly represents Crane's sense of the individual's isolation in a menacing world, and could, indeed, be his own epitaph. Owen begins his setting[34] with a repeated piano figure in the hypnotic march rhythm of the blindly moving "procession." The empty, parallel fifths drawn from the Phrygian mode lend an ancient quality to the universal tale, and the ingenuous little stepwise eighth note motif introduced here will later expand to a dramatic vocal series of leaping fourths ("There was one"). (See Ex. 3.14a and Ex. 3.14b, page 142.)

Halfway through the song, the parallel fifth figure intensifies and broadens with the addition of the upper octave, and in the final phrase, it is transposed down a half step to match the somber verbal irony. The latter finds

Example 3.14a, measures 1-5. Copyright 1966, General Music Publishing Co.; used by permission.

Example 3.14b, measures 19-21. Copyright 1966, General Music Publishing Co.; used by permission.

vocal representation through a slower, triplet rendering of the leaping fourth figure, suggesting the weariness of bitter reflection.

Example 3.15, measures 28-32. Copyright 1966, General Music Publishing Co.; used by permission.

In Stephen Crane's parable "I saw a man pursuing the horizon," he draws close to the allegorical mode of his literary forefathers, Hawthorne and Melville. This poem has been mentioned above as an updated parallel to the search for the Ideal in "Eldorado," although in this case, unlike the knight's encouraging "shade," the observer states "It is futile" with merciless clarity. Owen's setting[35] provides in musical terms a sense of the protagonist's ceaseless running, a physical activity which at once embodies his cosmic helplessness, and Existential dedication to courageous movement through life. The 6/8 "perpetual motion" figure, and circular shapes of the vocal and piano lines both contribute to this effect.

Example 3.16, measures 1-6. Copyright 1966, General Music Publishing Co.; used by permission.

At the climactic moment of confrontation, the composer stops the motion somewhat in "freer" recitative. The anguished rebuttal ("You lie") rises to the song's largest vocal leap, and touches off a frantic renewal of motion which fades dynamically in representation of a visually receding form.

143

Example 3.17, measures 16-22. Copyright 1966, General Music Publishing Co.; used by permission.

In 1966, the year in which the Crane settings had appeared, Richard Owen also published "The Impulse,"[36] to a poem by Robert Frost. (The reader is referred to Chapter 3, Volume II of this series, for a major treatment of Frost in connection with John Duke's settings.) "The Impulse" was originally included in the collection Mountain Interval, which Frost published in 1916, soon after he returned from England to receive America's belated recognition and to take up his life on the farm at Franconia, New Hampshire. The pressure was gone from his farming now, for he was in great demand as a teacher and lecturer and no longer depended on the land for a living. But his eye for nature and its interactions with man remained as keen as the ear which had raised the New England idiom "to the dignity of a literary language."[37] In poem after poem, he records the many faces of mountain life: its beauties, and its terrors.

"The Impulse" is the last of five sections in a longer poem called "The Hill Wife." The titles of the first four sections, "Loneliness," "House Fear," "The Smile," and "The

144

Oft-Repeated Dream," partially suggest the state of mind of the protagonist whose spirit is crushed by years of isolation with only her husband for company. In "House Fear" and "The Oft-Repeated Dream," surrounding trees and eventually the house itself come to be seen as increasingly malevolent, until in "The Impulse" she is driven to a sudden, unexpected flight through the woods from which she never returns.

The poem is in seven stanzas, exhibiting Frost's favorite four line verse form in an unusual pattern of alternating four and two stress lines. For the most part, Owen's setting treats the stanzas as consisting of two lines with six stresses each, and creates a rhythmic scheme based on the quarter note in groupings of 4, 6, 2, and 3 per measure. An exception to this is the pictorial effect of a single 4/8 measure which uses the smaller note values and an even faster moving triplet to suggest the woman's flight.

Example 3.18, measures 40-43. Copyright 1966, General Music Publishing Co.; used by permission.

The overall style of "The Impulse" is similar to Owen's Crane settings, in which a declamatory vocal line, with many repeated notes, is supported by a lightly textured accompaniment. This piano writing also contains a recurrent melodic motif (F, E, B) which is first stated just before the voice enters (see Ex. 3.19, page 146), reappears many times in transposition, inversion, and its original form, and finally transfers to the vocal line at a moment of profound emotion ("he looked ev'rywhere") (see Ex. 3.20, page 146).

Free use of tonal elements characterizes the harmony, with considerable polytonal juxtaposition of simultaneous D and D flat structures. The resulting dissonance is occasion-

Example 3.19, measures 5-7. Copyright 1966, General Music Publishing Co.; used by permission.

Example 3.20, measures 44-46. Copyright 1966, General Music Publishing Co.; used by permission.

ally parted by a clear diatonic function, such as in Example 3.21 where the widely spaced cadential chords on "felled tree," give a Copland-esque, "American" sense of the spacious natural environment.

Example 3.21, measures 20-22. Copyright 1966, General Music Publishing Co.; used by permission.

146

Six years after the Crane and Frost songs, Richard Owen published a setting of "Patterns,"[38] a widely-known poem by Amy Lowell who is originally discussed in Chapter 1, Volume II. "Patterns" was written in the spring of 1915, at a time when Amy Lowell and her championship of free verse were a subject of attack and ridicule in many circles.[39] One weekend, when Lowell's devoted companion, the former actress Ada Dwyer Russell, was out of town, the poet composed "Patterns" with an easy flow and mounting excitement. On Ada's return, she insisted on reading it to her at once, after which they agreed that Lowell had made a masterful statement against literary conservatism, armed conflict between nations, and the restricted lives of women, beneath the cloak of an eighteenth century historical romance. Sensing that "the piece was a trifle risqué for the general public,"[40] the poet sent it off to the Little Review, one of the foremost "little magazines"[41] of the period, whose editor, Margaret Anderson, readily accepted it for the August issue. The poem was an instant success, and a year later was printed as the opener to Lowell's poetry collection called Men, Women and Ghosts, published in the fall of 1916. It is still widely quoted and anthologized more than any other Amy Lowell poem, and among its recent appearances, was included in a 1972 anthology of anti-war poetry.

Written with an irregular but carefully controlled rhyme scheme, "Patterns" is a dramatic monologue in which a woman who has just learned of her betrothed's death in battle, cries out against the stiff materials which confine her body and the rigid mores of society which have destroyed her life. Richard Owen had already written three operas when he undertook to set this poem, and treated the text as he would have one of his own libretti, cutting where compression seemed necessary for heightened musical effect. Out of an original 107 lines, approximately 66 remain in an extended "scena" of operatic dimensions which Owen, not surprisingly, dedicated to his wife.

The vocal style of the work is a flexible arioso which ranges from recitative-like passages to widely spaced lyrical contours that seem to break loose from their restricted "patterns" at climactic moments. The piano writing is more expansive and more orchestrally conceived than in the settings treated above, and from the outset, establishes a motivic life of its own.

Example 3.22, measures 1-8. Copyright 1973, General Music Publishing Co.; used by permission.

The device of "word painting" is also employed by the composer in this dramatic context as he uses rapidly repeated vocal notes to suggest drops of water

Example 3.23, measures 25-27. Copyright 1973, General Music Publishing Co.; used by permission.

148

and ornamented piano tremolos to portray the visual distortion wrought by the terrible import of the Duke's letter.

Example 3.24, measures 82-89. Copyright 1973, General Music Publishing Co.; used by permission.

C is the tonal center which Owen holds as a reference point, and the song begins (see Ex. 3.22) and closes in its minor mode. The final phrase, set in the rhythmic freedom of an a capella cry of anguish, ends tellingly with the unresolved despair of the second scalar degree.

Example 3.25, measures 123-125. Copyright 1973, General Music Publishing Co.; used by permission.

<u>Jean Eichelberger Ivey</u> (1923-)
Sara Teasdale (1884-1933)

It is interesting to observe the several parallels that exist
between the life of Jean Eichelberger Ivey and that of Mary
Howe, another outstanding woman composer who is treated in
Volume II, Chapter 1 of this series. Both of these women
centered the major part of their lives in the Washington-
Baltimore area; both were professional pianists before they
became established composers; and both had important con-
nections to the Peabody Conservatory, where Howe received
a diploma in composition, and Eichelberger Ivey an M.M. in
piano as well as subsequent major faculty appointments (see
below).

The Eichelberger family's Baltimore roots extend back
to colonial times, and the composer has celebrated this pater-
nal heritage in a vocal chamber work called <u>Notes Toward</u>
<u>Time</u>, which premièred in March, 1984, having been commis-
sioned by the Baltimore Chamber Music Society for the 350th
anniversary of the founding of Maryland. "Although I have
written for virtually every medium" says Ivey, "my favorite
medium is the voice,"[42] and she attributes this fact to early
influences from her mother, a semi-professional singer, and
from two of her father's sisters, who were voice teachers.

Like many musically gifted children, the young Jean
quickly became fluent at the keyboard, and by the age of
eleven held a position as organist at St. James Church in
Mount Rainier. In this capacity, she was able to experiment
with the building of timbres on the parish's Hammond organ,
an interest which would expand in later life to the composi-
tion of electronic music and to her establishment of Peabody's
Electronic Music Studio. The development of her precocious
talent, however, was seriously threatened by the Depression,
which brought about the demise of <u>The Woman Patriot</u>, an
anti-feminist newspaper which her father had edited for a
number of years. Fortunately, she was able to win a full
tuition scholarship at Trinity College in Washington, and
her 1944 bachelor's degree was soon followed by the master's
in piano at Peabody mentioned above, and a second master's
degree in composition earned during the summers at the
Eastman School in Rochester.

Jean Eichelberger Ivey
(Photo: Wayne Sourbeer)

Over twenty-five years were to intervene before
Eichelberger Ivey was awarded a Doctorate of Music in com-
position by the University of Toronto, whose music school at
that time (1972) was a leading center of electronic music in

North America. The years between had been crowded: with a marriage that lasted "long enough to establish her professional reputation as Jean Eichelberger Ivey"[43]; with teaching appointments in piano, organ, and theory at middle-Atlantic colleges such as Peabody, Trinity, and Catholic University; and with recital tours as a concert pianist to Mexico, Germany, and Austria as well as the United States.

A review by Paul Hume, writing for the Washington Post in June, 1956, attested to the young performer's technical and interpretive talents as well as to her musical taste and versatility in a program which included the Haydn F minor variations, Beethoven sonata opus 109, and her own promising composition titled Prelude and Passacaglia.[44] Increasingly, with the passage of years, the pianist gave way to the composer. Ivey gained renown for performances by soloists and orchestras of her works in many media.[45] In 1969 she returned to Peabody as a major teacher of composition, and in 1982 acceded to her present position as coordinator of the composition department.

The 1983/84 season was a memorable one for the composer, as her sixtieth birthday occasioned all-Ivey concerts at Trinity College, Peabody Conservatory, and at the convention of the Music Teachers' National Association in Louisville. Surrounding these were performances of major Ivey works by the Oakland Symphony, Fort Wayne Philharmonic, and Peabody Chamber Orchestra. Currently, Ms. Ivey is composing a work for cello and orchestra, assisted by a grant from the National Endowment for the Arts. She hopes that it will be performed upon completion by the Baltimore Symphony which premièred two of her earlier works: Testament of Eve for mezzo, tape, and orchestra (1976) and Sea-Change for tape and orchestra (1982).

Musical sounds, both traditionally and electronically generated, have long created a comfortable ambiance for Jean Eichelberger Ivey. She is equally at home in the world of words, and has published a number of journal articles. These include "The Contemporary Performing Ensemble"[46] which describes American college groups dedicated to new music; "Electronic Music Workshop for Teachers,"[47] a review of the goals and achievements of this pioneering effort held at Peabody in 1967; and "The Composer as Teacher,"[48] in which Ivey's own keen pedagogical insights are revealed. She has herself been the subject of many articles by others, as well as of radio interviews and a half-hour television documentary filmed by WRC-TV (NBC) in Washington for their series <u>A Woman Is</u>.

Poetry is another preferred literary medium of the composer's. "I have always loved poetry," she says, "and have written a fair amount of it, including texts for some of my vocal works, notably <u>Solstice</u> (1977) and <u>Testament of Eve</u>. I have also set to music poems I have come upon and liked,"[49] and one of the earliest of these, written for medium voice in 1956, is an attractive, lyric-dramatic setting of "Morning Song" from <u>Senlin</u> by the poet Conrad Aiken (see Volume II, Chapter 4). This song received its Baltimore première on April 10, 1984 in a performance by Wayne Conner, tenor, and Ernest Ligon, pianist. Surprisingly, it has never been published, but is available from the American Music Center which holds a complete collection of Ivey works.[50]

As the composer points out, her attention has often been captured by the work of women poets, such as Carolyn Kizer's text for <u>Hera, Hung from the Sky</u> which setting has been recorded by CRI, and which treats the ancient myth from the woman's point of view. Ivey interprets this poem as describing the goddess' punishment "for daring to question the established male-dominated order of things,"[51] and her own text for <u>Testament of Eve</u> sees Eve non-traditionally as a heroic figure "choosing knowledge and growth for herself and her children."[52] Perhaps the earliest feminine poetic voice to capture Ivey's attention was that of Sara Teasdale, who has been treated at length in Volume II, Chapter 3. The composer explains: "I became interested in Sara Teasdale's poetry in college and later read a biography of her.... In the case of <u>Woman's Love</u> I was interested in the fact that she brought a special, feminine point of view to love poetry--not the only woman poet to do so, of course."[53]

<u>Woman's Love</u> is Ivey's title for a cycle of five songs composed in 1962, from which two have been published in Galaxy Music's American Artsong Anthology, Volume I.[54] The first of these, "I Would Live in Your Love," has a text taken from <u>Helen of Troy</u> (1910), Teasdale's second volume of poetry, and the one which established her reputation. The second song, "To One Away," plus the three which remain unpublished ("The Kiss," "The Old Maid," and "Peace")

all set poems from <u>Rivers to the Sea</u>, which appeared in 1915, the first year of the poet's marriage to Ernst Filsinger in a seemingly fulfilling resolution to "her search for the love that would justify the giving up of the separate self."[55] That the separate self eventually reasserted its claims appears unmistakably clear both from the poet's divorce of Filsinger in 1929 and from the internal evidence of the later poetry. "It was myself that sang in me"[56] writes Teasdale in <u>Dark of the Moon</u> (1926) which contains some of her finest work, and again, "Let them think I care, though I go alone.... Who am self-contained as a flower or stone."[57] But in the 1910 and 1915 poems, the point of view that Ivey found so typically feminine was that of a young woman in love, longing for a sense of completion by and absorption into the object of that love, and focusing her energies toward response to the other's needs and emotions.

The musical language and devices of <u>Woman's Love</u> show a sensitive adaptation by the composer to serve the expressed meaning and implications of the texts. In "I Would Live in Your Love," both the voice part and linear accompaniment are dominated by lines of scalar eighth notes, moving variously in unison, imitation, inversion, and/or contrary motion. These lines carry both an aural and visual suggestion of the waves that draw the sea-grasses in their wake:

Example 3.26, measures 4-8. Copyright © 1982, Galaxy Music Corp. New York, N.Y.; used by permission.

They also create, through their harmonic ambiguity (C major combined with Aeolian modal elements) and through their never-ending undulations of pitch, a sense of almost a hypnotic process at work, in which the protagonist is drawn up and down as though by an outside will.

This process is intensified at the emotive climax of the song by a shortening of the "wave" length to half a measure each at the end of the line "I would empty my soul of the dreams that have gathered in me." Suddenly, then, it is shattered by a subito forte, and a series of "heart beat" accents on the strong beats of the piano accompaniment. It is as though the submerged will had suddenly broken free to commit an impassioned act of total self-dedication.

Example 3.27, measures 12-16. Copyright © 1982, Galaxy Music Corp., New York, N.Y.; used by permission.

"To One Away" presents a sharp musical contrast to the flowing, tranquillo atmosphere of its companion piece. Here the tempo is agitated, and the unease of lovers separated takes the form of an unrelenting chromatic ostinato in the left hand of the accompaniment. The urgency of this figure is further underlined by the syncopated accent patterns of both the vocal line, and the piano's right hand chords.

Example 3.28, measures 4-9. Copyright © 1982, Galaxy Music Corp., New York, N.Y.; used by permission.

The "cry in the night" is not actually heard in musical terms until measure 10, when "my name" is set with a sudden dynamic increase imitated and confirmed by the piano an octave higher, and then repeated quite softly, in the awed whisper of overwhelming emotion.

Example 3.29, measures 10-12. Copyright © 1982, Galaxy Music Corp., New York, N.Y.; used by permission.

The second verse of this modified strophic form sets "I know," which is the woman's answer to her lover's call, with

156

a similar three part repetition, followed by yet another high, soft chordal echo of never-ending response.

Example 3.30, measures 22-25. Copyright © 1982, Galaxy Music Corp., New York, N.Y.; used by permission.

Of the three remaining unpublished songs,[58] "Peace" is a particularly attractive setting which demonstrates a changing metric organization well adapted to textual needs and the composer's always sensitive and fresh harmonic structures. Woman's Love was performed in a New York recital on April 8, 1984, by Dilly Patrick, soprano, and Daniel Ragone, pianist, and was called "an exquisitely crafted song cycle" by the New York Times reviewer.[59]

NOTES

1. Most of the biographical information on Beeson's early life is drawn from: David Ewen, American Composers (New York: Putnam, 1982), pp. 48-50.

2. Author's interview with Jack Beeson, on December 1, 1982.

3. Ibid.

4. Jack Beeson, "In Memoriam: Douglas Moore," Perspectives of New Music, VIII (Fall/Winter 1960), pp. 158-160.

5. Jack Beeson, "Virgil Thomson's Aneid (The Operas)," Parnassus, V:2 (Spring/Summer 1977), pp. 457-478.

6. Beeson interview.

7. Beeson, "Virgil Thomson's Aeneid," p. 471.

8. Beeson interview.

9. Jack Beeson, "Eldorado" in: John Belisle (ed.), American Artsong Anthology, Volume I: Contemporary American Songs for High Voice and Piano (New York: Galaxy, 1982).

10. Robert E. Spiller; Willard Thorpe; Thomas J. Johnson; Henry Seidel Canby; and Richard M. Ludwig (eds.), Literary History of the United States (New York: Macmillan, 1963), p. 338.

11. Floyd Stovall, ed. The Poems of Edgar Allan Poe (Charlottesville: The University Press of Virginia, 1965), p. xxvi.

12. From "Emelia (an Essay on the Material and Spiritual Universe)," quoted in Spiller, et al., p. 337.

13. Another interesting comparison in connection with "Eldorado" is John Duke's setting, "The Mad Knight's Song," of a poem by John Heath-Stubs (Southern Music, 1959). Both describe an endless journey, but whereas "El Dorado's" knight seeks for gold, "the Mad Knight's" quest is to escape the searing pain of unrequited love.

14. Jack Beeson, "Indiana Homecoming" (New York: Boosey and Hawkes, 1973). Baritone.

15. The letter and poem are in: Nathaniel Wright Stephenson, comp., An Autobiography of Abraham Lincoln (Indianapolis: Bobbs-Merrill, 1926), pp. 57-59.

16. Only three were actually written.

17. Beeson interview.

18. Marie Hénault, Peter Viereck (New York: Twayne, 1969), p. 18.

19. Ibid.

20. Ibid., p. 34.

21. Ibid., p. 36.

22. Jack Beeson, "Big Crash Out West" (New York: Mills Music Co., 1963). Baritone. Dr. Beeson is hopeful that Boosey and Hawkes may reissue this song.

23. Hénault, p. 38.

24. Jack Beeson, "To a Sinister Potato" (New York: Boosey and Hawkes, 1973). Baritone.

25. Beeson interview.

26. Jack Beeson, "The You Should of Done It Blues" (New York: Boosey and Hawkes, 1973). Soprano.

27. Richard Owen, "Husband, Father, Attorney, Composer," Music Journal, XXV (April 1967), p. 37ff.

28. Lynn Owen, "Wife, Mother, Opera Singer," Music Journal, XXV (April 1967), p. 36f.

29. Cf. "I Hear an Army," a strikingly similar James Joyce poem set by Samuel Barber. This setting is found in the Schirmer collection of Barber's songs (see Note 8, Chapter 1 of this volume).

30. Quoted in John Berryman, Stephen Crane (New York: Octagon Books, 1975), p. 266.

31. Daniel Hoffman, The Poetry of Stephen Crane (New York: Columbia University Press, 1956), p. 4.

32. Berryman, p. 269.

33. Hoffman, pp. 262-264.

34. Richard Owen, "There were many who went in huddled procession" (New York: General Music Publishing, 1966). Medium voice. This song, together with "I saw a man pursuing the horizon," has been recorded by John Reardon, baritone, and Bliss Hebert, pianist, on the Serenus label (SRE-1019/SRS-12019).

35. Richard Owen, "I saw a man pursuing the horizon" (New York: General Music Publishing, 1966). Medium high voice.

36. Richard Owen, "The Impulse" (New York: General Music Publishing, 1966). Medium voice.

37. Malcolm Cowley, "The Case Against Mr. Frost," in Robert Frost, ed. James M. Cox (Englewood Cliffs, N.J.: Prentice-Hall, 1962), p. 39.

38. Richard Owen, "Patterns" (New York: General Music Publishing, 1973). Medium high voice.

39. e.e. cummings had quoted from Lowell's "Grotesque" in his Harvard commencement address on the "New Art." The effect on the audience was mostly shock and embarrassment on behalf of Harvard's president, Abbott Laurence Lowell, who was Amy's brother.

40. Jean Gould, Amy (New York: Dodd, Mead, 1975), p. 181.

41. See the Introduction to Volume II of this series for a discussion of the "little magazines" and their contribution to the "poetic renaissance."

42. Letter to the author dated August 26, 1983.

43. "Jean Eichelberger Ivey--a Retrospective," Peabody News, July 1983.

44. This review is reprinted in the chapter on Jean Eichelberger Ivey which appears in: Jane Weiner LePage, Woman Composers, Conductors and Musicians of the Twentieth Century (Metuchen, N.J.: Scarecrow Press, 1980).

45. A complete listing of her works with publishers is available from: Nancy Shear Music Services, 180 West End Ave., N.Y.C. 10023.

46. Jean Eichelberger Ivey, "The Contemporary Performing Ensemble," College Music Symposium, VIII (Fall 1968), pp. 120-128.

47. Jean Eichelberger Ivey, "Electronic Music Workshop for Teachers," Music Educators Journal, LV (November 1968), pp. 91-93.

48. Jean Eichelberger Ivey, "The Composer as Teacher," Peabody Conservatory Alumni Bulletin, XIV:1 (Fall/Winter 1974).

49. Letter of August 26, 1983 to the author.

50. The American Music Center's address is 250 W. 54th St., New York City, 10019.

51. "Ivey Retrospective" (see note 43 of this chapter).

52. Ibid.

53. Letter of August 26, 1983.

54. See note 9 of this chapter.

55. Ruth C. Friedberg, American Art Song and American Poetry, Volume II (Metuchen, N.J.: Scarecrow Press, 1984), p. 91.

56. From "On the Sussex Downs" to be found in: Sara Teasdale, Collected Poems (New York: Macmillan, 1966).

57. From "The Solitary," also in Teasdale's Collected Poems.

58. Available from the American Music Center.

59. Tim Page, "Music-Debuts in Review," The New York Times, Sunday, April 8, 1984.

IV. THE THIRD DECADE 2.

William Flanagan (1923-1969)
Edward Albee (1928-)
Howard Moss (1922-)

Throughout his crowded, intense, and tragically shortened
life, William Flanagan was slightly out of step. Not only
was he marching to a different drummer, but indeed it must
often have seemed to him as though he was part of a whole
different parade than the one which engaged the rest of his
world. To begin with, he was born in Detroit to a non-
musical family, and received little early training besides ex-
posure to Max Steiner's scores in the movie-houses of the
thirties which he then reproduced "by ear" as chapel organ-
ist for the University of Detroit High School.[1] Having begun
his college work in Detroit and Ann Arbor aiming at a more
"acceptable" career as a journalist, Flanagan capitulated,
after two years, to the strength of his inner pull toward
music. It was only at this point, at the age of twenty,
that he started, in his own words, "to learn musical nota-
tion, and to grapple with the bare concept of imposing con-
trol over my random improvisations."[2]

     The youthful talent ripened in three years of study at
the Eastman School under Burrill Phillips and Bernard Rogers.
By the late forties, Flanagan had shown sufficient promise to
be taken on as a scholarship student at the Berkshire Music
Center where he studied under Arthur Honegger, Samuel
Barber, and Aaron Copland. Settling in New York City, he
sharpened his compositional technique in two years of work

162

with David Diamond, and also began to share a Greenwich
Village apartment with a young man named Edward Albee
who was trying to find his place in the world of literature.

Except for a brief stint as instructor at the now de-
funct School of American Music, William Flanagan was to earn
his living for the next twenty years primarily as a journalist,
his supposedly abandoned profession, while trying to come to
terms with his own conclusion that "only three classical com-
posers in the United States today ... can make a living from
their music: Barber, Copland, and Thomson."[3] As a fur-
ther irony, it was Flanagan's sending The Zoo Story (Edward
Albee's first major play) to David Diamond in Italy, that
eventually led to its German and American productions, and
to the meteoric rise of Albee's theatrical career. Yet Flana-
gan's composing career could, it seemed, gain little luster by
creative association with his friend. Their collaboration on
the opera Bartleby, based on a Melville story, opened in 1961
to a cool reception by the New York critics; Albee's dramatic
adaptation of James Purdy's novel Malcolm, with Flanagan's
music, fared no better in 1966; and a final collaboration,
commissioned by the New York City Center, on an opera
called The Ice Age, remained uncompleted at the composer's
death. The single exception to this discouraging list re-
ceived comment in Flanagan's rueful article written in 1963
and titled "How to Succeed in Composing Without Really Suc-
ceeding." Here he describes how seven minutes of incidental
music for Albee's one-act play, The Sandbox, had, since its
1961 opening, earned him two thousand dollars in royalties,
"at least as much," he says, "as the many performances and
recordings of my music have over the thirteen years of my
career as a professional composer."[4]

Albee and Flanagan had, in fact, moved to separate
living quarters after the late fifties, but had remained
friends and continued to work together. Despite their di-
verging fortunes, the composer commented in an interview
with John Gruen that although "people have often thought
it odd ... to this day I have never known a moment of
jealousy about Edward's fame (and) have always taken great
pride in his success."[5] One of Gruen's own memories which
confirmed Flanagan's generosity of spirit concerned a night
when both were writing concert reviews for the New York
Herald Tribune, and Flanagan "had left his own review wait-
ing in the typewriter"[6] to ease Gruen's anxiety on this, his

first encounter with a deadline. Other of Gruen's recollections portray William Flanagan as "one of the most intellectually stimulating people I have ever known," as well as a "deeply unhappy, somewhat sullen and bitter person," who was prone to periods of heavy drinking during which, "as he lived alone, it was often difficult for him to call for help."7

Although peripheral by his own perceptions, Flanagan's position in the New York musical scene of the fifties and sixties was actually quite central. He was music essayist for many magazines and newspapers and served as an important critic and reviewer for successively, Musical America, the New York Herald Tribune, and Stereo Review; he wrote well over a hundred "sleeve" commentaries for almost a dozen record companies; and between 1959 and 1962 he was heavily involved in a concert series called Music for the Voice by Americans which presented and often premièred major songs by Ned Rorem, Virgil Thomson, David Diamond, Daniel Pinkham, John Gruen, and Lou Harrison as well as Flanagan himself.

This series was, according to Edward Albee, William Flanagan's "brainchild,"8 but the actual work of organization and implementation was, from the outset, shared by Ned Rorem, who was his "close, if competitive ally for twenty-three years."9 Rorem's diaries contain numerous references to dinner parties and correspondence shared, and an article about his friend published in Critical Affairs suggests how alike they were in their fundamental musical convictions. "We were the same age," says Rorem, "and of similar convictions, namely that there was still blood in tonality, breath in the simple line, and that the flesh of music could be grafted onto the skeleton of poetry and given life by the singing voice, with a feeling of heightened naturalness for the listener."10

Lester Trimble, still another American composer of about the same age, had known William Flanagan at Tanglewood, in Paris, and as a fellow critic for the Herald Tribune. In his memorial tribute, written two months after Flanagan was found dead in his New York apartment from an overdose of barbiturates, Trimble recounted the twofold "nature of the battle Flanagan was fighting in his creative and professional life."11 The first major strain he delineates was the composer's refusal to adopt the seemingly mandatory serial techniques of the successful avant-garde. The second was the advantage held by composers only five or six years older than Flanagan, whose careers had been solidly established before the traumatic interruptions of World War II. "I have no doubt," added Trimble "that the special obstacles posed against his generation have produced special inner tensions which ... were the underlying cause of his death." As a final irony, the last decade of William Flanagan's life had brought him the National Institute of Arts and Letters Award, a Pulitzer nomination, several major recordings, and commissions and performances of his works by leading orchestras. Out of step to the end, Flanagan, on the threshold of the recognition he had long desired, brought it all to a crashing halt.

Song had remained a favorite medium of William Flanagan's ever since his early settings, in 1946, of poetry by W.B. Yeats ("After Long Silence") and Siegfried Sassoon ("The Dugout").[12] He explained its early appeal as stemming from his lack of technique adequate to longer forms,[13] but as time went on, his innate vocal orientation became apparent even in the symphonic and chamber works,[14] as did his dedication to the art of word-setting in a growing body of songs. "The vocal line" wrote Flanagan "is a song's most elusive property. Its curves, its metrical pulse should be one with the rhythmic flow of the language."[15] The comments were scarcely surprising coming from an artist who, in a 1967 article, had listed Mozart, Mahler, Debussy, Poulenc, and Britten as among his ten favorite composers.[16]

On examining a complete listing of Flanagan's vocal works, one finds settings of a number of American poets, including Gertrude Stein,[17] e.e. cummings,[18] Herman Melville,[19] and Walt Whitman.[20] The composer also collaborated twice in this medium with Edward Albee, once in 1959, in a long cantata-like work for two singers and seven instruments called "The Lady of Tearful Regret," and on another occasion, nine years earlier, in a small masterpiece for solo voice and piano called "Song for a Winter Child."[21]

Edward Albee had been born in Washington, D.C. to natural parents whom he never knew, for at the age of two weeks he was adopted by millionaire Reed Albee and taken to Westchester County, N.Y. Here he grew up in the midst of

Edward Albee

physical luxury but almost unrelieved emotional poverty.
His adoptive father was a silent man, twenty-three years
older than his wife, Frances--a strong-willed former fashion
model who dominated the marriage. As a child, Edward was
not very close to the Albees, and also harbored deep-seated
resentment towards his natural parents. The only warmth
in his early years stemmed from his relationship with "Grand-
ma Cotta," Mrs. Albee's mother, who would leave him the in-
heritance that supported his decade of artistic struggle.[22]

       School represented a series of traumas for the "spoiled
... plump, precocious and unhappy" youth.[23] Expelled from
boarding school in Lawrenceville, New Jersey and from Valley
Forge military academy, Edward finally found a congenial at-
mosphere at the Choate School in Connecticut, where he be-
gan to write seriously and to turn out large quantities of
prose and poetry. After a short interlude at Hartford's
Trinity College, Albee ended his formal education and got a
job writing continuity for musical programs on radio station

WNYC. This position reflected a strong interest in music which had first surfaced at Lawrenceville and which would eventually carry over into his concepts of playwriting. "I always find," said Albee from a later vantage point, "a great association between plays and musical composition, [and] composer friends of mine have told me that my work is related very strongly to musical form as they understand it."[24]

At the age of twenty, Albee left home after a family argument, settled in New York, and held a series of odd jobs until the production of The Zoo Story in 1959 (see p. 163) brought him recognition as a major young dramatic talent. For nine years of this unsettled period, Albee and Flanagan shared an "airy and comfortable ... floor-through flat"[25] in the Village. On one occasion in 1950, Albee recalls, "Flanagan asked me to write a brief poem, which I did, which he set."[26] This, then, was the genesis of "Song for a Winter Child."

The poem, which is metrically free with a subtle rhyme scheme, and full of compelling imagery, has not, to this writer's knowledge, ever been published. Its message is that of welcome to a new infant whose coming has set "winter to flight as new grasses crack the hoping winter earth." One cannot help wondering whether Albee, who was himself born on March 12th, 1928, was not perhaps imagining on some level a poetic welcome for his own birth from all of spring-intoxicated Nature, having been denied by harsh circumstance the celebrations of mother and father as traditional welcomers.

Flanagan's setting, written only four years after he had begun composing, certainly demonstrates "a melodic style that is part and parcel of the language"[27]--his own description of a goal he felt had already been achieved by "popular" composers and should be imitated in serious music. Flexible quarter note groupings of 2, 3, 4, or 5 to the bar follow the poetry's changing accents; the prosody shows a keen ear for the rhythms of American speech; and the vocal contours rise and fall convincingly to the emotive context of the words. (See Ex. 4.1, page 168.)

The diatonic dissonances of the harmony, and largely chordal accompaniment with broadly arching counter melodies attest to Flanagan's years of study with David Diamond (see

Example 4.1, measures 1-8. © Copyright 1964, Peer International Corp.; used by permission.

Chapter 2). But the key movements (E to F to F sharp major with a brief interlude in C) are the ascending half-step relationships of Broadway, and the synthesis of all these elements with Flanagan's unerring instincts in text setting produces a new and exciting flavor that is unique in mid-twentieth century American song. Although the overall orientation of "Winter Child" is dramatic, with little lied-like verbal correspondence, there is one very effective instance of musical pictorialism in the last phrase. While the piano moves in legato augmentation, the voice sings a dropping line of tender eighth notes to set "And gentle rain will fall tonight." (See Ex. 4.2, page 169.)

On March 11, 1962, the fourth yearly concert in the Music for Voice by Americans series was given in Carnegie Recital Hall. There were nine composers represented and the conclusion of Musical America's reviewer was that "Flanagan's new cycle, Moss, was the strongest collection of songs

168

And gen-tle rain will fall to - night.

Example 4.2, measures 19-23. © Copyright 1964, Peer International Corp.; used by permission.

at the concert."[28] Indeed, in Howard Moss, William Flanagan appeared to have found an ideal poetic counterpart and the five products of this combination, still barely known to the American public, are a major contribution to the genre.

There were two important contrasts in Howard Moss' early life which broadened his world view beyond that of the average American schoolboy. The first was cultural, and stemmed from the "old country" influence in the house of his paternal grandparents, whom his father had brought over from Lithuania after himself "making it," as an immigrant, into middle-class American society. The second was geographical, for the family had settled in Rockaway Beach (a brief train ride from Manhattan) as a healthful place to raise a child, thus providing Howard's growing years with an ambiance that was "half sea-soaked, half citified."[29]

Well-nourished by all the gifts of nature, family tradition, and the metropolis, Moss began to write in grammar school, and in high school was already producing short stories and poetry. Reversing William Flanagan's progression, he left the New York area to spend his college years in the Middle West which beckoned with a "romantic aura."[30] He attended the University of Michigan for one year, and finished his B.A. at the University of Wisconsin, where, as a sophomore, his first poem was accepted for publication by Accent.

Finding his proper niche in the literary world, however, involved a number of "tries." Even before graduation

Howard Moss
(Photo: Copyright © 1983 Thomas Victor)

from college, he had had a dazzling rise from copy-boy to
book-reviewer during a period of employment by <u>Time</u> maga-
zine.   After graduation, there was a short stint with the
Office of War Information as World War II came to a close;
some graduate work at Columbia never completed; two years

teaching English at Vassar College; and a year as fiction editor of Junior Bazaar. In 1948 he joined the editorial staff of the New Yorker, where he has remained as poetry editor ever since 1950.

His own poems had brought him Poetry magazine's Janet Sewall David award in 1944, as the first of many subsequent prizes. Two years later he published his first book, The Wound and the Weather, a volume of poems which would be followed by ten more in the ensuing quarter of a century. In Selected Poems of 1971, he made choices from the seven preceding volumes, and for this collection he was co-winner of the 1972 National Book Award in poetry. Moss says he has given up fiction, since "none of it is any good,"[31] but he has written a number of plays which have had small productions. Interestingly, his The Palace at 4 A.M. was produced in the summer of 1972 at the John Drew Theater in East Hampton with Edward Albee as its director.

In 1975 Moss described having lived in the same garden-terraced Greenwich Village apartment for the past twenty years. Moving no doubt, in the same Village circles as Flanagan and Albee in the fifties, the poet and his work evidently had come to the attention of the composer, and the flood of Flanagan-Moss settings began in 1959. William Flanagan's attraction to Howard Moss' poetry might well have been predicted, for Flanagan's resistance to the stylish musical fads of his time was paralleled by Moss' stated position that "Schools of poetry (and) insistences on the way to write or not to write are deadening."[32] Stylistically, too, they were well-matched, for Moss' ability to "convey complex states of feeling"[33] in his poetry was equalled by Flanagan's plastic and subtle command of rhythmic, melodic, and harmonic nuance.

William Flanagan in a 1968 article had credited Leonard Bernstein with "more influence on popular music than any other composer of his time. What he did" added Flanagan, "was to take the vocabulary of Copland and Stravinsky and sneak it onto Broadway [which] filtering through of these sources has created a whole new musical vocabulary."[34] In the Moss cycle, Flanagan takes this new vocabulary and brings it back into the art song, with its Broadway experience still clinging to it--a direction that Paul Bowles had begun to explore some fifteen years earlier (see Chapter 2). The influences are clearly seen in the theatrical waltz background and sudden dynamic spurts, plus the added sixth and seventh chords of "Planets Cannot Travel"[35] (written in 1959).

Example 4.3, measures 1-6.   Copyright 1963, C.F. Peters Corp.; used by permission.

The text of this song is a single ten-line verse of a longer, seven-sectioned poem called "Cliché's for Piano and Orchestra," and the pervasive accompaniment figure (see Ex. 4.3) could be easily related to the pianist's contribution in a theater orchestra.   This verse, which echoes the e.e. cummings preoccupation with love as the universe's enabling mystery, suggests that love's "miracle" can invest the natural world with at least the appearance of consciousness.   The rest of the "Cliché's," however, turn toward doubt and depression, thus making Flanagan's abruptly joyful vocal leaps followed by a swift descent of pitch and dynamics appropriate to the overall poetic context.

Example 4.4, measures 14-29. Copyright 1963, C.F. Peters Corp.; used by permission.

The other four Moss settings were all composed in 1961 and 1962 and published two to three years thereafter. For the text of "If You Can,"[36] Flanagan used a complete poem, without change or deletion, taken from <u>A Winter Come</u>, <u>A Summer Gone</u>, which was Moss' third volume of poetry, published in 1960. The form of this poem is interesting, having a complicated rhyme scheme which interrelates the four four-line stanzas, plus a refrain which adds one line after each stanza to achieve its final form:

> For I have loved
> But not loved well
> If I have loved
> At all.

The theme of the poem is closely tied to that of "Plants Cannot Travel" and the two songs were originally published together. This time the poet sees the physical world as a mystery which can be given meaning and reality only through love--an emotion which he is not certain he has ever truly experienced. Here, in one of his strongest settings, Flanagan demonstrates his dramatic flair and lyrical gifts, as musical-theater derived modulations and chordal constructions are subsumed in a fabric of inspired prosodic choices and motivic manipulation.

Having begun in F sharp major, a favorite Flanagan key, the thematic construction eventually lowers into a quasi-operatic contour in C major. (See Ex. 4.5, page 174.) It then combines the germinal motivic intervals of a minor second and major sixth into a final vocal phrase ("I have loved at all") that blossoms as a piano postlude. (See Ex. 4.6, page 174.)

Example 4.5, measures 35-36. Copyright 1963, C.F. Peters
Corp.; used by permission.

Example 4.6, measures 44-52. Copyright 1963, C.F. Peters
Corp.; used by permission.

As a final elegant detail, the last two measures (see Ex.
4.6) are a transposed repetition of the voice line's opening
melody on "Country-man, tell me if you can." The resulting
sense of formal and conceptual unity has been masterfully
achieved.

The March, 1962 concert (see p. 168) which premiered
the Moss songs had included two settings of his poem "See
How They Love Me," one by Flanagan,[37] and another by Ned
Rorem. As indicated in a letter from Howard Moss to the
author, "'See How They Love Me' was originally a poem on
its own [and] was then incorporated as section 7 of a much

longer poem, 'King Midas.'"[38] Setting aside its later inclusion into the myth of the "golden king," the poem standing alone is a succinct, moving lyric which juxtaposes human rejection to the poet's loving acceptance by natural elements ("green leaf, gold grass ... blue sea," etc.).

The 1962 reviewer had found it "interesting to compare the strophic-like setting by Rorem with the freer improvisatory one by Flanagan."[39] Evidently he missed the equally strophic flavor lent by Flanagan's basic motif which, with only slight pitch or rhythmic changes, begins each of the song's four verses (measures 1 and 2).

Example 4.7, measures 1-3. Copyright 1965, C.F. Peters Corp.; used by permission.

It is true, however, that the piano accompaniment markedly changes in figuration as the verses gain in intensity, and that the third verse culminates in a dramatic a cappella line beginning with a high subito piano on F sharp, Flanagan's frequently encountered "note of ecstasy."

Example 4.8, measures 16-18. Copyright 1965, C.F. Peters Corp.; used by permission.

175

The fourth and final verse introduces a nervous sixteenth note triplet into the piano part which seems to contrast the niggardly human emotion of "rebuke" with the more expansive eighth note triplet of nature's warmth (see Ex. 4.7).

Example 4.9, measures 22-24.   Copyright 1965, C.F. Peters Corp.; used by permission.

"Horror Movie"[40] is a setting of a poem from A Swimmer in the Air, Moss' third collection, published in 1957.   In this setting, both artists prove themselves thoroughly at home in contemporary farce: the poem's rhymed couplets frequently recall Ogden Nash ("You took the gold to Transylvania / Where no one guessed how insane you were") and the piano figurations are a send-up of melodramatic movie music from the silent films on out.   (See Ex. 4.10, page 177.)   Most of the vocal writing is declamatory in the interests of the text's narrative emphasis, while the form is through-composed and sectional with motivic interweaving suspended as inappropriate.   An especially notable moment is the pianistic tango figure which emerges rather suddenly to set the stage for the appearance of two exotic figures: the Spider Woman and Dracula.   (See Ex. 4.11, page 177.)

"The Upside Down Man"[41] was completed in January, 1962, just two months before its concert première.   Although written earlier, the poem was first published in a Moss collection when it appeared in Finding Them Lost (1965).   The interesting thesis of this poem is that man, formed as he is, suffers from having his feet "chained to earth," and the poet here imagines the soliloquy of a more fortunately formed being

Example 4.10, measures 1-5. Copyright 1965, C.F. Peters Corp.; used by permission.

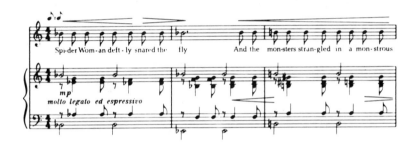

Example 4.11, measures 22-24. Copyright 1965, C.F. Peters Corp.; used by permission.

who experiences the world in positional reverse. The needs of the text give rise to a very angular, leaping vocal line, as well as a mostly linear accompaniment in which the hands frequently imitate each other at the interval of an octave or a tenth. (See Ex. 4.12, page 178.) Most of the song is in C major with much overlay of chromatic dissonance, but a single passage of diatonic lyricism pulls to one of Flanagan's favorite heavily-laden sharp keys, in this case B major. (See Ex. 4.13, page 178.)

Example 4.12, measures 5-7. © Copyright 1964, Peer International Corp.; used by permission.

Example 4.13, measures 24-26. © Copyright 1964, Peer International Corp.; used by permission.

In 1970, a memorial concert of Flanagan's music took place at the Whitney Museum. Ned Rorem accompanied some of his songs, Albee's Sandbox with music by Flanagan was presented, and the late composer's talents were praised by no lesser figures than Aaron Copland and Virgil Thomson. Shortly before, Thomson had written in American Music Since 1910 that although "the English art song is not yet a major form" and "has never achieved psychology or drama as we know these qualities through the German or French," the songs of William Flanagan nevertheless "have a soaring intensity all unusual to the English language."[42] Bill Flanagan's songs, it seemed, had conquered even the redoubtable Virgil Thomson. It is past time for their rediscovery by the rest of us.

Ruth Schonthal (1924-)
Walt Whitman (1819-1892)

Ruth Schonthal belongs in that category of American compos-
ers who were not born in this country, but who, like Charles
Loeffler and Sergius Kagen, emigrated here as young adults,
and soon became firmly woven into the fabric of the American
musical scene. Schonthal's birthplace was Hamburg, Germany.
Her parents were Viennese, and they actively encouraged
their precociously talented daughter, who began to compose
at the age of five and in the same year became the youngest
student ever accepted at the Stern Conservatory in Berlin.

In 1937, the Schonthals fled Hitler's Germany, leaving
everything behind. The composer's father, who had a weak
heart, would never thereafter discuss this extremely painful
loss of home, friends, and possessions. Stockholm provided
a temporary and uneasy refuge as Schonthal continued her
studies there at the Royal Academy of Music, but the family
moved again just three months before the completion of her
degree. This time they located in Mexico City (where Schon-
thal's mother still owns a shop) and the young woman was
taken on as a composition student by Manuel Ponce.

While traveling in Mexico on a concert tour, Paul Hinde-
mith heard about Ruth Schonthal's talent, and shortly there-
after arranged for her to study composition with him on
scholarship at Yale University. She came to the United
States in 1946, earned a Bachelor of Music degree at Yale,
and remained to become a U.S. citizen, marry, and raise a
family of three boys. Her husband is a painter and lithog-
rapher and one son followed in his artistic parents' foot-
steps by attending Juilliard and becoming a violist and com-
poser.

Ruth Schonthal is a concert pianist as well as composer
and she has had an active teaching career in the areas of
piano, composition, and music literature. In 1973, after a
number of years of private teaching, she joined the faculty
of Adelphi University. Three years later she began to teach
at Westchester Conservatory and eventually bought a home
in New Rochelle after constantly missing trains back to her
Manhattan apartment because of her unwillingness to cut a
lesson short. At the time of the author's interview with Ruth

Ruth Schonthal

Schonthal (December 3, 1982), she had also held a part-time position teaching "period" and "genre" courses at New York University for four or five years. She described this as a difficult situation, due to lack of tenure and fringe benefits plus the financial uncertainty of a teaching load tied to unpredictable course enrollments.

Schonthal is a small, vital, personable woman with black, slightly graying hair and dark, intense eyes. She and the writer met on the steps of Carnegie Hall, talked in a nearby coffee-house, then drove to Town Hall to pick up programs for an upcoming concert in the International Chamber Artists series which would include a world première of her chamber work "Aranjuez." The composer maintains humor and perspective despite the many struggles of her life which have included the raising of her mentally retarded oldest son, now living in a group home. Nor has recognition of her creative work come easily, for as Schonthal explains, she "does everything herself for her career and it is hard to get the music out to publishers."

During the last decade, however, Ruth Schonthal's reputation as an important contemporary composer has become firmly established. For her one-act opera, The Courtship of Camilla, she became a finalist in the 1980 New York City Opera Competition, and the previous year she was nominated for the Kennedy Center-Friedheim Award for In Homage of.... (a set of 24 piano preludes). She has won a number of ASCAP music awards and "Meet the Composer" grants; her music is being played in major American and European music centers, and she herself is in demand for lectures, workshops, and guest appearances on radio and television. Her song cycle Totengesänge, which sets her own poetic texts, has been recorded by Leonarda Records, and Capriccio Records has recently released her piano works performed by pianist Gary Steigerwalt.

Four publishing houses are currently issuing Schonthal works, and facsimiles of unpublished scores are available from the American Music Center and the composer herself. [43] Her catalog includes instrumental works for orchestra, solo instruments, and chamber groups; works for solo voice and vocal chamber music; one opera (see above); and the film score for Lantern Love. When asked about the influence of other composers on her work, Schonthal mentions Beethoven's structural method of working, Brahms' warmth, and the emotional styles of Schubert and Wagner. She feels that Hindemith, from whom she learned harmonic and contrapuntal control, influenced her composition only during the time she was studying with him.

Ruth Schonthal is fluent in five languages: the German, French, Spanish, and English gleaned from her world travels, and the Italian which she taught herself. It is interesting, therefore, that the texts of her vocal works are all either in German (she set Rilke at the age of fourteen) or in English (the majority of these are British, such as the poetry of Yeats and Wordsworth). Commenting on the different problems in setting German and English texts, Schonthal says:

> Of course the language changes the style of the music because of its sound qualities and accents. But besides this, I change my personality and the tempo of my speech when I change languages. Even English and American speech are different: English is more elaborate, mannered, civilized with a sheen, while American is open, direct, and deliberate. After all, American immigration was self-selected--those who wanted to get away from traditions to a more open society.

Given this view of America, it is not surprising that Walt Whitman is the single American poet that Schonthal has thus far chosen for setting. She explains that she "loves Whitman, and when [she] wanted to write an American work, felt that he was typically American." Schonthal was also drawn to "the conciseness of the short poems" since she "loves conciseness in general" and found a strong appeal in the "emotional climate"[44] of this writing. The poems to which she refers come from the section of Leaves of Grass that is subtitled "By the Roadside" and this is the same title that Schonthal assigned to a remarkable ten page song cycle which sets six of them.[45]

Earlier volumes of this author's series have discussed Walt Whitman's life,[46] as well as settings of Whitman texts drawn from the exultant, life-celebrating Song of Myself (1855)[47] and from the more reflective, sometimes somber poetry of Inscriptions[48] and Drum Taps,[49] written ten years later. Thomas Crawley, in his structural analysis of Leaves of Grass postulates that a bridge "was needed between the exuberant story of material and social development and success of 'Song of Myself' ... and the dark, critical experiences of 'Drum-Taps' " (Whitman's Civil War poetry). "To perform this function," he continues, "scattered poems of doubt and turmoil were collected under 'By the Roadside.' "[50] It is also true, that in this transitional phase of Whitman's

verse, the expansiveness and the catalogs of the earlier
writing give way to sharply focused portraits, delineated
with the conciseness that Schonthal found so appealing.
And perhaps, too, this composer, whose youth had been
traumatized by man's inhumanity to man, felt herself to be
on familiar ground with Whitman's increasingly pessimistic
view of America's capacity for self-delusion and destruction
as the country moved uneasily toward and over the brink
of war.

The six poems that Schonthal selected are all very
short (between one and four lines in length), all unrhymed,
and with varying poetic meters, although there is a prepon-
derance of three and six stress lines. They are not all
alike in mood, however, and seem to fall into two distinct
groups: those written in 1860 ("Thought," "Visor'd," "To
Old Age") which are philosophical reflections on man's con-
dition and behavior; and those from 1865 ("Mother and
Babe," "A Farm Picture," "A Child's Amaze") which pre-
sent vignettes of American life drawn from observation or
memory. Schonthal has not opted for a chronological ar-
rangement in the cycle, but for an artistic one, which re-
sembles a circular structure. She opens with the pictorial
"Mother and Babe," continues with the three reflective
verses of 1860, and concludes with the Americana pieces
"A Farm Picture" and "A Child's Amaze."

In "Mother and Babe," the poet sees a mother nursing
her infant, and gazes at them "long and long" in a state of
"hush'd" contemplation which suggests his awed tribute to
the miracle of life and its processes. Schonthal sets this
text and begins her cycle with an appropriately soft dy-
namic level and gently rocking 6/8 (or 9/8) meter.

Example 4.14, measures 1-6. Copyright 1979, Oxford University Press; used by permission.

In a middle section marked "Quasi doppio movimento" the eighth notes move twice as fast in contrary motion, hinting at a rush of emotion arising in the poet as he "studies them."

Example 4.15, measures 14-18. Copyright 1979, Oxford University Press; used by permission.

As can be seen in Example 4.14, the opening harmonic scheme uses the superimposed tonalities of C major and E

major in the piano part, with the voice joining in the right
hand's E major but at mostly dissonant intervals to the ac-
companiment. The vocal line by itself is an arching diatonic
contour, as are the individual lines of the "doppio movimento"
which nevertheless clash in consort. Similarly, the song
ends with warm, softening B major chords, and their ambig-
uous echoes of dissonant minor seconds. The combined ef-
fect of all these harmonic juxtapositions is that of a timeless
lullaby filtering through a contemporaneous and possibly
threatening haze.

   "Thought" is the most pessimistic poem of the whole
"By the Roadside" series and contains Whitman's discouraged
observation, no doubt occasioned by pre-Civil War politics,
of how easily men could be led by demagogues "who do not
believe in men." Schonthal begins this setting in dramatic
contrast to number one with a forte, accented, sixteenth to
quarter note accompaniment pattern of consecutive fourths,
with the two hands almost on top of each other as they clash
angrily in the bass register.

Example 4.16, measures 1-4. Copyright 1959, Oxford Uni-
versity Press; used by permission.

   As the soprano enters softly in the bottom of her
range the piano remains in its depressed lower octaves, and
the tempo changes to a musing andante. Gradually then,
the vocal and right hand pitches rise (over a grimly repeti-
tive D pedal point) while the tempo accelerates to a climactic
point of despair.

185

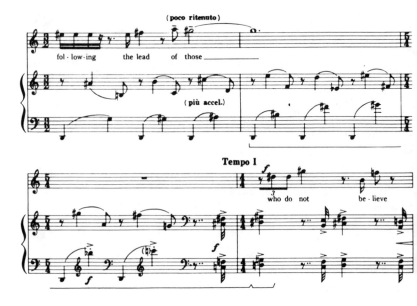

Example 4.17, measures 12-15. Copyright 1959, Oxford University Press; used by permission.

Now the battering fourths of the introduction return (see Example 4.16), again serving to escalate the original poetic negativity from sorrow to disgust.

Number three of the cycle sets "Visor'd," Whitman's evocation of a woman whose face was always a changing mask of concealment, even in sleep. Schonthal takes off brilliantly from the text line "Changes and transformations every hour, every moment" to create a musical climate of constantly altering meters, tempos, vocal rhythms, and broken chordal structures. "Even when she sleeps" the changes continue, now in a whispered pianissimo dynamic with tiptoeing staccato accompaniment. (See Ex. 4.18, page 187.) Interestingly, this song contains the only instance of the composer's changing Whitman's original texts. In the line "a perpetual natural disguiser of herself," she chooses to omit the word "natural," probably in pursuit of a more forceful vocal contour which is rising at that point to a climax in solo recitative. (See Ex. 4.19, page 187 and page 188.)

Example 4.18, measures 13-20. Copyright 1959, Oxford University Press; used by permission.

Example 4.19, measures 1-6. Copyright 1979, Oxford University Press; used by permission.

In the fourth poem, "To Old Age," the poet compares the late years of human life to an "estuary that enlarges ... as it pours into the great sea." This powerful metaphor for Whitman's concept of the individual soul preparing to return to universal consciousness gains further strength in its musical mating. Large-interval arpeggios, with the right hand climbing into the upper register, create an appropriate pianistic context of expansion as the voice also rises to the climactic moment of fulfillment:

Example 4.20, measures 4-13. Copyright 1979, Oxford University Press; used by permission.

There is greater consonance between voice and accompaniment in this setting, and a clear D major is carried upward in scalar fashion by the vocal line to the very moment of transformation ("grandly"), signified by the sudden appearance of D flat major. Thereafter the original key quietly reasserts itself, as the soul loses itself in God (see Ex. 4.20).

"A Farm Picture," painted by Walt Whitman in number five, was a scene of daily life to the poet, but "the peaceful country barn" and "sunlit pasture field" take on the aspect of a nostalgia piece in the face of late twentieth century encroachments on the farmer's tranquillity. The setting enhances this flavor, with its forthright C major opening in a swinging 6/8 folk-like pattern. Towards the end, a sudden slowing of tempo and rhythmic movement, and a drift to "hazy" A major/minor key references set up the musical "fading" of the picture into the "far horizon" of the past.

Example 4.21, measures 7-15. Copyright 1979, Oxford University Press; used by permission.

In the final song, "A Child's Amaze," Schonthal adds her lively sense of humor to Whitman's irony and creates a bravura ending to the cycle. The verse is a recollection of the poet's boyhood amazement while listening to the preacher speak of God as though "contending against some being or influence." Schonthal surrounds this text with a pseudo chorale-prelude accompaniment as it would be played by a bad church piano player on a worse instrument ("non legato, clangy, with much pedal"):

Example 4.22, measures 1-3. Copyright 1979, Oxford University Press; used by permission.

The voice then enters timidly ("hymnlike, as sung by a child") but as the memory unfolds, begins to imitate the pomposity of the preacher, while the piano pounds away with increasing vigor:

Example 4.23, measures 19-25. Copyright 1979, Oxford University Press; used by permission.

As the Ivesian scene draws to a close, the piano player strikes the triumphant final chord and hits a few wrong notes out of sheer exuberance (see Ex. 4.23).

Richard Cumming (1928-   )
Philip Minor (1927-   )

Richard Cumming's early life was centered in the West coast and the Orient which it faces. Born in Shanghai to American parents, he was brought back to the States to settle in California and graduated in 1945 from George Washington High School in San Francisco. For the next six years he attended the San Francisco Conservatory of Music, spending the summers of 1947 and 1948 at the Music Academy of the West in Santa Barbara and those of 1949 and 1950 at the Griller Quartet Summer School in San Francisco. During these same years he studied the piano with Herbert Jaffe and Lili Kraus, and, as a talent for composition began to emerge, was able to develop it through lessons with three towering figures who were teaching nearby: Roger Sessions, then professor of music at Berkeley; Ernest Bloch who left his Oregon retreat each summer to teach, also at Berkeley; and Arnold Schönberg who was at that time seeing just a few private students in his Los Angeles home.

From 1951 to 1956, Cumming did a great deal of per-

191

Richard Cumming

forming as a concert pianist. There were solo recitals, ap-
pearances as soloist with a number of West coast orchestras,
and as chamber player with the Griller and San Francisco
Quartets and the Corinthian Piano Quintet. During the early
fifties, he spent several summers at Aspen where he contin-
ued piano study with Rudolph Firkusny, and in the summer
of 1954 served as assistant to the directors of the Aspen
Institute (Victor Babin and Richard P. Leach). Through
all these formative years, a strong empathy for the vocal
repertoire was developing and in 1950 Cumming began a
twenty-five year stint as concert accompanist during which
he would play for Phyllis Curtin, Donald Gramm,[51] Frank
Guerrera, Florence Kopleff, Martial Singher, Jennie Tourel,
and many others.

Around 1955, Richard Cumming met Philip Minor, who

at that time was spending his summers acting and directing with the Princeton University Players. As Minor puts it, he "got Richard Cumming into the theater,"[52] and from that point on, Cumming turned his talents increasingly to use in musical/dramatic contexts. He, too, joined the Princeton University Players (as composer-in-residence) through the summers of 1957 to 1960, and for the three following years served as an assistant conductor at the Santa Fe Opera in New Mexico. From 1963 to 1967 he alternated winters and summers as composer-in-residence for the Milwaukee Repertory Theatre, and the Marin Shakespeare Festival at San Rafael, California. In 1966 he moved his home and the center of his artistic activities, to Providence, Rhode Island. There he has remained composer-in-residence at the Trinity Square Repertory Company for almost twenty years, besides serving as their director of educational services until 1980, when he became the company's literary manager. Since taking up residence in Rhode Island, Cumming has also taught in the Providence Arts Magnet Program and the Rhode Island Governor's School for Youth in the Arts, and has spent several years as both a music and a theater consultant to the Rhode Island State Council on the Arts.

Richard Cumming's impressive catalog of works includes scores for nearly seventy-five plays, ranging from Euripides and Shakespeare to Brecht and Saroyan. By the 1970's, having had wide experience with the literary demands of the dramatic situation, he became the co-author and adaptor, with Adrian Hall, of a number of dramatic pieces for stage, radio, and film (such as Ethan Frome, an adaptation of the Edith Wharton novel). As regards the non-dramatic areas of his composition, it is interesting to note that, outside of a sizable group of piano works,[53] almost all the rest are text-oriented. The large majority of his chamber and orchestral works are for voice plus instruments, and the catalog also shows seventeen choral settings and over seventy songs.[54] Of the seventy, fully half are based on the work of American poets. There are two settings of Robert Frost, two of Muriel Rukeyser, five of Walt Whitman, and a number by less familiar writers some of whom, like Philip Minor, are primarily known for their work in other fields.

Philip Minor was born, one year earlier than Richard Cumming, in the town of Butler, Pennsylvania. His parents lived, for the first twenty years of their married life, in various countries of South America, and in Mexico. The longest period in one place was 1935 to 1944 in Buenos Aires, where Minor attended an American school, fulfilling the Argentine government's curriculum while preparing to enter an American college. In 1944, he graduated from high school, came to the States, and attended Princeton University for one year. Minor was then drafted into the United States Army Air Force where he claims to have spent "thirteen totally unproductive months, but as the first lengthy exposure to life in these United States," he adds, "it was quite an eye opener."[55] He then returned to Princeton, and graduated in 1950 with a degree from the Woodrow Wilson School of Public and International Affairs.

At this point occurred one of those complete changes of direction often made by people who are beginning to feel impelled toward an artistic career. This is how Minor describes what happened:

> The next few years were spent in an attempt to carve out some sort of a career as an actor, and eventually, as an actor-director. I lived in Greenwich Village--where else?--and did the usual things: odd jobs to keep body and soul together; small productions hither and yon. I attended the Royal Academy of Dramatic Art in London, 1952-53. On returning, I began to work with the University Players in Princeton, New Jersey, for approximately seven summers, which is where I received whatever real theatrical training I have.[56]

Minor has lived in New York since 1951, except for the time spent in London while at the Royal Academy. He has worked extensively with the APA-Phoenix Lyceum Theatre and the Sheridan Square Playhouse in New York City, and has also traveled around the country to such regional theaters as the Guthrie Theater in Minneapolis, Alley Theater in Houston, and the Trinity Square Repertory Theater in Providence. He continues to both act and direct, but admits to spending most of his time and energy on the latter. Teaching has been another phase of his career. Besides shorter appointments at New York University, Circle in the Square, and the American Academy of Dramatic Art, his most important academic connection was to Bennington College, which continued, off and on, from 1970 to 1980.

On the occasion of his meeting with Richard Cumming in 1955, Minor, who says he is "not a musician, but plays the piano,"[57] recalls that the two of them "played four-hand Mozart, Haydn, and von Weber, and listened to a recording of Strauss' Four Last Songs with Elizabeth Schwarzkopf."[58] He also disclaims the title of poet and says he does not write verse very often, but admits that the muse may strike again at any time, adding that he is currently involved in translating the libretto of a little known Donizetti opera into English.

Richard Cumming has a different view of Minor's poetic talents, and describes the genesis of the song cycle on which they collaborated in these terms:

> Philip Minor has been an old, dear, and valued friend of mine for almost thirty years. In 1959, he made his own translation of Jacinto Benavente's The Bonds of Interest which was produced in New York City. Act III of that play closed with a ravishing serenade, the words of which I liked so much I asked him to think of writing me some more poems for concert songs. Other Loves[59] resulted. They were written for Helen Vanni and first sung by her in 1974 at the Cleveland Institute of Music.[60]

The première of Cumming's other song cycle, We Happy Few,[61] had been presented in 1964 by Donald Gramm who had commissioned the work through the Ford Foundation Program for Concert Soloists. Reviewing it, Musical America called Richard Cumming a "notable vocal composer" who, in all the songs, found "interesting things for the voice to do, and things which set the voice off well."[62] Nineteen years later, in his liner notes for the 1983 issuance of Cambridge Records' retrospective Cumming disc (see Note 51c), Ned Rorem describes his songs similarly, but more colorfully, as "delectably singable goodies." Rorem further characterizes Cumming as "a survivor, being of that handful of Americans who were writing first-rate tonal songs 35 years ago, and who, in their madness, persisted in writing such songs to this day." Finally he recalls his first meeting with Richard Cumming, now a long-time friend, in New York in 1956, and discovering that "we and only a few others (Flanagan, Daniel Pinkham, who else?) were playing the game."

The impressive degree of skill with which Richard
Cumming continues to "play the game" is clearly evident in
Other Loves. "First rate tonal songs" they are, but with a
tonality constantly adapting to the needs of the text and the
times, and with a buoyant, effortless clarity of texture that
is a Cumming trademark. The three free-verse poems which
provide the text of this mini-cycle immediately invite musical
setting with their titles: "Summer Song," "Night Song,"
and "Love Song." As it happens, the unity of this set is
found mostly in the titles. All, it is true, are "Songs," but
of a riveting diversity, with the first a languid portrait of
fulfillment, the second a lament for lost love, and the third
a rollicking celebration by a "torch carrier"[63] who is about
to drop his torch.

Minor's "Summer Song" is haiku-like in feeling, if not
in form, with its images of satiated bees, lolling catfish, and
branches barely moving in a light breeze. Striving is
erased and meaning is implicit in the moment as the poet in-
tones "Now. Now!" Cumming rises to this challenge with a
series of choices that effectively annihilate musical drive.
His triplet piano figures circle back on themselves, and the
"lento e languido" 5/4 meter incorporates long, lazy pauses
on beats two, four, and five.

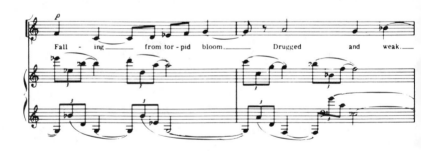

Example 4.24, measures 3-4. Copyright © 1982, Galaxy
Music Corp., New York, N.Y.; used by permission.

"G" is clearly the tonal center, but it is softened with
desultory lowerings of the third and sixth degrees (see Ex.
4.24). More importantly, the seventh scalar degree appears
most prominently as F rather than F sharp, thus sacrificing
its pull to the tonic.

Example 4.25, measures 19-23. Copyright © 1982, Galaxy
Music Corp., New York, N.Y.; used by permission.

Notice that as the song ends (Ex. 4.25), the measures length-
en from five quarter note beats to six, and then the triplet
figures disappear. It is as though time itself has stopped.

"Night Song" is a poignant farewell to a lover who was
so "eager to be gone" that the poet has been left with "un-
claimed treasures in [his] weeping hands." It is unclear
from the poetry whether it is a rival or death whose hand
now "lies softly" on the absent one's throat, but Cumming's
"blues" setting seems to opt for the lesser tragedy of the
former. Over a recurrent chordal background full of the
sixths, sevenths, ninths, and thirteenths of "popular" har-
mony, the composer sculpts an artfully contoured vocal la-
ment which rises and falls in the familiar framework of two
choruses, verse, and chorus: (see Ex. 4.26, page 198).
One may find, in this song, some parallels to Paul Bowles'
settings such as "Sugar in the Cane" and "Once a Lady was
Here" (see Chapter I). It is worth remembering that Bowles,
like Cumming, composed heavily in the areas of musicals and
theater scores, both of which have become increasingly
strong and vitalizing influences on the American art songs
of recent decades (see p. 171 for a discussion of William
Flanagan's participation in this trend).

Example 4.26, measures 1-5. Copyright © 1982, Galaxy
Music Corp., New York, N.Y.; used by permission.

Cumming and Minor end their trilogy with a nicely con-
trasting touch of sophisticated humor. "Love Song" proves
to be an ironic title, for the poet's heart is longing to be re-
leased, "like a rampant kite" that is constantly pulled back
by the "candied chains" of his passion. The bright, brassy
tone of Broadway is never far from the surface as Cumming
writes a jazzy, syncopated introduction, simple but propul-
sive chordal piano part, and a voice line that borrows the
rhythmic emphasis and dramatic leaps of the musical comedy
idiom.

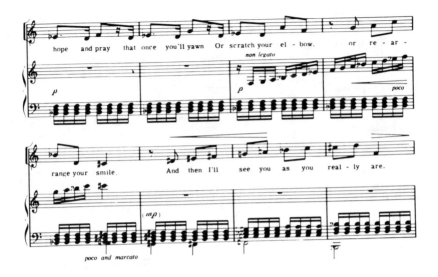

Example 4.27, measures 1-12. Copyright © 1982, Galaxy Music Corp., New York, N.Y.; used by permission.

The agitated speed of the "allegro commodo" keeps a steady pace with the lover's desperation. As he begins his vision of freedom, the intensity is increased by a tango-like syncopation in the melodic line that releases into an unmeasured "liberamente" declaration and a final, child-like shout of glee.

Example 4.28, measures 38-44. Copyright © 1982, Galaxy Music Corp., New York, N.Y.; used by permission.

NOTES

1. Edward Albee, "William Flanagan," Bulletin of the American Composers' Alliance, IX:4 (1961), p. 12.

2. Lester Trimble, "William Flanagan (1923-1969)," Stereo Review, XXIII (November 1969), p. 118.

3. Peter Reilly, "William Flanagan," Stereo Review, XXI:5 (November 1968), p. 134.

4. William Flanagan, "How to Succeed in Composing Without Really Succeeding," Bulletin of the American Composers' Alliance, XI:1 (1963), p. 8.

5. John Gruen, The Party's Over (New York: Viking, 1972), p. 114. This is an excellent series of memoirs of New York artistic life in the fifties by John Gruen who is himself a writer, composer, and art historian.

6. Ibid., p. 110.

7. Ibid., p. 110 and 118.

8. Albee, p. 12.

9. Ned Rorem, Critical Affairs (New York: George Braziller, 1970), p. 119.

10. Ibid.

200

11. Trimble, p. 118.

12. A complete listing of Flanagan's works up to that date can be found in the following article: Ned Rorem, "(William Flanagan) and his music," Bulletin of the American Composers' Alliance, IX:4 (1961), pp. 13-19.

13. Trimble, p. 118.

14. Rorem, p. 14.

15. Ibid., p. 15.

16. William Flanagan, "My Ten Favorite Composers," Hi Fi/ Stereo Review, XIX (September 1967), pp. 68-69.

17. a) William Flanagan/Gertrude Stein, "Valentine to Sherwood Anderson" (New York: Peer International Corp., 1948). Mezzo-soprano.
      b) William Flanagan/Gertrude Stein, "A Very Little Snail" (New York: American Composers' Alliance, 1949). Soprano.

18. William Flanagan/e.e. cummings, "Buffalo Bill" (New York: American Composers' Alliance, 1947).

19. William Flanagan/Herman Melville, Times Long Ago (New York: Peer International Corp., 1951). Cycle of six songs for soprano.

20. William Flanagan/Walt Whitman, "Goodbye, My Fancy" (New York: Peer International Corp., 1959). Soprano, flute, and guitar.

21. William Flanagan, "Song for a Winter Child" (New York: Peer International Corp., 1964). Medium voice.

22. Information in preceding paragraph from: John Wakeman, World Authors, 1950-1970 (New York: H.W. Wilson, 1975), p. 22.

23. Ibid.

24. Richard E. Amacher, Edward Albee (New York: Twayne, 1969), p. 37.

25. Ibid., p. 18.

26. Letter from Edward Albee to the author, dated November 30, 1983.

27. Back cover notes to: William Flanagan, "See How They Love Me" (New York: C.F. Peters, 1965). High voice.

28. John Ardoin, "Rorem-Flanagan Concert," Musical America, LXXXII (May 1962), p. 37.

29. Wakeman, p. 1038.

30. Ibid., p. 1037.

31. Ibid., p. 1038.

32. Howard Moss, Writing Against Time, Critical Essays and Reviews (New York: Morrow, 1969), p. 194.

33. Wakeman, p. 1038.

34. Reilly, p. 134.

35. William Flanagan, "Plants Cannot Travel" (New York: C.F. Peters, 1963). High voice. This song, together with "Horror Movie," "If You Can," and "See How They Love Me," has been recorded by Carol Bogard, soprano, and David Del Tredici, pianist, on the Desto label (DC-6468).

36. William Flanagan, "If You Can" (New York: C.F. Peters, 1963). High voice.

37. See note 27.

38. Letter dated August 18, 1983.

39. Ardoin review.

40. William Flanagan, "Horror Movie: (New York: C.F. Peters, 1965). Medium high voice.

41. William Flanagan, "The Upside Down Man" (New York: Peer International Corp., 1964). Medium high voice.

42. Virgil Thomson, American Music Since 1910 (New York: Holt, Rinehart, and Winston, 1970), p. 88.

43. Ruth Schonthal, 12 Van Etten Boulevard, New Rochelle, NY 10804.

44. All the foregoing Schonthal quotations are from the December 3, 1982 interview.

45. Ruth Schonthal, By the Roadside (New York: Oxford University Press, 1979).   Soprano.

46. See Vol. I, p. 64 and vol. II, pp. 159-160.

47. See Vol. I, pp. 65-67--"Walt Whitman" (Charles Ives) and Vol. II, pp. 172-174--"I think I could turn" (Sergius Kagen).

48. See Vol. II, pp. 162-163--"The Ship Starting" (Charles Naginski).

49. See Vol. II, pp. 160-162--"Look down, fair moon" (Charles Naginski).

50. Thomas Crawley, The Structure of "Leaves of Grass" (Austin: University of Texas Press, 1970), p. 219.

51. Richard Cumming appears as pianist accompanying Donald Gramm on the following recordings:
     a) Recital by Donald Gramm--Music Library Recordings MLR 7033.
     b) Songs by American Composers--Desto DS 6411B.
     c) Cycles and Songs by Richard Cumming--Cambridge Records CRS 2778.

52. Telephone conversation with the author on June 15, 1985.

53. Cumming's Piano Sonata was published by J. & W. Chester in 1953, and recorded by the composer on Music Library Recordings MLR 7053.   His Twenty-Four Preludes were published in 1971 by Boosey and Hawkes and recorded by John Browning on Desto DC 7120.

54. The major recordings of his songs are the disc listed in

Note 51c, and <u>Art Song in America, Volume 2</u> (John Hanks and Ruth Friedberg) which contains "Go, Lovely Rose," "Memory, Hither Come," and "The Little Black Boy." <u>Art Song in America</u> is published by Duke University Press.

55. Letter from Philip Minor to the author, dated June 25, 1985.

56. Ibid.

57. Phone conversation of June 15, 1985.

58. Letter of June 25, 1985.

59. Richard Cumming, <u>Other Loves</u> (New York: Galaxy Music Corp., 1982). High voice. The work is included in the volume titled <u>American Artsong Anthology</u>, edited by John Belisle.

60. Letter from Richard Cumming to the author, dated September 9, 1984.

61. <u>We Happy Few</u>, which appears on the record described in Note 51c, is a cycle of ten songs based on mostly British poetry, the majority of which relates to war. American poets are represented by two of the settings: Walt Whitman's "A Sight in Camp" and Archibald MacLeish's "The End of the World."

62. "Reviews," <u>Musical America</u>, LXXXIV:34-5 (February 1964).

63. The author is using the term "carry a torch" in the colloquial sense of trying to hang on to a failed or failing love affair.

V. NED ROREM (1923-   )

Ned Rorem would probably be the first to agree that his life
has been founded in a series of contradictions, some of
which have proved forceful, if occasionally painful, spurs
to artistic creativity. To begin with, although raised in
geographically insular Chicago, Rorem's earliest musical al-
legiance was to the sophisticated nuances of French Impres-
sionism. Secondly, this son of Quaker converts whose
strongest values were intellect and discipline, spent his
youth as the dissolute, often guilt-ridden (but always in-
dustrious) "golden boy" of Paris and New York artistic so-
ciety. And finally, after becoming, in his maturity, one of
the best known names in American art song, Ned Rorem has,
during the last two decades, written increasingly in the in-
strumental forms, and turned much of his energy toward
building a notable reputation as a musical journalist.

In his diaries and journal articles, Rorem describes
with warm affection his parents' supportive role in his de-
veloping talent. "Although not specifically musical, [they]
exposed my sister Rosemary and me to concerts, mainly
high-class piano recitals"[1] says the composer who, at the
age of seven, began a decade of keyboard study under a
series of seven teachers. Notable among these were Nuta
Rothschild, who introduced him to the magic of Debussy;
Margaret Bonds, who "played with the authority of a pro-
fessional and showed [him] how to notate [his] ramblings"[2];
and Belle Tannenbaum whose instruction was supplemented
by harmony classes in the Loop with Leo Sowerby. Writing
in 1969 at the time of Sowerby's death, Rorem recalled that

Ned Rorem
(Photo: © Jack Mitchell 1984)

"his encouragement during my adolescence was the spring-
board of my career."[3] Having emerged from high school
at the age of sixteen, Rorem turned toward the area of mu-
sic which was increasingly absorbing him and entered North-
western University's School of Music as a composition major.
This plan had the full cooperation of his father (a vigorous
91 at this writing), who was America's leading medical

economist, the founding father of Blue Cross, and a "not so sublimated baritone"[4] as well.

Dr. Alfred Nolte, a former protégé of Richard Strauss, now became Rorem's professor of composition, but he remembers less about those lessons than about his piano instruction with Harold Van Horne. Setting out to enlarge his keyboard repertoire beyond its heavy emphasis on Debussy and Stravinsky, Rorem learned "all thirty-two Beethoven sonatas and the entire keyboard catalogue of Bach and Chopin"[5] in his two years at Northwestern. A Curtis scholarship brought him to Philadelphia in 1943, but Rosario Scalero's counterpoint exercises proved too limiting to the young composer. Against the advice of his parents, who cut off his allowance, Rorem moved to New York the following year to become Virgil Thomson's copyist in exchange for twenty dollars a week and orchestration lessons.

The New York experiences in "the real world of music"[6] came thick and fast, punctuated by pilgrimages to Aaron Copland's tutelage at Tanglewood in the summers of 1946 and 1947. Rorem became the accompanist for Martha Graham's dance classes, studied composition with Bernard Wagenaar at the Juilliard School where he earned a Master's Degree in 1948, and began to establish some long-lasting friendships. In the New York Diary, Rorem remembers 1947 in Mary's Bar on Eighth Street, noting that "it is already eleven summers ago that John Myers and Frank Etherton worked there, whining the tunes Paul Goodman and I composed for them: Bawling Blues, Jail Bait Blues, Near Closing Time."[7] Paul Goodman, then, was already an artistic collaborator and important force in Ned Rorem's life. Looking back from the 1960's, the composer would refer to him as "my Manhattan Goethe,"[8] and indeed, it was Rorem's setting of a Goodman poem ("The Lordly Hudson") that won recognition as the best published song of 1948. In the same year, Rorem received the Gershwin Award for the Orchestral Overture that was his Master's thesis at Juilliard, and by 1949 he was off to Paris, having been awarded a Fulbright scholarship to study there with Arthur Honegger.

After only a few months in France, Ned Rorem followed the path to Morocco pioneered by Paul Bowles. Although this move had nothing to do with Bowles, it is also true that the older composer had fascinated him from their first meeting in Taxco when Rorem was sixteen. He stayed in Morocco for two years, and even after his return to Paris, would be drawn back at intervals to the colorful, mysterious ambiance of Fez, Marrakech, and Tangier. France, however, remained his principal residence until 1958, and he spent most of his time in the luxurious homes maintained in Paris and Hyères (on the Mediterranean coast) by the Viscountess Marie Laure de Noailles, his patroness. During these years in France, Rorem won acceptance in the artistic circles headed by Poulenc, Auric, and Cocteau, but did not allow the active and brilliant social life of Marie Laure's "salon" to deter him from serious application to musical composition in many forms, including a large number of song settings.

In the John Gruen collection of "fifties" reminiscences, Ned Rorem made some interesting observations on his decade as an expatriate. "I was always attracted by things French," said the composer, "so I didn't become French by living in France. I was already French at home in Chicago, and later in New York ... I went to France for the same reason everybody else in America went to France--we went looking for what were then stylishly called 'our roots.' I found out," he added, "that my roots were not in France but America."[9] In the same memoir, Rorem commented on The Paris Diary, the book which began his flourishing literary sub-career as journalist and critic. He recalls that Marie Laure had encouraged him to keep a diary, and states his feeling that what this early writing reveals is "terribly fifties ... full of self-pity and self-advertisement."[10] He is quick to note, however, that his diary also "reflects the fact that ninety percent of my time was spent at home working hard, writing music, and not out getting drunk or crying or lacerating myself for love."[11]

During the mid-fifties, Rorem made several trips to America for premières of major symphonic works. He was beginning to realize that, unlike Frederic Prokosch (see Chapter 1), who had confided that he needed to live far from America's "vulgarity," Rorem himself wanted "more and more to leave the France [he knew]."[12] In 1958, he resettled in New York City, having come to believe that "an American composer must live here whether he likes it or not ... [for] it is here that his most interesting problems will at least be presented if not solved."[13] One of the problems which did present, and which is movingly delineated in the

New York Diary, is a form of early mid-life spiritual crisis
that began to envelop the thirty-five-year-old composer.
Entry after entry speaks of boredom, uncaring, joylessness,
the failures of religion, and the consideration of suicide.
Alcohol, perhaps as an antidote to meaninglessness, had be-
come a friend and enemy (says Rorem, "the fifties to the
sixties was my drinking decade"[14]) bringing both surcease
of pain, and guilt-laden aftermath.

Work, however, remained a driving and salutary force.
In the decade following his return to America, Rorem added
to his catalog of works several song cycles, two operas, and
many choral, orchestral, and chamber works. Other direc-
tions opened up as well, with teaching appointments at the
University of Buffalo (1959-61) and Utah (1966), and the
publication of the Paris Diary (1966), The New York Diary
(1967) and the essay collection Music from Inside Out (1967).
Yet another venture, this time in behalf of the song litera-
ture which was always close to the composer's heart, was
recorded proudly in 1959: "Last February, Bill Flanagan
and I ... inaugurated to Standing Room Only the first in
what we hope will be a series called Music for the Voice by
Americans"[15] (see p. 164).

The Later Diaries chronicles the years from 1961 to
1972 and is crowded with the names and events of the ar-
tistic life of the period. In New York we follow Rorem's
interactions with such literary figures as John Ashbery,
Frank O'Hara, Paul Goodman, Edward Albee, and James
Purdy, as well as an endless stream of conductors, singers,
instrumentalists, and fellow composers. On visits to France
we see him with Nadia Boulanger and the Milhauds, and in
Morocco with Paul and Jane Bowles. One name which recurs
constantly is that of Bill Flanagan, whom he reports in a
1964 entry seeing daily, and whose many hospitalizations and
final solitary death in a losing battle against drugs and al-
cohol are a historically valuable while personally tragic as-
pect of this journal. The overall tone of this diary, despite
the mourned losses to mortality of important friends such as
Flanagan, Goodman, and Marie Laure, is far more positive
than the earlier two. By the end of the volume, Rorem has
stopped drinking, and reports his mental condition on a num-
ber of occasions to be that of "happiness, [a state in which]
nobody is much interested."[16]

During the late sixties and early seventies, Rorem published three more volumes of essays, which were mostly drawn from lectures delivered in university settings, or articles previously printed in various periodicals. Music from Inside Out (see p. 209) had devoted a fourth of its content to the composer's valuable insights on vocal music in the section titled "Variation Two: Music for the Mouth." The newer collections revealed his continuing literary preoccupation with the philosophy of and contributors to art song in articles such as "Poetry of Music" and "Bill Flanagan" in Critical Affairs (1970); and "Paul Bowles" and "Remembering a Poet" in Pure Contraption (1973).

Rorem's most recently published books are An Absolute Gift (1978) and Setting the Tone (1983), which combine some personal memoirs with criticism, reviews, and the author's unique observations on the contemporary artistic scene. Both of these volumes are dedicated to James Holmes, a fellow musician whose friendship had become one of the stabilizing factors in a life which the composer described in 1974 as no longer incorporating "a strong need for novelty [or] for possibilities around the corner."[17] This author's interview with Ned Rorem, previously quoted in Volume I, took place at just about this time (April, 1975) in the composer's pleasant apartment in Manhattan's West Seventies. The interview had been graciously granted, with little advance notice. Rorem not only patiently answered questions, but also contributed generously to the interviewer's grasp of her subject, by putting her in touch with Alice Esty, who commissioned so many American art songs of the sixties,[18] and with a whole group of younger song composers who will be represented in Chapter Six of this volume.

In 1982, an interesting and useful summary of the composer's lifelong thinking about the art song appeared as a conversation with Ned Rorem reported in the November/ December issue of the NATS Bulletin. Herein Rorem reiterated that for song texts he chooses "whatever, as the Quakers say, speaks to my condition," and that in his settings he adheres "to two moral principles: follow a natural prosodic flow [and] never repeat words not repeated by the poet."[19] Asked about French influences on his songs, he replied "I'd like to suppose that after years and years ... of emerging into myself I finally speak my very own dialect,"[20] and he underlined his continuing advocacy of

American songs sung by American singers. "We Americans," said Rorem, "now lead the world in weaponry, but still follow sheepishly in artistic standards. Yet the future will judge us not by our destruction but by our creation."[21]

Towards the end of this conversation, Rorem states that his earliest songs "were made not from love of the human voice but from the love of poetry, and from a need to meld two passions--music and literature--into one entity."[22] Discounting those composed at the age of eleven while studying with Margaret Bonds, he feels that "the first songs of any quality at all were written ... when [he] was a student at Northwestern ... mostly on poetry of e.e. cummings."[23] His literary "passion" then, had, by 1939, already become attached to American poetry as an important focus. In the years to come, the focus would grow even stronger as Rorem's single songs and cycles came to include settings of a long list of American poets. Paul Goodman, Theodore Roethke, Howard Moss, Walt Whitman, Kenneth Koch, John Ashbery, Elizabeth Bishop, Wallace Stevens, Sylvia Plath, and Witter Bynner were all grist to his mill, as Rorem continued to prove his own claim, that "in general a composer prefers to set poetry of his national contemporaries."[24]

Paul Goodman (1911-1972)

Paul Goodman, one of Rorem's major poetic sources, was a complex and dramatic figure whose poetry formed a little-known but critical part of a wide-ranging literary output. He was born in New York City's Greenwich Village, the fourth child in a remarkably atypical middle-class German Jewish family. Goodman's father, having failed in business, abandoned the family before Paul was born; his mother, a "bourgeois gypsy,"[25] was a traveling saleswoman, seldom at home; and he was mostly cared for, even through his college years, by his sister Alice, who was ten years his senior.

Though unconventional, the atmosphere of his childhood was clearly a nurturing one. Goodman later described himself as "an orphan who had had a home" and as a "fatherless [child] free on the streets of the Empire City and the wild rocks along the Hudson River."[26] The rich resources of New York's free educational opportunities fed his developing mind, and he proved an exceptional student of literature and languages at Townsend Harris Hall High School, and of philosophy at the City College of New York (A.B., 1931). During his college years, he not infrequently hitchhiked to Cambridge to sit in on courses at Harvard, and observed the same process of "informal audit" at Columbia University during the five years after graduation when he was an unemployed writer living with his sister.

From 1936 to 1940 he was a graduate student, research assistant, and part-time instructor in literature and philosophy at the University of Chicago, but did not complete his doctoral dissertation (published as The Structure of Literature) until 1954. In 1940 he returned to New York City and for the next two decades attracted a small but dedicated group of young intellectuals who followed his career as editor and contributor to Partisan Review, Kenyon Review, Commentary and other journals; as teacher at Manumit, a progressive boarding school, and at Black Mountain College; and as author of novels, plays, short stories, and many essays. These essays, considered by some critics to be among his finest work, included forays into social criticism, such as Communitas, a description of the ideal city written with his architect brother, Percival, and a volume on psychoanalytic process called Gestalt Therapy, drawn from his own experiences in analysis and later as a practicing therapist. Even music did not escape this Renaissance mind for Goodman not only wrote critically and philosophically on musical subjects, but also, from time to time, tried his hand at composing.

An earlier common-law marriage of five years to Virginia Miller had produced a daughter, Susan, in 1939. From 1945 to the end of his life, Goodman was married to Sally Duchsten who often functioned as his secretary and informal bibliographer. They had two children (a son Matthew Ready born in 1946, and a daughter, Daisy, born seventeen years later) and family life followed the "bohemian" model of artistic struggle and material poverty. In 1961, however, the successful publication of Growing up Absurd (subtitled "Problems of Youth in the Organized Society") brought not only many requests for lecturing and teaching engagements and a substantially increased income, but the adulation, as well, of a whole generation who saw Goodman as their hero and spokesman.

During the last decade of Goodman's life, a number of volumes of poetry were added to the novels, short stories, and social criticism which he continued to publish. In 1962 his first volume of verse, titled The Lordly Hudson, appeared, and was soon followed by Hawkweed (1967), North Percy (1968), and Homespun of Oatmeal Gray (1970). The seemingly new literary mantle was no surprise to his friends, in whose company there would always "come a moment when he handed around five or six sheets of new poems"[27]; in fact, he had been a frequent contributor to Poetry magazine during the forties and fifties, and had published poems in small editions throughout his life. His final decade also encompassed tragedy, for Goodman's son Matthew was killed in a 1967 mountaineering accident, and the writer's lifelong charismatic vitality gave way to depression and ill health. He died of a cardiac ailment at his New Hampshire farm in August, 1972, having spent the summer working on a new collection of poetry, Little Prayers and Finite Experience, as well as the editing of his Collected Poems, both of which were published posthumously.

Goodman historians are for the most part in agreement as to the major influences on his thinking. Alicia Ostriker lists "Aristotle, who taught him to observe human institutions and Kant, who taught him the moral imperative"[28] as well as Freud, Reich, John Dewey, William James, Maimonides, Buber, and Marx (Goodman was not a Communist, but an anarchist). There is less critical consensus, however, on the position of the poetry in his work, or, indeed, in American letters. Kingsley Widmer finds him to have "had little sense of poetry and an absurdly wooden sense of language"[29] while Robert Merideth calls Goodman "a major American poet, though almost completely ignored," partly because "his technical skill and knowledge are so considerable as to be nearly invisible."[30] Ostriker, another advocate, opines that "there has not been a thoughtful and passionate personal voice like this in our poetry since Robinson Jeffers" and sees him being criticized as too pragmatic to be a good poet because he writes "without decorum and the manners which protect the private self."[31]

Emile Capouya adds that the power of Goodman's rhetoric which is "direct and hopelessly unsophisticated" draws upon strong, fundamental emotions like patriotism, and he offers as proof a quotation in entirety of "The Lordly

Hudson," calling it the greatest poem about New York since Walt Whitman.[32] This poem had been published with the Goodman selections in the second series of Five Young American Poets in 1941. Three years before, Ned Rorem, who was then fourteen years old, had met Paul Goodman, a graduate student at the University of Chicago, and the two had formed part of a group that attended Thursday evening Poetry Sessions at Monroe Library.[33] In the essay "Remembering a Poet,"[34] written in the month of Goodman's death, Rorem recalls that, in the years after their meeting, the writer became his "most pertinent influence, social and poetic," and that he (Rorem) "never in the following decades wearied of putting his words to music."

In the 1975 interview, Ned Rorem told the present author that when he wrote "The Lordly Hudson"[35] he knew no other American songs, and only later became familiar with settings by Chanler, Diamond and Bacon. It is interesting, however, to learn that the French song literature played a crucial part in the inspirational genesis of this seemingly prototypical piece of Americana. In The Paris Diary, Rorem describes a New York Christmas party of 1946 during which he was much taken by his first hearing of Poulenc's "C," particularly the vocal interval which sets "de la prairie." The next day, moved to compose a song himself, he fastened on "The Lordly Hudson" (then called "Poem") which he had already tried unsuccessfully to set. "In one sitting," says Rorem, "I wrote the song ... deciding on 6/8 because that means 'water,' I suppose. I first wrote the vocal phrase 'home, home' and 'no, no'--skipping a seventh and rising in the sequence, because Poulenc had skipped a fifth and dropped. Then I decided on the accompaniment pattern, and for the rest of the words I simply used taste and a melodic stream of consciousness."[36]

Rorem then gave the song, without changes, to Janet Fairbank, a young soprano who during the forties presented concerts of new American songs, and it was she who premièred the setting of "Paul's soaring words that still so grandly extol his beloved Manhattan."[37] It was sung first under the title of "Poem," later "Driver, What Stream Is It?" (the opening line); and finally, when Richard Dana offered to print it, was given its present title by the author. The song was dedicated to Janet Fairbank who died in 1947 on the day it was published, and who was mourned by the whole community of poets and musicians whose work she had fostered.

Although an early song, "The Lordly Hudson" already demonstrates the composer's highly developed instinct for poetic setting. Using melodic variations on the original seminal interval, Rorem allows the welcoming rush of feeling to expand vocally in arpeggiated ninths, and pianistically in a similar, chordally amplified line.

Example 5.1a, measures 40-42. Copyright 1947, Mercury Music Corp.; used by permission of the publisher.

215

Example 5.1b, measures 50-56. Copyright 1947, Mercury
Music Corp.; used by permission of the publisher.

As is true in many Rorem settings, the more intricate and
developed melodic structure is carried by the piano. In this
case, the slower rhythms and frequent pauses in the vocal
line seem to suggest the protagonist's attempt at control ("Be
quiet, heart!") while the accompaniment releases the over-
whelming flood of emotion.

Harmonic usage, too, feeds textual needs. The basic
tonality of F minor appears in its modal form (Aeolian) for
the cloudy, dreamlike opening and contrasts with the raised
pitch and greater brilliance of A minor for each impassioned
setting of "Home! Home!" (see Ex. 5.1b). In the last three
measures, Rorem sets an F pedal point in two voices against
a wandering, downward scale in the Phrygian mode which
finally and joyfully comes "home" to the brightness and reso-
lution of an F major chord (see Ex. 5.1b).

Paul Goodman's poetry was in a continual state of revi-
sion throughout his life and "The Lordly Hudson" as it ap-
pears in the Collected Poems shows changes which, in this
writer's opinion, are weaker than the original version (for-
tunately that of Rorem's setting). The same is true of
"Absalom," another poem published in the Five Young Amer-
ican Poets of 1941, and a prime example of the prodigious
albeit invisible technical skill that Robert Meredith claims for
Goodman. "Absalom" presents three verses of five lines each
in which the second and third lines rhyme, as do the first,
fourth, and fifth. The use of language is strong and original,

216

and paints a dramatic picture of the dead, blood-stained prince hanging from his hair amid frightened birds in the agitated oak tree.

As is often the case, Rorem's 1946 setting of "Absalom"[38] swallows the original metric structure, and replaces it with a plastic, freely flowing alternation of 3/4 and 4/4. Once again, as is his custom based on conviction, Rorem sets the text precisely as given (the word repetition in the final line is Goodman's) but creates dramatic space by devices like the two-measure vocal hold on the climactic word "blood." Perhaps the most interesting aspect of this remarkable song is that it is entirely built around the motif of two conjunct descending scalar steps, first announced in the introduction:

Example 5.2, measures 1-5. Copyright 1946, Boosey and Hawkes; used by permission.

This motif continues to appear in the piano, often in sequence, throughout the song, but is never taken into the voice part until it becomes the father's despairing cry:

Example 5.3, measures 39-45. Copyright 1946, Boosey &
Hawkes; used by permission.

    In 1949, newly arrived in Paris, Rorem set a short,
charming lyric of Goodman's called "Rain in Spring,"[39] which
he appropriately completed and dated on the seventh of June.
This poem recalls a season when a "clear and refreshing rain,
falling without haste or strain" marked the very moment when
spring began.   Taking his cue from the text, Rorem creates
a "very languid" (his indication) setting whose double-dotted
accompaniment figures seem to hold back any urge toward
"haste," while the simple diatonic voice line and thinly tex-
tured piano chords suggest the clarity of the water:

Example 5.4, measures 1-7. Copyright 1949, Boosey and
Hawkes; used by permission.

Influences of the French cabaret and jazz scene filtered through Poulenc seem to hover in this song around the pianistic figurations as well as the heavy sprinkling of seventh, ninth, and thirteenth chords. One is reminded of the mood, if not the meter, of "Hôtel" from Banalités.

An entry dated October 28, 1972 in The Later Diaries recalls that twenty autumns earlier, Rorem had returned from France for the first time to spend three months in New York's Chelsea Hotel. "My 1952 agenda shows," he writes, "... that Paul Goodman handed over thirteen new poems (which I made into songs the next summer)." The next seven Goodman settings which Rorem published (all completed during the fifties) are drawn from this group, and the first five to be treated below bear the legend "Hyères, September 1953."

The poem which Rorem sets in "The Midnight Sun"[40] had originally appeared in Poetry magazine[41] under the title of "Stanzas." It is a strange, haunting poem wherein a dream of floating people, droning bagpipes, and a midnight sun takes on a mystical air uncommon to Goodman through the line "I hastened to behold him there." Rorem's setting enhances this mystical quality with its chant-like melody full of repeated notes and melismas set off against the bareness of single or superimposed empty fifths in the accompaniment:

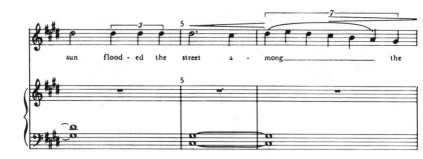

Example 5.5, measures 1-6. Copyright 1968, E.C. Schirmer
Music Co., Boston. Reprinted with permission.

Harmonic treatment intensifies the strangeness of the atmos-
phere in the final phrase ("and where the shadows fell they
lay") by means of soft, polytonal chords that create a power-
ful, though whispered dissonance with the vocal line in the
last two measures:

Example 5.6, measures 28-31. Copyright 1968, E.C. Schir-
mer Music Co., Boston. Reprinted with permission.

"The Midnight Sun" forms an interesting pair with
"The Tulip Tree."[42] In the text of the latter, an apparent-
ly straightforward story is told of a boy in a tree tossing
blossoms to the girls below and then engaging in a game of
catch-ball with the poet as a thunder storm gathers. Liter-
alness fades, however, as the composer, again using a single,
constantly recurring, accompaniment motif as announced in
the introduction

Example 5.7, measures 1-2. Copyright 1968, E.C. Schirmer
Music Co., Boston. Reprinted with permission.

changes and amplifies it, sometimes to exuberant heights, to
match the mood of the text:

Example 5.8, measures 29-31. Copyright 1968, E.C. Schir-
mer Music Co., Boston. Reprinted with permission.

This device serves to unify the song, and also seems to
hold the suggestion of an ongoing event in which the boy
and the poet become symbolic figures, woven into the fabric
of eternity.

    "Sally's Smile" appeared in Goodman's first published
collection of poetry (The Lordly Hudson, 1963). Included
in the section called "Love Poems," it is the poet's tribute
to the compelling smile and presence of his wife. Allusions
to "caution and resentment, both my wardens," and their
connection with the Miami grave of the mother he rarely saw,
hint that a strong maternal influence has been overcome by

the nuptial alliance. In any case, Rorem opts for a light-
handed treatment[43] suggested by the endearment "Sally-o"
and by the fact that the two stanza poem is one unbroken
sentence. He makes it a fast-moving patter song with a
mostly diatonic scalar melody in the voice part and in the
elaborated sixteenth note piano figurations. There is only
one major break in the two page vocal line, and the whole
effect is of breathless, unabashed joy.

The last two of the "Hyères, 1953" Goodman settings
are "For Susan" and "Clouds," both published in 1968 to-
gether with "What Sparks and Wiry Cries" under the head-
ing of Three Poems of Paul Goodman.[44] "For Susan" com-
pares Goodman's older daughter as a child to a "wildflower
untended among garden flowers no fairer" and praises the
"wild strain of blood and wit" that is somehow nourished by
nature, even in our "disastrous homes." Rorem looses his
lyrical vein on this fatherly fancy, in a vocal line whose
frequent chordal leaps seem a musical representation of the
young lady's labile nature as poetically portrayed:

Example 5.9, measures 13-15. Copyright 1968, Boosey &
Hawkes; used by permission.

"Clouds" is a technically interesting eight-line poem in
which lines three and four rhyme, as do five and six, while
the other four do not. It is a skillful portrayal of the move-
ment of clouds as they gather, pile into great heights, and
disperse, without effort or desire. The composer captures
the emotionless, "now-centered" atmosphere of the poem in
one of his most impressionistic settings. With perhaps a

subconscious nod to Debussy, his earliest musical mentor, and his "Clouds" (i.e., the orchestral "Nuages"), Rorem writes a "highly pedaled" piano part full of non-resolving chords built in fourths and fifths. To the singer, whom he instructs to begin "in a 'half-voice,'" he gives two musical stanzas whose melodic contours emphasize and end on the suspended second degree of the E major scale. Thus all musical elements serve the textual aspects of haziness, lack of effort, and an endless cycle of becoming.

The notation that concludes "What Sparks and Wiry Cries" is "France, 1952-1956," and from this we learn that Rorem took somewhat longer to complete what emerged as possibly the strongest setting of the Three Poems group. Goodman had titled this poem "1943" when it appeared in The Lordly Hudson collection, and one assumes that it was inspired by a failed love affair of that year. The rather unique idea therein expressed is that the sorrow of parting is tempered by the "furious joy" of a "heart [now] undivided by hope or fear." This is presented in harshly powerful verbal images of a "skirl of glee" being played with a "pick of flint" on "twangled ... iron strings." In Rorem's setting, the twangling of these strings is clearly heard in the accompaniment, and the folk-like contours and modal context of the vocal melody deepen the atmosphere of an ancient, keening troubadour.

Example 5.10, measures 1-5. Copyright 1968, Boosey &
Hawkes; used by permission.

In the middle, recitative-like section of this ABA form, the
remembered pain of separation becomes a growing lament. It
rises to a despairing cry on a sudden, triple forte high B
flat, by which the composer may be letting us know that the
poet's "furious joy" is self-delusion.

Example 5.11, measures 15-20. Copyright 1968, Boosey &
Hawkes; used by permission.

The last of the Goodman settings, "Such Beauty as Hurts to Behold"[45] was completed at Hyères, in July 1957, when Rorem was soon to leave France for his return to New York. The poem, which also appeared in the "Love Poems" section of the 1963 collection, describes a passion so deep as to be beyond desire, giving rise to a muttered prayer of thanks for the existence of the beloved. The tone here is far more serious than "Sally's Smile" and Rorem accordingly sets it with an arioso-like vocal line ("very slow, very free") over a mostly chordal background. Metric insertions of 5/4 and 3/4 into the basic 4/4 combine with melodic contours that sensitively follow the inflexional rise and fall of the language. The result is to throw the emphasis on the poetic text in a kind of musically heightened speech that relates to what Debussy achieved for the French language in Pelléas and the late songs.

Theodore Roethke (1908-1963)[46]

Roethke, like Ned Rorem, spent his formative years in the mid-west. He was born in Saginaw, Michigan, where his grandparents had settled in 1872 as immigrants from East Prussia. Theodore was a small and sickly child who would in maturity attain a height of six feet and the physical stamina to become a skilled tennis player and coach. Artistic leanings surfaced early, and Roethke recalled "an intense period of pleasure in nursery rhymes in English and German and songs my mother and nurse sang me."[47] He became an avid reader when quite young and began subscribing to the Dial in the seventh grade.

Roethke's father, who inherited the family greenhouse and gardening business, died when the boy was fifteen, but remained a strong influence throughout the poet's life. Although drawn to Harvard, Roethke enrolled at the University of Michigan to placate his mother's fears of "the mysterious East"[48] and received his B.A. in 1929. He had begun to write short stories and poetry while still at Ann Arbor. During an abortive post-graduate year at Harvard Law School, he was encouraged by Robert Hillyer to begin marketing his poetry, and thereafter turned gratefully to a career as teacher and writer.

By the time Roethke received his M.A. from the University of Michigan in 1936, he had taught English for four years at Lafayette College, for less than a semester at Michigan State University, and had been hospitalized with the first of the periodic mental breakdowns that were to afflict him all his life. At the 1967 inauguration of the Theodore Roethke Memorial Foundation in Saginaw, Stanley Kunitz recalled "the outbreaks and absences and silences that he had to cover up, partly because he realized what a threat they offered to his survival in the academic world."[49]

Despite this ever-present threat, Roethke proceeded to forge a name for himself in academic circles. He held faculty positions at Pennsylvania State University (1936-1943) and Bennington College (1943-1946), and by the time he came to the University of Washington (1947), where he would remain for the rest of his life, he had become "the greatest teacher of poetry in the country."[50] His friends also remember that Roethke had "a girl" every place he taught, but no serious alliances occurred until 1953, when on a trip to New York, he ran into Beatrice O'Connell, a former Bennington student. They were married a month later.

With the publication in 1941 of Open House, his first poetry collection, Roethke's position as a major American poet began to be recognized. He was awarded a Guggenheim fellowship in 1945, and a second one followed after the publication of The Lost Son in 1948. The Waking brought him the Pulitzer Prize in 1954, and the remaining decade of his life was crowded with European travel and lecturing made possible by Fulbright and Ford Foundation grants. Continuing to write and publish (including several books for children) during these years, Roethke had barely returned to the United States as Poet-in-Residence at the University of Washington when his life abruptly ended. On the fourth of August, 1963, Ned Rorem wrote "Theodore Roethke has dropped dead in a Seattle swimming pool. Is no one immune? Who will write my songs now? and those others he'll never hear?"[51]

Paul Goodman had been characterized by Ostriker as a poet with "a bias toward the literal [who] sees the world as ethics, not metaphysics."[52] When Rorem began to set Theodore Roethke in the late fifties, it was almost like a turning to the opposite principle, for all of Roethke's life and work seem in retrospect to take on the aspect of a metaphysical journey. William Heyen described him as "an artist who experienced moments of deep religious feeling and almost inexpressible illumination [whose] choice was not traditional Christianity or Atheism, but a reliance upon the mystic perceptions of his own imagination."[53] Neil Bowers in a recent study[54] sets forth the further premise that it was Roethke's manic-depressive illness that produced a propensity for mystical insight, and the poet himself, according to Kunitz, "eventually more than half believed that the springs of his disorder were inseparable from the sources of his art."[55] From the reader's viewpoint, however, the precise relationship between Roethke's illness and his poetic gift is immaterial. Of far greater moment, is the incredible power and concision of his verbal imagery as he chronicles his descent into his own unconscious, followed by emergence and growth toward loving union with the finite and the Absolute.

Alice Esty, "a soprano of style and means"[56] together with her knowledgeable pianist, David Stimer, had performed and recorded twentieth-century French and American songs during the years 1954 to 1959. In the latter year, she began commissioning major cycles which she premièred in Carnegie Hall to an eventual total of nine by American and seven by European composers. (For a listing of the former, see the source cited in Note 56.) Ned Rorem's Eight Poems of Theodore Roethke was the first of the American cycles. It was presented on April 3, 1960, and Rorem marks its completion with an entry in The New York Diary written from the University of Buffalo where he was, at that time, Slee Professor of Composition.

"After a labyrinthine correspondence with Theodore Roethke, letters of practical suspicion and mutual praise, the settings of his eight poems are finally completed for Alice Esty. Because--and not despite the fact that--my heart wasn't in them, they've turned out to be great songs. (For musicians, the heart is a dangerous vulgarian.)"

Five of the eight poems that Rorem had chosen for setting came from Roethke's collection The Lost Son. In this volume the poet turned from the more formal structures of Open House to the liberating cadences of free verse as he sought the origins of his life and thought. "Root Cellar" and "Orchids" borrow their imagery from memories of his father's greenhouse, and in them the poet is struck by the stubborn and strong attachment to life of plant forms. It is interesting to observe how Rorem in his settings dramatizes this attachment and suggests its menacing aspect. He does this in "Root Cellar"[57] through a series of highly dissonant chords harshly struck on the piano, while the voice intones repetitively, as though hypnotized by fear.

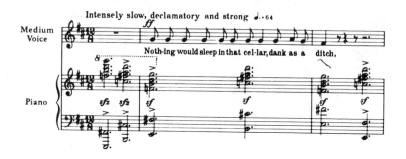

Example 5.12, measures 1-3. Copyright 1963, Henmar Press, Inc.; used by permission of C.F. Peters Corporation.

The terror rises as the contours of the vocal line take on the shape of the shoots which "dangled and drooped,"

Example 5.13, measures 7-8. Copyright 1963, Henmar Press, Inc.; used by permission of C.F. Peters Corporation.

and ends in a muffled whisper at the recognition that even the dirt seems alive.

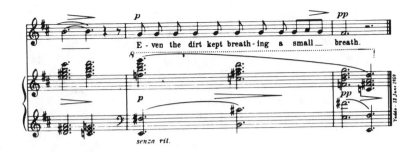

Example 5.14, measures 19-21. Copyright 1963, Henmar Press, Inc.; used by permission of C.F. Peters Corporation.

In comparison to "Root Cellar," "Orchids"[58] is a more gently insinuating horror story. The orchids are very beautiful, but therefore more dangerous, and the vocal lines take on a more arching contour, like the graceful flowers as they "lean, addermouthed, over the path." The chordal background, too, is different here. Softly struck, less dissonant harmonies built often of superimposed fourths and fifths exploit the extreme ranges of the piano, to create an impressionistic, seductively enveloping haze of sound.

Example 5.15, measures 1-2. Copyright 1969, Boosey & Hawkes; used by permission.

"Night Crow" is a short, evocative eight line poem which explores levels of awareness. Seeing the "clumsy

crow" in flight causes the image of a "tremendous bird" to
rise from the unconscious, but the poet barely grasps its
meaning before it retreats again into the "moonless black."
In Rorem's "Night Crow,"[59] musical device expands the ver-
bal suggestion. The piano prelude, postlude, and interludes
with their restlessly moving triplets and sixteenth note fig-
ures become the seething, fertile contents of the unconscious
mind (see Ex. 5.17). Over this, a lyrical vocal line employs
a recurrent melodic formulation, moving in the slower, more
controlled cadences of the conscious mind, while the piano
sinks back to sustaining chords:

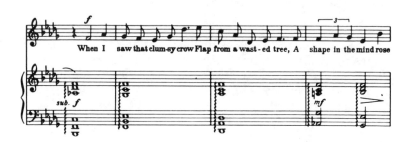

Example 5.16, measures 4-7. Copyright 1963, Henmar
Press; used by permission of C.F. Peters Corporation.

The two levels are masterfully joined at the song's climax.
As the image of the bird recedes, Rorem moves up a major
third from D flat to F major. In the more brilliant key, the
voice line repeats the melodic pattern but in agitated rhythms
over an accompaniment now in moving eighth notes. Con-
scious and unconscious have come together for a brief mo-
ment, only to give way again to the separation announced
by the piano postlude.

Example 5.17, measures 13-20. Copyright 1963, Henmar Press, Inc.; used by permission of C.F. Peters Corporation.

Since the Eight Poems were intended to be performed as a cycle, contrast was essential. "My Papa's Waltz" differs from the other seven in that it is not metaphysically oriented but a clearly held memory of being waltzed off to bed by an intoxicated but beloved father. The poem is four verses of iambic trimeter with rhymes or half-rhymes linking lines one/three and two/four. Rorem's setting[60] maintains the verse divisions with pianistic interludes of swooping arpeggios that propel the wild gyrations of the dance.

We romped un - til the pans Slid __ from the

Example 5.18, measures 18-28. Copyright 1963, Henmar Press, Inc.; used by permission of C.F. Peters Corporation.

The three stress line which Roethke used to suggest a waltz easily becomes a 3/4 meter as Rorem expands the accented syllables to half notes (see Ex. 5.18, measures 25-28). Although the tempo is the fastest of the cycle, the composer makes it clear by his marking that this is not a totally happy situation ("very fast but joyless, breathless, crude and free"). The boy's ambivalence, torn as he is between fear and excitement, is musically clear in the strong dissonances on pianistic downbeats, and the octave vocal leaps which suggest "papa's" drunken lurches (see Ex. 5.18).

"I Strolled Across an Open Field,"[61] the last of the Lost Son texts, carried the original poetic title of "The Waking." It was no doubt changed because another song in the cycle sets another poem called "The Waking"--that one the title poem from the Roethke collection published in 1953. From this it becomes clear that the idea of "waking" (i.e., the coming of understanding or sudden illumination) was important to Roethke's thought. In "I Strolled Across an Open Field" the mechanism of illumination is an early morning walk through spring fields full of flowers and singing birds, and its effect is the sense of merging the poet's own identity with the rich life around him ("and all the waters of all the streams / sang in my veins that summer day"). Notable also is the presence of the river in verse six of this poem, which can be compared with the even greater prominence of the symbol in "Song"--a Douglas Moore setting of Theodore Roethke discussed on page 97, Volume I of this series.

Rorem's setting of this poem deals more with the physical than the metaphysical aspects of the stroll. His tempo

marking is "fast and exuberant" and a steady eighth note
motion in pianistic cluster chords establishes the rapid pace
of the walker, while a filigree of sixteenth notes in the
right hand breaks loose in joyful roulades.

Example 5.19, measures 4-9. Copyright 1969, Boosey &
Hawkes; used by permission.

In the middle section of the ABA form, Rorem moves from
the brighter key of A major to the greater warmth of D flat
and lets his voice line take on jazz-like syncopations as the
flowers jump "like small goats." The returning A material
brings a resumption of purposeful walking, which continues
without abatement until with the closing pianissimo scale the
"stroller" vanishes from sight. (See Ex. 5.20, page 234.)

The Roethke volume called The Waking (see above)
included poems written between 1933 and 1953. Its title
poem demonstrates a technically impressive command of form:
six stanzas of three lines each in strict iambic pentameter,
wherein all second lines, and all first and third lines through-
out share a single rhyme (or near rhyme). Further there is

Example 5.20, measures 36-38. Copyright 1969, Boosey &
Hawkes; used by permission.

a poetic "motif" built of two separate lines that come to-
gether at the end in refrain and recapitulation. "I wake to
sleep and take my waking slow. / I learn by going where I
have to go." As always with Roethke, the language is sim-
ple, but the thought complex. The poet appears to be say-
ing that in sleep comes the real waking, when the uncon-
scious mind delivers its uncensored messages. He goes on
to celebrate intuition over cerebration ("we think by feel-
ing") and experience over analysis (see second line of re-
frain). When Ned Rorem chose to set "The Waking,"62 he
wisely selected a musical style which would highlight rather
than compete with this intriguing text. The rhythmic struc-
ture is a square, steadily moving 4/4 with the voice in con-
stant quarter notes and the pianist's left hand in chordal or
arpeggiated eighths. The right hand of the accompaniment
either doubles the voice or engages in a complementary
counterpoint which opens up as the voice holds the last note
of the refrain lines.

Example 5.21, measures 16-23. Copyright 1961, Henmar Press, Inc.; used by permission of C.F. Peters Corporation.

The song opens and closes with simple C major chords, but in between employs free chromatic movement, with many poly-harmonies and other forms of dissonance. The intuitive state, it seems to say, is clear and organically whole, but the mind (witness this poem) weaves tangled webs trying to attain it.

Words for the Wind was published in 1958, and its section designated "Love Poems" reflects a new area of Roethke's growth stemming from his marriage five years earlier. "Memory" is from this group, and seems to bear out Bower's contention that Roethke's love poetry "functions simultaneously on sensual and spiritual levels" with his lady often becoming the embodiment of his striving toward the Absolute (see Note 54). The poem, which is three four-line stanzas of free verse, begins (again) in the dream-world with the lovers merged into one ("we breathe in unison"). The woman turns, then, and moves away toward a doe and her fawn, as everything becomes frozen in the eternal mo-ment ("the grass changes to stone"). Rorem's "Memory"[63] captures the alluring strangeness of the poetic atmosphere quite remarkably, with restricted but highly appropriate musical means. The repetitive melodic motifs which center around an open fifth and derive from the pentatonic scale create an exotic, Oriental feeling, as does the overall spare-ness of the setting. (See Ex. 5.22, page 236.) Notice, also, that the earlier, "together" part of the dream unfolds in smooth, diatonic harmonies. As separation and uncer-tainty take over, the vocal melody repeats strophically but the accompaniment incorporates increasing dissonance and polytonal ambiguity.

Example 5.22, measures 1-8. Copyright 1961, Henmar Press, Inc.; used by permission of C.F. Peters Corporation.

    "Snake,"[64] the last of the Eight Poems, comes from the section in Words for the Wind called "Voices and Creatures." It is a masterful verbal portrait of the appearance and movement of a young snake whose "pure, sensuous form" raises the poet's longing "to be that thing" and the hope that he might be, in some way, at some time. As B. Middaugh has pointed out,[65] Ned Rorem's setting employs three ostinato figures, and it is interesting that despite the composer's expressed disdain of musical "word-painting," two of these take on the coiled, circular contours of the reptile in question. The "Presto" tempo marking and recurrent opposition of F minor voice patterns to A flat chordal outlines in the bass (See Ex. 5.23, page 237) lend a possibly humorous note which this writer has heard over-emphasized in performance. This was clearly not Roethke's intent, and it is doubtful that it was Rorem's, since he assigns two and a half lines at the song's end to a pianistic spinning out of the philosophical speculation on the possibilities of reincarnation.

236

Example 5.23, measures 1-5. Copyright 1963, Henmar
Press, Inc.; used by permission of C.F. Peters Corporation.

In 1965, Ned Rorem published a song cycle called
Poems of Love and the Rain[66] which was without precedent
in the literature.   The composer begins this cycle with set-
tings of eight poems, and after an "Interlude" (number 9)
proceeds to contrasting settings of the original eight, in
reverse order.   The pair which appears as numbers five and
thirteen sets a Roethke poem "Apparition" from The Far Field,
a collection published posthumously in 1964.   Although the
poet's mysterious references to "the softfooted one" make it
uncertain as to whether the apparition is a spirit, fantasy,
or dream figure, the three verses of conventionally rhymed
four lines each, have the unmistakable flavor of a folk bal-
lad.   Rorem's second setting (number 13) picks up this at-
mosphere with a flowing 9/8 meter, a lyrically contoured
voice line doubled in the accompaniment and a largely homo-
phonic texture.   (See Ex. 5.24, page 238.)   In the first
setting, however (number 5), he adopts the always arresting
theatrical device of "playing against the mood."   Now the
voice line becomes highly angular, with much chromatic move-
ment and many jagged leaps.   The singer is sometimes alone,

Example 5.24, measures 1-3. Copyright 1965, Boosey &
Hawkes, Inc.; used by permission.

recitative style, and at other times shares a polyphonic,
even imitative texture. The tempo is allegro agitato, the
dynamic level mostly fortissimo, and the effect, one of
dramatically portrayed desperation.

Example 5.25, measures 1-6. Copyright 1965, Boosey &
Hawkes, Inc.; used by permission.

Number 9, which Rorem calls "Interlude," sets a Roethke poem by that same title, and is the only poem that Rorem ever used from Roethke's first published collection, Open House. In rich verbal images, and the tight formal structuring of the poet's early period, it describes the time of anxious waiting for a threatening thunderstorm which does not "come to pass." The Rorem "Interlude" has two distinct sections. The first is an unaccompanied vocal recitative in the chromatic, angular style of the first "Apparition." The second is a solo piano passage in rapidly moving chromatic figurations which reach a towering dynamic climax at the upper range of the keyboard and then recede. Each section alone and the combined effect are skillful musical portrayals of gathering excitement with a disappointing end.

Ned Rorem's next to last Roethke setting was written in 1971 and dedicated to Phyllis Curtin, one of the singers whom he has most admired and who has given many performances of his songs. This was "The Serpent,"[67] a poem published in Words for the Wind in the section titled "Lighter Pieces and Poems for Children." In these amusing verses, we see an entirely different side of the obscure and mystical Roethke, and indeed this story of the "serpent who had to sing" is attracting settings by a number of composers who appreciate its possibilities for musical humor. As a matter of fact, the humorous is an unaccustomed area for Rorem, too, but he rises magnificently to the occasion. A lively, "perpetual motion" figure in the piano mocks the reptile's urge toward a "Singing Career," while the vocal line modifies its strophes with occasional melismas of an appropriately operatic contour.

Example 5.26, measures 47-52. Copyright 1974, Boosey & Hawkes; used by permission.

Although Rorem's vocal lines become increasingly chromatic into the seventies, this one remains largely diatonic, in keeping with the ingenuous nature of the text. Notice also the jazzy, syncopated vocal rhythms which contribute to the light-heartedly contemporary atmosphere.

The final Rorem/Roethke setting opens the cycle called The Nantucket Songs,[68] which was commissioned by the Elizabeth Sprague Coolidge Foundation and premièred in 1979 by Phyllis Bryn-Julson and the composer at the Library of Congress. Rorem titles this opening piece "From Whence Cometh Song," a phrase that serves as the first line of a poem called simply "Song" in Roethke's collection The Far Field.

In his jacket notes for the CRI recording of the cycle, the composer tells us that it was written at his house on Nantucket Island, and that the songs "are emotional rather than intellectual," being aimed "away from the head and toward the diaphragm." Roethke's compressed, dramatic exploration of the sources of song, love, and death was an inspired poetic choice to establish the desired "emotional" ambiance of the work. The setting has an equally visceral impact, as the wide-ranging vocal line, highlighted against a spare accompaniment, poses and answers Roethke's uneasy questions in stark, unrelenting contrasts of pitch, dynamics, and contour.

NOTES

1. Ned Rorem, "The Piano in my Life," Setting the Tone (New York: Coward-McCann, 1983), p. 18.

2. Ibid., p. 20.

3. Ned Rorem, The Final Diary (New York: Holt, Rinehart and Winston, 1974), p. 310. Reprinted by North Point Press under the title, The Later Diaries.

4. Rorem, Setting the Tone, p. 20.

5. Ibid., p. 22.

6. Ibid., p. 23.

7. Ned Rorem, The New York Diary (New York: George Braziller, 1967), p. 174. The three songs are now printed in a private edition as Paul's Blues (Red Ozier Press).

8. Ned Rorem, Critical Affairs (New York: George Braziller, 1970), p. 32.

9. John Gruen, The Party's Over (New York: Viking, 1972), p. 74.

10. Ibid., p. 80.

11. Ibid., p. 81.

12. Rorem, The New York Diary, p. 105.

13. Ibid., p. 155.

14. Gruen, p. 81.

15. Rorem, The New York Diary, p. 184.

16. Rorem, The Later Diaries, p. 144.

17. Rorem, Setting the Tone, p. 85.

18. See Setting the Tone, pp. 230-231, for a listing of these commissions.

19. Ned Rorem, "Interview," The NATS Bulletin, XXXIX:2 (1982), p. 5. This interview ends with a complete catalog of Rorem songs to date plus a discography. A recent addition to the latter is Rosalind Rees and the composer performing Ned Rorem's songs (GSS 104), and the record includes ten of the twenty-one Goodman and Roethke settings discussed in this chapter.

20. Ibid., p. 46.

21. Ibid.

22. Ibid., p. 47.

23. Marvin Robert Bloomquist, "The Songs of Ned Rorem" (Kansas City: The University of Missouri Dissertation, 1970), p. 2.

24. Quoted in: Philip L. Miller, "The Songs of Ned Rorem," Tempo, CXXVII (December 1978), p. 25.

25. George Dennison's "Memoir" in: Paul Goodman, Collected Poems (New York: Random House, 1973), p. XIII.

26. Kunitz and Haycraft, eds. Twentieth Century Authors, First Supplement (New York: H.W. Wilson, 1961), p. 372.

27. Dennison, p. XV.

28. Alicia Ostriker, "Paul Goodman," Partisan Review, XLIII:2 (1976), p. 286.

29. Kingsley Widmer, Paul Goodman (Boston: Twayne, 1980), p. 23.

30. Robert Meredith, "Everywhere a Single Voice," Poetry, CXXVIII:2 (1976), p. 105.

31. Ostriker, p. 294.

32. Emile Capouya, "The Poet as Prophet," Parnassus, III:1 (1974), p. 30.

33. See The Later Diaries, p. 432.

34. Ned Rorem, Pure Contraption (New York: Holt, Rinehart and Winston, 1974), pp. 97-101.

35. Ned Rorem, "The Lordly Hudson" (New York: Mercury Music Corp., 1947), Medium high.

36. Ned Rorem, The Paris Diary (New York: George Braziller, 1966), p. 10.

37. Rorem, Pure Contraption, p. 101.

38. Ned Rorem, "Absalom" (Boosey and Hawkes, 1972). Medium voice.

39. Ned Rorem, "Rain in Spring" (Boosey and Hawkes, 1956). Medium voice.

40. Ned Rorem, "The Midnight Sun" (Boston: E.C. Schirmer, 1968). Medium high.

41. See Daryl Hine and Joseph Parisi, eds., The "Poetry" Anthology (Boston: Houghton Mifflin, 1978), p. 275.

42. Ned Rorem, "The Tulip Tree" (Boston: E.C. Schirmer, 1968). Medium high.

43. Ned Rorem, "Sally's Smile" (New York: Henmar Press, 1957). Medium high. C.F. Peters is the selling agent for Henmar Press.

44. Ned Rorem, Three Poems of Paul Goodman (New York: Boosey & Hawkes, 1968). Medium high.

45. Ned Rorem, "Such Beauty as Hurts to Behold" (New York: Henmar Press, 1961). Medium high.

46. The reader is referred to Volume I, p. 97, of this series for a brief discussion of Roethke in connection with a song by Douglas Moore.

47. Kunitz, and Haycraft, p. 837.

48. William Heyen, comp., Profile of Theodore Roethke (Columbus, Ohio: Charles E. Merrill, 1971), p. 5.

49. Ibid., p. 13.

50. Ibid., p. 8.

51. Rorem, The Later Diaries, p. 65.

52. Ostriker, p. 292.

53. Heyen, p. 101.

54. Neil Bowers, Theodore Roethke (Columbia, MO: University of Missouri Press, 1982).

55. Heyen, p. 13.

56. Rorem, "The American Art Song" in Setting the Tone, p. 230. Although listed here as a cycle, Ned Rorem points out in a November 20, 1985 letter to the author, that the Eight Poems of Theodore Roethke were not necessarily intended to be performed as a group and have never been done that way since their première.

57. Ned Rorem, "Root Cellar" (New York: Henmar Press, 1963). Medium high.

58. Ned Rorem, "Orchids" (Boosey and Hawkes, 1969). Medium voice.

59. Ned Rorem, "Night Crow" (New York: Henmar Press, 1963). Medium high.

60. Ned Rorem, "My Papa's Waltz" (New York: Henmar Press, 1963). Medium high.

61. Ned Rorem, "I Strolled Across an Open Field" (Boosey and Hawkes, 1969). Medium high.

62. Ned Rorem, "The Waking" (New York: Henmar Press, 1961). Medium high.

63. Ned Rorem, "Memory" (New York: Henmar Press, 1961). Medium.

64. Ned Rorem, "Snake" (New York: Henmar Press, 1963). Medium high.

65. Bennie Middaugh, "The Songs of Ned Rorem," The NATS Bulletin, XXIV (May 1968), p. 36.

66. Ned Rorem, Poems of Love and the Rain (Boosey and Hawkes, 1965). Mezzo-soprano.

67. Ned Rorem, "The Serpent" (Boosey and Hawkes, 1974). Medium high.

68. Ned Rorem, The Nantucket Songs (Boosey and Hawkes, 1979). Soprano.

VI. THE FOURTH DECADE

<u>Richard Hundley</u> (1933-   )
Kenneth Patchen (1911-1972)
James Purdy (1923-   )

Richard Hundley's early life straddled the states of Ohio
and Kentucky. He was born in Cincinnati, into what the
composer describes as a "very emotional, Protestant-revival-
type"[1] family. Two weeks after his birth, the Hundleys
moved to Kentucky, and it was here that young Richard
learned the fundamentals of music from a Hungarian teacher,
and began piano study with a Mrs. Wyman whose fee was a
dollar an hour. The composer recalls performing at a ladies'
tea party, and being unable to finish the piece through lack
of self-discipline in his preparation. "I started writing my
own pieces," says Hundley, "so I'd be able to finish!"[2]

When he was eleven years old, Hundley began commut-
ing from his home in Kentucky to the Cincinnati College Con-
servatory. Here he came under the imposed discipline of a
teacher who dismissed him from lessons when assignments
were not completed. By the age of fourteen he was able to
perform a Mozart piano concerto with the Northern Kentucky
Symphony Orchestra, and at sixteen, he soloed with the Cin-
cinnati Symphony under Thor Johnson's conducting.

In 1952 came his first visit to New York, a city which
he quickly came to love because there he "could be free and
not have to conform." For most of the fifties, he traveled
back and forth between New York and the Cincinnati

Conservatory. Finally, at the death of his grandmother, Hundley severed his last emotional tie to the Midwest and, with fifty dollars in his pocket, took up residence in Manhattan.

While growing up in Kentucky, Hundley's musical gods had been Stravinsky, Beethoven, and Wagner, but a chance hearing of Samuel Barber's "Knoxville, Summer of 1915," had effected a radical change which steered him toward the voice as a medium of expression. By the time he settled in New York, he had already begun to compose songs, and to center the rest of his musical activities on singers, as a vocal coach and accompanist. Hundley, himself, possesses a very pleasant singing voice, and after performing with various choral groups, he took and passed an audition in 1960 for the Metropolitan Opera Chorus. To prepare for the position he "went to school to learn ten operas in four languages," and in retrospect, Hundley feels that his concept of writing vocal music is strongly related to the bel canto influence from his four years with the Met chorus.

During this period, Hundley wrote music in the summertime and studied counterpoint with Israel Citkowitz and harmony with William Flanagan, both of whom were strongly oriented toward vocal composition. He also began to show his music to some of the leading Metropolitan singers, and soon Annaliese Rothenberger was singing his "Softly the Summer" (see below) all over the country. Anna Moffo, too, was taken with the songs that Hundley played for her while she was changing in her dressing room. When she started to program them on recitals, the composer felt that "[he] was made."

For the next twenty years, however, Hundley's reputation was to achieve a steady, but frustratingly slow growth. One notable event in this growth was an Overseas Press Club concert in 1966 at which the tenor Paul Sperry, who is a well-known specialist in American song repertoire, was so favorably impressed by two of the composer's works, that he has been singing and promoting Hundley's songs ever since. By the early seventies, the songs were also appearing in concerts by members of the Metropolitan Opera Studio[3] and by many stars of the opera such as Judith Blegen, Rosalind Elias, and Giorgio Tozzi.

It was not until this decade of the eighties, however, that the recognition which has taken him thirty years to achieve seems finally to be descending on Richard Hundley. Frederica von Stade has performed his "The Astronomers" on a 1982 CBS recording (Digital 37231); his Eight Songs were selected for inclusion in the repertoire for the 1982 International American Music Competition for vocalists; and his work has been featured at the Newport Music Festivals of 1983 and 1984 (at the latter, he was the festival's first composer-in-residence). In August, 1983, the Eight Songs, originally published two years earlier, had gone into their third printing, and were finding their way, along with other Hundley songs, onto recital programs throughout the United States.

A small amount of support for his creative activity had come to Hundley through the years in the form of scattered ASCAP and "Meet-the-Composer" awards as well as three summer fellowships at the MacDowell colony in New Hampshire (see Volume II, Chapter I). Nevertheless, Hundley has paid a price for being what he terms a "maverick" and for forging an "independent career outside of academia and [the] grants" that are available to those pursuing conventional teaching careers and writing in the large forms acceptable to the musical establishment. Hundley continues to live very modestly in the apartment at West Street and Bethune where the author interviewed him. It is an artists' low rent housing project, located one truck-laden and trash-littered block from the East River. Here, a huge yellow-brick building whose entrance is guarded by security policemen, has been cut up into large, loft-like spaces, which the residents divide into sleeping, working, and eating areas.

The piano was not a grand, but Hundley made it sound like one as he played his songs and sang them in a pure, lyric tenor voice. He was anxious to communicate his feelings about the texts he sets and how he sets them, and the author was struck by the warmth of his personality. "What I am interested in," said Hundley, "is the crystallization of emotion. I memorize a text and live with it, then set it according to how I feel about the poem. I have to tell the listener what it's about when the pianist starts--like a short story."

Hundley went on to say that what he looks for in a poem is "something [he] can identify with" and that he "finds much contemporary poetry unsuitable for setting because it is alien to nature." He reads a great deal of poetry, recites it at the drop of a hat, and knows "by heart" every text he has ever set. He mentions James Purdy, who is a close friend, as one of his favorite poets, and points out that Dorothy Parker had thought him the wittiest writer in America.

Questioned about influences on his compositions, he lists Barber as the first, and continues "Harris, Copland, and the young David Diamond were the reasons I went into serious music. Virgil Thomson's wit was also an influence, and his use of simple chords for interesting effects. William Flanagan, of course--his music had a kind of pre-Sondheim 'gorgeousness' about it"--and sadly adds, "no one knows exactly how he died."

Richard Hundley's list of compositions includes, besides the many songs, some choral works, a piano sonata, some chamber music for winds, and a few songs with orchestra. He also has the draft of an opera with a text by James Purdy. Hundley believes that the uniquely American musical theater has had a strong influence on the country's art song, and he also feels that "the academic serial school that dominated American music in the 1960's simply lost its audience."[4] This means, therefore, that with "the subsequent resurgence of romantic feeling, tonal harmony, and melody, conservative composers like himself are the new 'avant garde.'"[5]

There is, however, a caveat about Hundley's conservatism, for, as he explains, he "uses conventional harmonic and melodic material but rethinks it so that it comes across freshly in the contemporary spirit." A more apt description could hardly be made of "Softly the Summer,"[6] one of the earliest, and still one of the composer's most successful songs, which Hundley wrote to his own text. It had been begun in the unsettled year of 1954, was completed on moving to New York City in 1957, and finally published in 1963. Around 1956, Hundley had showed it to "an academic" who called it a popular song. Conversely, "the popular folks said it was too serious" for their categories. Once discovered by Rothenberger, however, (see p. 247) it has been sung with enjoyment by many sopranos who simply and correctly saw it as an art song with an unusual flavor.

The poem describes the moment when the "lovely green" of summer begins to fade into darkness, and the key to the composer's "crystallized emotion" in this setting is in the first line: "Softly the summer lies down in sleep." Hundley wanted a gentle, hushed atmosphere to prevail from the first word, and so he "wrote 'softly' on the high A flat so that singers couldn't sock it."

Example 6.1, measures 4-9. Copyright 1963, General Music Publishing Co.; used by permission.

In the fourth stanza of the modified strophic form, the soft, sustained A flats extend to B flats in an exquisitely shaped contour that sets "High in the heav'ns" with a shimmering quality appropriate to the verbal description of silver light. It need hardly be pointed out that the tessitura and expressive demands of the vocal line are not only totally foreign to the realm of "popular" music, but in the author's experience require the artistry of a highly trained singer.

The song, indeed, is a brilliantly conceived wedding of sophisticated art song procedure to musical theater elements such as the simple, recurring waltz bass patterns of the left hand, and the encouraged freedom in performance of all the colla voce sections (see Ex. 6.1). As in all Hundley settings, the vocal writing is extremely grateful, the texture is classically transparent, and the piano writing extremely idiomatic as the right hand weaves its graceful filaments of sound around the sleeping figure of personified Summer.

Kenneth Patchen (1911-1972)

Life as a dedicated artist would have seemed a most unlikely result from Kenneth Patchen's origins. He, too, was born in Ohio but not into the metropolitan environment of Hundley's Cincinnati. Patchen's birthplace was Niles, a town which typified the mining and industrial atmosphere of the Mahoning Valley. Descended from English, Scotch, Irish, and French forbears, Patchen had one grandfather who had worked in the coal mines and another as a farmer-blacksmith. His father was a "roller" in the steel mills of the area for over twenty-five years, and Patchen never lost his youthful memories of grimy houses and the daily struggles of the workers against weariness, fear, and boredom.

In his early childhood, Patchen moved with his family to nearby Warren where he, a brother, and two sisters attended school. His mother, a devout Catholic, raised the children in her faith and cherished the hope that Kenneth would become a priest. Instead, he became a poet, whose lifework was infused with the priestly qualities of compassion and visionary hopes for mankind. He began to write in his twelfth year, at fourteen had two sonnets published in the New York Times, and became a frequent contributor to school publications until his graduation from Harding High School.

In order to pay for a college education, Patchen had worked alongside his father and brother in the steel mills for two summers. Entering the University of Wisconsin in 1929, he was accepted, after a battery of tests, into Alexander Meiklejohn's experimental college, the aim of which was to educate by focusing on a single great period of cultural history. The subject for Patchen's class was Athens in the fifth century B.C., "an exposure to a civilization that

251

Patchen never forgot and which influenced his work decisively in terms of social viewpoints."[7]

During his year at Wisconsin, Patchen continued to play football, an activity begun in high school partially to promote his acceptance in a milieu which took a dim view of writers. Nevertheless, the break with home and family was complete after 1929. He transferred for one semester to Commonwealth College in Mena, Arkansas, into another experimental program, run by Meiklejohn's son; then turned to the self-education often preferred by artists, for a four-year period of writing, working at odd jobs, and wandering across the United States and Canada.

Patchen, like his father before him, was a powerfully built man with a passionate ideological commitment to pacifism. The strain was no doubt inherited from a family ancestor, Sir Aaron Drake--a British general who had deserted during the Revolutionary War to marry a Pennsylvania farm girl. When Patchen's wanderings found him in Boston on Christmas Eve of 1933, Destiny arranged his meeting with Miriam Oikemus, an attractive University of Massachusetts coed who had been involved that year as an anti-war organizer at Smith College. "We met at a party," she later remembered. "He was very rude and unsociable. He looked ... sad and thin ... and I was very impressed with him. Five months later we were married."[8]

Thus began a marriage which was to prove the poet's chief sustenance through a lifetime of prolific writing and almost constant pain. The pain resulted from a series of back injuries and operations which began in 1936, and left him crippled and bed-ridden from 1959 'til his death thirteen years later. The Patchens began their married life in Greenwich Village, and lived in and around it from 1934 to 1950 except for two periods of travel. The first of these was to Santa Fe in 1936, a trip made possible by the Guggenheim Fellowship awarded after the publication of Before the Brave, Patchen's first book of poetry. The second was a short time spent in Hollywood in 1937, where the lure of quick money to be earned in film writing could not allay the couple's unease in the "sordid small town with the psychology of a big city."[9]

Returned to the East, Patchen was an important

presence in the avant-garde Village environment, which included e.e. cummings, Henry Miller, William Carlos Williams, and Stephen Vincent Benét. In 1950 Patchen left for the West Coast, moved into the north bay area of San Francisco, and soon formed ties to Kenneth Rexroth, Lawrence Ferlinghetti, and the West Coast literary movements. His defiance of academia and his anti-war, anti-materialist philosophy made him an immediate and important influence in "Beat" circles, but he fought to maintain his unique artistic identity since the nihilism of the "Beat" credo was totally foreign to him.

In 1956, the Patchens moved to the house in Palo Alto which would be the last home they shared. The next year, Patchen began his pioneer work in the Poetry-and-Jazz movement. For three years, before the final disabling injury, he toured the U.S. and Canada reading his poetry to the music of such jazz players as Charlie Mingus, the Alan Neil quartet, and the Chamber Jazz Sextet. Incredibly, the stream of writing never stopped. Between 1936 and the heart attack which killed him in 1972, Patchen produced an average of a book a year, in the genres of poetry, poetry-prose, concrete-poetry, "anti-novels," and "picture-poems," most of which he created as radically new forms.

Two of these genres came into being because Patchen, like his friend e.e. cummings, was strongly gifted in visual as well as verbal art forms. Concrete poetry was based on reduced elements of language, with an emphasis on arrangement and appearance on the page of the selected elements. The "picture-poems" and "painted-books" which he increasingly fashioned in his isolating disability, took on sufficient stature to merit a one-man show of Patchen graphics, held at the Corcoran Art Gallery (Washington, D.C.) in 1969.

With the passage of time, Kenneth Patchen, who had started out as a proletarian poet in protest against society and its ills, enlarged his focus to perceive a vision of individual growth and universal love. Love had indeed been one of the most powerfully sustaining forces in his life of physical torment. He had dedicated all his books "For Miriam" and had written a group of poems to her, through the years, that are perhaps his best known work, and which have appealed to a number of composers as texts for setting.[10]

The poem of Richard Hundley's choice, "O Sleeping Falls the Maiden Snow," had first appeared in <u>Pictures of Life and Death</u> (1946), and was reprinted in the little volume called <u>The Love Poems</u> which City Lights Books of San Francisco published twenty years later. It is a short, free-verse poem of three three-line stanzas whose deep feeling is heightened by the tightness of structure deriving from the preponderance of four-stress lines and the repetition of the opening one. Within this confining but enabling form, Patchen's characteristic perceptions unfold: the sharp visual image of the cold, clean snow on the "bitter roofs of the world"; the hostile world's menace in the "rush of dark wings"; and the impassioned commitment to protect the love who lay "safe in [his] arms."

The setting of this poem,[11] which Hundley dedicated to Anna Moffo, is dated December 27, 1960, and shows the composer's early mastery of serious, dramatic writing. Now titled "Maiden Snow," it is far removed from his light, sophisticated vein, and combines the expressive intensity of a short Puccini aria with the subtle interweaving of voice and piano that is characteristic of art song. The vocal line has many arioso-like repeated notes but the tension thus created always breaks out into a lyrically curving contour:

Example 6.2, measures 1-7. Copyright 1961, General Music Publishing Co.; used by permission.

The piano, which begins with the unobtrusive chordal sup-
port of a recitative, grows to full partnership in measure 6
(see Ex. 6.2) with an inspired rhythmic suspension in the
right hand serving to delay the instrumental motivic thrust.

Strong dissonance is used sparingly but effectively as
major and minor seconds fall with anguished force at the be-
ginning of measures 14 and 15.

Example 6.3 measures 14-17. Copyright 1961, General Music
Publishing Co.; used by permission.

The setting of the final phrase uses musical device most
skillfully to create two levels of meaning. The vocal line
resolves to "safety" in a C minor/major context, reiterated
by the uppermost chords of the piano postlude, while the
rest of the accompaniment holds to the stolid G minor of
the outside world's continuing threat. (See Ex. 6.4, page
256.)

Patchen's Collected Poems of 1968 includes "O Sleeping
Falls the Maiden Snow" which seems, in the Paul Goodman
manner, to be a later version of the poem Hundley set.
There are major changes here, in the direction of increased
vulnerability ("Upon the bitter place of our shelterlessness"),
and the result is weaker in both form and content. Inter-
estingly, Hundley, too, is preparing a revised version of his
original setting, which incorporates only minor rhythmic and
harmonic changes.

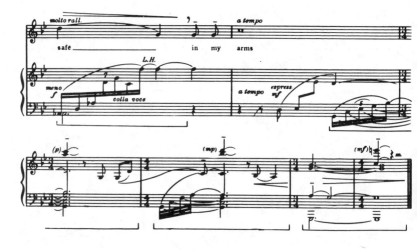

Example 6.4, measures 24-29. Copyright 1961, General
Music Publishing Co.; used by permission.

James Purdy (1923-   )

James Purdy is also a fellow Ohioan of Richard Hundley's,
having been born ten years before the composer near the
town of Fremont. He was educated at the University of
Chicago in 1941 and 1946, and also spent some time studying
at the University of Puebla in Mexico. Purdy worked as an
interpreter in Latin America, France, and Spain, and taught
at Lawrence College in Appleton, Wisconsin, from 1949 to
1953. Since that time he has devoted himself to full-time
writing, except for a Visiting Professorship held in 1977 at
the University of Tulsa, Oklahoma.

   Purdy has been the recipient of a number of major
awards: a National Institute of Arts and Letters grant in
1958; Guggenheim Fellowships in 1958 and 1962; and a Ford
Fellowship for drama in 1961. His most recent novel, On
Glory's Course, has been nominated for the William Faulkner
Pen Award. His works include short stories, novels, plays,
and poetry and he is widely considered to be a contemporary
master of the short story genre. The writer has lived at the
same Henry Street address in Brooklyn for many years and
has been an integral part of the literary and musical New

York scene which Ned Rorem chronicled in his Diaries (see Chapter IV). A sense of this can be gleaned from two items of the Rorem-Purdy correspondence dating from the middle sixties. In 1965 Rorem writes: "Edward A. tells me he's deep in work on Malcolm. No doubt, if the production ultimately requires music, this will be allotted to Bill Flanagan, since he's Albee's official composer. But it goes without saying that I'd also love to do it if you want me!"[12]

The reader will recall (see p. 163) that Bill Flanagan did write the music for this ultimately ill-fated production. Two years later, Rorem wrote again to congratulate Purdy on the publication of a new novel:

> Yesterday, in 2 fell swoops, I finished Eustace Chisolm and the Works and was overwhelmed. And though I'm a fan of almost everything you've written, this novel I like even better (if possible) than Cabot Wright Begins.... Everything pleased me: the horror and pity of love, the revival of my own adolescent Chicago years ... the "importance of your theme"--as reviewers say--and above all: your musical ear. It's the best so-called fiction I've read in an age.... Thanks for reviving what in me is ever rarer: excitement.[13]

The keen aural awareness that Rorem characterizes as Purdy's "musical ear" comes through in the writer's own comments on his artistic goals. "As I see it," he says, "my work is an exploration of the American soul conveyed in a style based on the rhythms and accents of American speech."[14] The result of his exploration has been, in the prose works, primarily a dark vision, of a commercial culture in which "anything is sacred which brings in money"[15] and where "love ... seems to be a sickness rather than a satisfaction."[16] Early in his career, Purdy had difficulty getting his writing published, and interpreted this, perhaps correctly, as a rejection by the literary establishment of his unconventional point of view. After Dame Edith Sitwell arranged British publication, however, his work rapidly gained recognition. Today he is regarded as a writer of extraordinary imagination who was able to mix realism, fairy-tale, and allegory in a unique combination of surrealism and a "meticulously rhetoric-free prose."[17]

Purdy's poetry, which shows many of these same qual-
ities, was initially published together with short stories in
collections titled An Oyster is a Wealthy Beast (1967), Mr.
Evening (1968), and On the Rebound (1970). In 1971 and
1973, two volumes of only poetry appeared, respectively
called The Running Sun and Sunshine is an Only Child.
Reading the poetry, one senses that Purdy has lightened
the weight of his satire to suit the compressed poetic form,
and indeed, the titles themselves of the two verse collec-
tions are steeped in sunshine and the suggestion of increas-
ing cheer.

In a December, 1967, letter, Hundley begins to speak
to Purdy of the settings he is making of his friend's poetry.
Marcia Balwin, a singer from the Metropolitan, has come to
his apartment and he has played "Sea Foams" (to a Purdy
text) for her, plus sketches for other songs. She is anxious
to have a cycle, and Hundley projects "the work will be a
much welcomed addition to the nearly non-existent repertoire
of humor in 'serious' music."[18] Curiously, the cycle was not
to be performed for another fifteen years, but was finally
premièred in 1982 in Alice Tully Hall, New York, under com-
mission from Clarion Concerts for its twenty-fifth birthday
celebration. It had by then become The Sea is Swimming
Tonight, a work scored for chorus, soloists, and four-hand
piano, with the composer still planning additions to the exist-
ing ten James Purdy settings.

In the summer of 1969, we can see from Hundley's cor-
respondence that he is beginning the process that would
lead to the Purdy settings for solo voice to be eventually
published in the 1981 Eight Songs[19] collection.

On August 3rd he writes to Purdy: "I read the poems
in the Mr. Evening book by Black Sparrow Press and liked
them again ... 'Come ready and see me, no matter how late'
is real Purdy."[20] On the sixth of August he begins a di-
rected study of their possibilities: "I'm working on the
Purdy poems--grouping them according to subject and char-
acter.... If there is poetry of such extraordinary imagina-
tion being written today, I have never heard or seen it."[21]
And on August 12th, he prepares to share his enthusiasm
with friends: "The poems are always a delight. Anne Cooper
Dobbins and a pupil of mine, Cynthia Fleming, an educational
editor, are coming here this evening and we will read you--
and 'feel out' the poetry."[22]

The first composed of the four Purdy settings which constitute half of the Eight Songs was "Come ready and see me." Hundley finished it in January, 1971, a year and a half after he had praised the poem extravagantly in the letters quoted above. In a flyer put out by the publisher, Boosey and Hawkes, in 1982, Hundley declared "My chief source of inspiration in these songs are the words themselves and I have tried to recreate in the music the emotion I experienced on first reading the poems.... 'Come ready and see me' concerns the poignancy of lost love."

A poignant poem it is, with its urgent plea to "come before the years run out," and its longing is in no way lessened by allusions to the contemporary scene such as "you must haste on foot or by sky." The ten-line poem is an unusual form, with lines three, five, and ten ending in the word "out," six and eight in "sky" and seven and nine in "forever." The lines are all short, and varyingly include two, three, or four stresses each. The particular combination of repetition and randomness gives the poem itself the feel of a song lyric, as does its verbal parodying of Tin Pan Alley.

Hundley's musical choices for this have the "inevitable" feel of skillful text setting. To underline the universality of the poetic message, he writes a spare, guitar-like accompaniment, and a simple 4/4 meter which the textual rhythm is stretched to accommodate by means of tied-over half notes. (see Ex. 6.5, below and page 260.)

Over this seeming simplicity are layered a broadly contoured vocal line of an octave and a half in compass, subtle use of lowered fourth and seventh steps in a basically diatonic context to emphasize "forever," and a masterful employment of formal repetition for dramatic purposes. The latter

Example 6.5, measures 1-6. Copyright 1981, Boosey and Hawkes; used by permission.

occurs when, after a piano "break" that restates the opening vocal material, Hundley brings the voice back, in popular ballad style, to repeat the entire chorus at a higher dynamic level, with quasi-hypnotic fervor. The modern-day incantation falls over into a coda which winds up from an elongated 3/2 measure, then continues to unfold after the voice ceases with a softly syncopated piano part. The final instrumental sound is a wistful, jazz-formula suspension signifying that the song, like the poet's years, has "run out":

260

Example 6.6, measures 43-53. Copyright 1981, Boosey & Hawkes; used by permission.

"Birds, U.S.A.," like "Come Ready and See Me" was published in Purdy's Mr. Evening collection of 1968. Birds seem to be a frequently reappearing theme in Purdy's prose. They are mentioned in the short story "Home by Dark," while the novel I am Elijah Thrush (1972) is, as Tony Tanner puts it, "full of birds"[23] and their symbolic reference to the pure innocence lost by verbalizing humans. This five-line poem is given a humorous cast by its longish listing of the "principal birds of the U.S.A." which takes place in a jazzy, heavily accented anapestic tetrameter. Even the disillusion of the penultimate line ("Aren't the songsters that delighted you at seven") doesn't seem to stop its rush of headlong gaiety.

Hundley creates a musical satire from this text by means of two principal devices. One is the heavy use of syncopation in the vocal line over a "four square" chordal accompaniment which recalls popular America's ragtime roots:

Example 6.7, measures 5-7. Copyright 1981, Boosey and Hawkes; used by permission.

In the other, as Hundley himself tells us, he "paraphrases certain patriotic songs." Although the references are subtle, a perceptive listener can detect the outlines of "O, Say Can You See" in measures one and two,

Example 6.8, measures 1-4. Copyright 1981, Boosey and Hawkes; used by permission.

and "the home of the brave" in measures 28 and 29 (just before the song's end):

Example 6.9, measures 26-30. Copyright 1981, Boosey and Hawkes; used by permission.

The "paraphrasing" piano carries out its task through the body of the song as well, and in measures 11 and 12 takes off on "My country, 'tis of thee" while the voice sustains a joyful crescendo on F. (See Ex. 6.10, page 263.)

"Birds, U.S.A." had been set by Hundley in 1972. "I do," which was completed in August, 1974, is based on a poem from The Running Sun. Its four verses of a short four lines each present an interesting mixture of a conventional metric and rhyme scheme with an e.e. cummings style rejection of capitalization. Hundley calls it "a vocal

Example 6.10, measures 11-14. Copyright 1981, Boosey & Hawkes; used by permission.

valentine," reading the poet's proposal as a straight-forward offer of delightful gifts in return for a promise to wed. This requires ignoring the tongue-in-cheek flavor of "This offer comes once in a lifetime or two" and of "pin on your wings (i.e., join the married establishment) and say 'I do.'" Be that as it may, the song "works" as a vocal valentine and Hundley seems to be tying it stylistically to both its predecessors by means of the running eighth note introduction and "tag" which recall "Come ready and see me" and the syncopated vocal line and chordal accompaniment which are a slowed-down, less accented, gentler version of those elements in "Birds, U.S.A."

Example 6.11, measures 1-7. Copyright 1981, Boosey & Hawkes; used by permission.

For the last of these Purdy settings, which he com-
pleted in November, 1978, Hundley used a text from Purdy's
1967 volume, An Oyster is a Wealthy Beast. In his conver-
sation with the author in 1982, Hundley had called this set-
ting a "Hallowe'en or All Souls' Day piece," and in the Boosey
and Hawkes brochure he mentions that he had "tried to cap-
ture the zany quality of [the] poem." The poem's title is
"Bartholomew Green" and it consists of four rhymed couplets
which center on four different, evocatively named personages:
Bartholomew Green, Corliss Hart, Amelia Swan, and Isadore
Gray. Following the composer's suggestion of a Hallowe'en
piece, one is able to put together their minimal treatments
into a ball scene in which the ladies flourish while the men,
like the lustreless Green, are "seldom seen."

The "zany quality" Hundley sought has indeed been
captured in this inspired setting which begins in the rapid,
scurrying 5/4 rhythm of Bartholomew's diffidence.

Example 6.12, measures 1-7. Copyright 1981, Boosey &
Hawkes; used by permission.

An emphatic waltz rhythm takes over (see Ex. 6.12) as

Corliss and Amelia enter, and continues until Isadore Gray's "fading away" which uses a transitional 3/2 meter on the way back to Green's awkwardly characteristic 5/4.

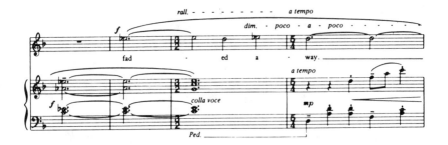

Example 6.13, measures 28-31. Copyright 1981, Boosey & Hawkes; used by permission.

Hundley chooses to repeat "faded away" for pictorial purposes and those of musical transition. He now creates a coda on three reiterations of "Bartholomew Green," with a soft, misterioso indication on the final one that supports the intriguing enigma of Purdy's rarely visible protagonist.

Example 6.14, measures 38-41. Copyright 1981, Boosey & Hawkes; used by permission.

It might also be mentioned that as recently as May, 1985, Richard Hundley premièred another work based on a James Purdy text. This one is an eight minute choral piece called "Ball" and was performed in Cleveland by the Robert

Page Singers who had commissioned the work for their final appearance of the season. The text describes a group of children tossing a ball, but the reviewer noted that "Hundley's music seems to imply that there are deeper levels of significance to be plumbed."[24]

Robert Baksa (1938-)
Emily Dickinson (1830-1886)

Robert Baksa grew up "with a European respect for the arts"[25] which he attributes to his Hungarian background. His mother, who had been born in the United States, went back to Hungary to marry, then returned with her husband four years before the birth of their son. Robert was born in New York City, but when he was seven and a half the family moved to Tucson, Arizona, seeking a better climate for his mother's asthma. Baksa sees the Hungarian influence in his life as having been a strong one. He still has a "Hungarian vocabulary"[26] and is very fond of the music of Kodály, as well as of Hungarian folk and popular traditions.

Baksa had started piano lessons at six, and with the passage of time studied violin, flute, oboe, clarinet, French horn, trumpet, trombone, viola, and cello as well. At the time of the move to Arizona, the Baksas could not afford a piano in the house. When, at the age of thirteen, Robert once again had a piano to use, he began to compose his first pieces, which were later published. Baksa calls himself a "self-taught composer," despite his academic credentials. Although he earned the degree of Bachelor of Arts in Composition from the University of Arizona, he recalls that his composition professor, Robert McBride, gave him "only two suggestions" during his entire course of study. Moreover, having won a scholarship to Tanglewood after graduation, he was assigned to Lukas Foss, whom he perceived as "very condescending" and was consequently "unable to write a note" during the entire summer.

As a result of these experiences, Baksa concluded that composition is largely a matter of "one's personal taste"

266

Robert Baksa

and that there were no hard-and-fast rules to be imparted. He settled in New York City in 1962, and during the ensuing years amassed a catalog of over 400 compositions which include keyboard, orchestral, and chamber works as well as text settings of British and American poetry for solo voice and chorus. Still other genres include documentary film scores and two very successful operas. The first of these was Aria da Capo, based on Edna St. Vincent Millay's well-known play, which premièred at the Lake George Opera Festival in 1969. The second, called Red Carnations (libretto by Glenn Hughes) was commissioned by Lincoln Center for the Metropolitan Opera Studio and toured for two years with the Miniken Opera of Delaware.

The author's interview with Robert Baksa took place on West End Avenue up several flights of stairs in the composer's small, modestly appointed apartment, which was richly crowded with books, scores, and recordings. Baksa had prepared afternoon tea to follow the interview, hospitably inviting two neighbors in the area to join the party who were friends of his and of the author: Carolyn Heafner, a soprano who has specialized in certain aspects of the American song repertoire,[27] and Michael Best, comprimario tenor of the Metropolitan Opera. Baksa's connections with the singers of New York City, it might be noted, stem not only from his work as a composer of vocal repertoire, but also from the fact that he has done professional chorus work and considers himself a "frustrated singer."

In the course of the interview, a clear picture emerged of another talented composer who, like Richard Hundley, had been struggling on his own for many years to make his music known. "Like most composers," said Baksa, "I have no time to sell my music, or even to copy it." Ironically, he has done a great deal of work as a free-lance copyist, and has spent many hours copying for others, music that he feels is less deserving than his own. During the past several years, however, Baksa's music seems to be coming into greater prominence. As indicated in a 1985 brochure, a large number of his vocal and instrumental works are now published by Composers Library Editions for which Theodore Presser is sole agent. (This is Baksa's own company, for which he himself does the printing.) Also, Musical Heritage Society has recently issued a recording of music by Robert Baksa which includes 12 Bagatelles for the piano, Overture for Clarinet, and the Quintet for Oboe and Strings.

Performances of his music are likewise on the increase. In a letter dated June 6, 1985, Baksa described the Merkin

Hall première in April, of his quintet for harpsichord and strings honoring Bach's tri-centennial year. "This week," he continued, "my Oboe Quintet was given its première in Norway in a broadcast concert. The New Jersey Youth Symphony toured England and the Low Countries with my early (1957) 'Meditation,' and the Dutch vocal ensemble 'Quink' will feature my [Shakespeare] madrigals on their American tour next season. I'm beginning to feel like a multinational conglomerate."[28]

When questioned about the relative importance of vocal and instrumental media to his composition, Baksa replied that they are about equal, but that "many people have the impression that I am mostly a vocal composer, because the public responded to my choral music and it sold well." As regards differences of word setting in opera and art song, there is, of course, "more chance to show the voice in opera," and he deliberately tries to "keep [his] art songs fairly low to let the words come through." Baksa, like many song composers, reads a lot of poetry looking for settable texts. About 75 percent of his songs have set the work of American poets, largely because "most available English poets are 100 years old" and lack the quality of "natural speech patterns" which is important to him. "Most of the twentieth-century poets I really enjoy are women," says Baksa, "such as Sara Teasdale, Lowell, and Crapsey." (He has unpublished songs setting all three.) "I find poetry by men interesting" the composer explains, "but not emotional, and I have to have an emotional climate in a poem."

Once the text has been chosen, Baksa first decides "what the piano is going to say." He gets a "couple of germ ideas," then goes through and looks for "shapes in the text that will give interesting vocal lines." He establishes accent patterns and the relative importance of words. "Then harmony has to underpin it all--its tension and resolution has to enhance the meaning of the text." Baksa recalls that about 1970 he sensed a sudden maturity in his ability to handle form, and feels that this is prefigured by the Emily Dickinson songs of the sixties.

The reader is referred to p. 105 of this volume for a discussion of Persichetti's Emily Dickinson settings as well as listings of Dickinson treatments in earlier volumes of the series. It is interesting that so many twentieth-century composers have been, and continue to be drawn to the verses of this poet, whose compassion, wit, imagery, and unconventionality they find highly appropriate to the contemporary scene. Curiously, when Robert Baksa came to set Emily Dickinson, he, like Persichetti, used the text versions from the older Martha Dickinson Bianchi edition, rather than Thomas H. Johnson's newer scholarly readings which became available in the late fifties. Quite probably, they were the versions he had known over a period of time and the Johnson work may not as yet have been widely distributed. In any case, the discrepancies are few and minor.

The years of Emily Dickinson's greatest creativity were 1858 to 1865, during which she produced forty-six of the forty-nine stationery "packets" of her poetry. Midway through this period, in 1862, came the crucial submission of her verses to Thomas W. Higginson, editor of the Atlantic Monthly, and his discouraging response to their stylistic unorthodoxy. It is not surprising, then, to note Thomas H. Johnson's observation that "a growing preoccupation with the subject of fame is a striking characteristic of the poems written between 1862 and 1865."[29] All of the texts selected by Robert Baksa for his Seven Songs to Poems of Emily Dickinson[30] date between 1859 and 1862, well within the "floodtide" years, and over half of them show the author trying to come to terms with her rejection by the literary establishment, and with the knowledge that her work would remain unknown in her lifetime.

Baksa's Seven Songs are arranged chronologically in the cycle in order of their composition: the first was written in 1963, second in 1964, third and fourth in 1965, and the last three in 1966. It would have to be fortuitous, therefore, that number one seems to serve as an introduction to the set. The poem, one of the 1862 group, is "Much madness is divinest sense," and embodies Dickinson's growing conviction that assent to majority opinion is society's requirement for acceptance, while those who "demur" are held to be "dangerous" and/or insane. The recurring theme has thus been struck of the poet's self-image as maverick and dissenter, and a unifying style characteristic of the set, which is its structural emphasis on small melodic and rhythmic motifs, is also unfolded here.

The motif chosen by Baksa for his opening is a simple

downward whole or half step formed by two eighth notes
which are followed by a leap upward of a third or more to
a longer quarter or half note value. The five measure piano
introduction is entirely constructed from a right hand chain
of these motifs in rising sequence, while the left carries the
motif in chordally amplified versions.

Example 6.15, measures 1-4. Copyright 1977, Composers
Library Editions; used by permission.

The piano writing continues to carry the questioning contour
of the motif behind a vocal line that is mostly written in
descending scale patterns of discouragement and token resig-
nation. In the final three measures, however, the piano ut-
ters what the singer (i.e., the poet) apparently cannot, and
with three attenuated statements of the motif, turns question
into pleading.

Example 6.16, measures 22-26. Copyright 1977, Composers
Library Editions; used by permission.

The fearful and macabre aspects of death were never
buried very far in Emily Dickinson's mind, and crop out
from time to time in the poetry as they force their way to
the surface of her consciousness. Number 2 sets such a

poem, written in 1859 and called "What Inn is this[?]"
Here, the Inn becomes a metaphor for a cemetery, the "curi-
ous rooms" are the graves, and the unspeakable answer to
the final question, "Who are these below?" appears to be
the dead themselves. Baksa's "germ idea" for this setting
seems to relate to his own ideas about the "rhythmic quality
in music" which he set forth in an article called "Man as
Music Listener."[31] Falling in line with the notion of the
strong physical impact of an insistent rhythmic pattern is
his recurring piano figuration of a menacing, upward-sweeping
thirty-second note run followed by three inexorable dotted
eighth and sixteenth notes.

Example 6.17, measures 1-3. Copyright 1977, Composers
Library Editions; used by permission.

This pattern is repeated many times, either whole or
separated into its elements, as the "landlord" is importuned
with rising agitation. Baksa then concludes the song with a
striking use of poetic repetition. He begins to reset the
last four lines of the poem, but eschews the final one in
favor of three hysterical reiterations of "landlord" and two
of "What Inn is this?" (See Ex. 6.18, page 273.)

Number three sets "I took my power in my hand,"
another of the 1862 poems, in which the author, like the
young David, "aims [her] pebble" and goes "against the
world." She sees herself as "the one who fell" and wonders
if it was because of the overwhelming size of the giant or
her own inadequacy. It is difficult not to imagine an under-
tone of irony in this masterful little poem since the proof of
its author's "power" is internally implicit. Baksa underlines

Example 6.18, measures 28-33. Copyright 1977, Composers
Library Editions; used by permission.

this suggestion with a gently mocking "power figure" which
is given out in the first measure by the pianist's right hand
and immediately imitated by the left. The vocal line then en-
ters within the harmonic and melodic parameters of the "power"
figure but breaks it up into timorous, repeated eighth notes
of feigned obsequiousness.

Example 6.19, measures 1-3. Copyright 1977, Composers
Library Editions; used by permission.

273

The two figures recur throughout the song, sometimes in contrapuntal juxtaposition, and sometimes with one temporarily dominating as does the timid eighth note pattern in the setting of "or only I too small?"

The fourth setting, "I died for beauty," is the expressive and conceptual as well as positional center of this cycle. In these concise opening words of the 1862 poem, Dickinson confesses that dedication to art was the fundamental meaning of her life, and in the rest of it she imagines an after-death conversation with a like-minded soul who also "failed." Baksa had stated, in the article quoted above, that mood is conveyed primarily by harmony.32 In this song, with a seemingly simple group of one major and two minor thirds derived from the melodic form of B minor, he perfectly captures the hazily wistful atmosphere of spirits in the process of giving up their earthly struggles and attachments.

Example 6.20, measures 1-5. Copyright 1977, Composers Library Editions; used by permission.

Over this, the composer's plastic and poignant lyricism expands in the vocal line to three octave leaps which mark the philosophical and emotional peak of the conversation. Notice also that Baksa has taken the liberty of moving Dickinson's "he said" to follow "truth" rather than "we brethren are," so that the prosody will align with the rising melodic curve. (See Ex. 6.21, page 275.)

"A shady friend for torrid days," written in 1861, is the poem set as number five. In this musing on friendship, no doubt drawn from disappointing personal experience, Dickinson notes that the storms of life drive "muslin souls"

Example 6.21, measures 31-40. Copyright 1977, Composers
Library Editions; used by permission.

away from us, while only those "broadcloth breasts" of
"higher temperature" continue their support. She extends
the fabric metaphor in wonderment at "the bewildering
thread" with which "the Weaver" concocts all the vagaries
of creation. Baksa's setting calls for a "bouncy" tempo
which is a needed contrast at this point in the cycle, and
maintains an objective, not too serious tone in its approach
to the subject matter. The "germ idea" for this song seems
to stem from "the Weaver" and his "tapestries," for a con-
stantly moving accompaniment triplet pattern in 9/8 time is
passed from hand to hand as it weaves around supporting
chords, or alternately, around the vocal line. At the cli-
mactic "Ah! the bewildering thread!" the voice adds its own
contrapuntal triplet line in a further addition to the texture.

Example 6.22, measures 34-39. Copyright 1977, Composers Library Editions; used by permission.

The sixth song sets the last, and one of the most forceful of the 1862 poems. In "The soul selects her own society," Dickinson achieves poetic revenge on the Establishment, and the rejected becomes the rejecter, who "shuts the door" on "chariots" and "emperors" at will. This is perhaps Baksa's most sweepingly lyrical setting of the group and contains some of its most developed and idiomatic piano writing. The basic elements, set forth in the introduction, are the little, self-contained, circular sixteenth-note motif on beat one, measure one, and the opposing figure of entreaty (3 eighths, quarter, and half) which finishes measure one and begins measure two. The latter is then expanded in the left hand figure (5 eighth notes, 2 halves) of measure two into three, as the scale line becomes energetic leaps and the suspended dissonance resolves from the greater tension of a half rather than a whole step.

Example 6.23, measures 1-3. Copyright 1977, Composers Library Editions; used by permission.

Following "on her divine majority obtrude no more," Baksa writes an expansive piano interlude, based on the "entreaty" figures of the introduction. As the text returns, with the soul "unmoved" by the blandishments of the world, the circular sixteenth note figure of self-containment is restated.

Example 6.24, measures 10-16. Copyright 1977, Composers Library Editions; used by permission.

The last of the Seven Poems is "I'm nobody," a parody on the hazards of fame written by Dickinson in 1861, before her full realization that she was, indeed, never to experience it. It is interesting to compare this setting with that of Vincent Persichetti's discussed in Chapter 2. One finds similarities in the brisk tempo and non legato phrasing, with the principal differences being Baksa's choice of triple rather than duple meter and Persichetti's greater use of jazz-like syncopation. It should also be noted that Baksa uses a recurring pianistic ostinato figure announced in the introduction: (see Ex. 6.25, page 278). If suspicion arises that this motif may be a pictorial device representing the unappealing frog who "tells his name the livelong day," it is borne out by the postlude filled with his escalating croaks of self-advertisement. (See Ex. 6.26, page 278.)

Example 6.25, measures 1-3. Copyright 1977, Composers Library Editions; used by permission.

Example 6.26, measures 19-24. Copyright 1977, Composers Library Editions; used by permission.

In 1967, Robert Baksa composed More Songs to Poems of Emily Dickinson.[33] This second set of seven had been commissioned by the American mezzo soprano, Carolyn Reyer, who like Janet Fairbank and Alice Esty before her, had devoted much of her artistic energy to the performance of new American songs. The strongest members of this group from the point of view of text setting are "Poor little Heart" in its use of an ingeniously plaintive rhythmic/melodic motif in the vocal line, and "When night is almost done," whose tonality contrast of B minor lifting to E major seems a more transparent, New World version of the dawn breaking in Hugo Wolf's "In der Frühe."

John Corigliano (1938-   )
William M. Hoffman (1939-   )

"My father did everything he could to discourage me from
being a composer,"[34] recalls John Corigliano--a not surpris-
ing paternal stance in mid-twentieth century America. It
becomes more surprising, however, given the added informa-
tion that his father, John Corigliano, Sr., was concertmaster
of the New York Philharmonic from 1943 to 1966, and his
mother, Rose Buzen Corigliano, was a pianist and teacher.
As a further curiosity of this unique path toward the mak-
ing of a composer, Corigliano never gained proficiency on a
musical instrument. A single piano lesson with his mother
"ended in a fight,"[35] and lessons begun on the clarinet with
Stanley Drucker of the New York Philharmonic finished when
the instrument was stolen from his locker at Midwood High
School in Brooklyn.

Although virtuosity did not interest him, music was
becoming a growing force in young Corigliano's life, as he
attended rehearsals and concerts of the Philharmonic, and
began to buy recordings and scores for his own study. De-
spite his father's disapproval, which was based on personal
observation of American composers' struggles for recognition,
he began to study composition with Otto Luening at Columbia
University and graduated in 1959 cum laude, with a B.A. in
music.

At that point, Corigliano was faced with the problem
of every young composer of serious music--how to "pay the
rent" as he puts it, with work that would leave him time to
write. "When I left college," says Corigliano, "I bought my
time to compose by working at other jobs. I was music di-
rector of WBAI, I worked on all the CBS TV music specials
and Young People's Concerts for 12 years, I produced rec-
ords for Columbia, I ran the Corfu Music Festival. Right
now I teach at Lehman College and the Manhattan School of
Music. If I had to live on what I earn as a composer...."[36]
The negative implication of the unfinished sentence is clear,
and Corigliano reiterates the discouraging fact, noted four-
teen years earlier by William Flanagan (see p. 163), that only
three or four American composers are able to live solely on
the income from their serious works.

John Corigliano
(Photo: Jack Mitchell)

While he was working in all the above capacities,
Corigliano started to make a name for himself as a young
composer to watch. In 1962 he began a period of composi-
tion study with Vittorio Giannini and a year later finished
the Violin Sonata that won first place in the Spoleto compe-

tition and effectively launched his career. Three other con-
cert violinists had already performed it when Corigliano's
father finally programmed the work on a New York recital
in 1966. Convinced at last that his son was going to suc-
ceed as a composer, Corigliano, Sr. became concertmaster of
the San Antonio Symphony after retiring from the New York
Philharmonic. In the new position, he led the violins in his
son's Concerto for Piano and Orchestra which had been writ-
ten in 1968 on a Guggenheim Fellowship, and which was per-
formed the same year by Hilde Somer for the inaugural con-
cert of the San Antonio Hemisfair.

Other major orchestral works by Corigliano followed in
the seventies. The Concerto for Oboe and Orchestra was
commissioned by the New York State Council on the Arts for
the bicentennial, and performed on November 9, 1975, by
the American Symphony in New York, with Bert Lucarelli as
soloist. A clarinet concerto was then commissioned by the
New York Philharmonic, and in December, 1977, Corigliano's
longtime friend and erstwhile "teacher," Stanley Drucker,
premièred it with Leonard Bernstein conducting.

Corigliano has also written several piano works, a
multi-media opera called The Naked Carmen, and the film
score for the 1980 movie Altered States. His catalog further
includes a number of choral compositions, one of the most
important being a trilogy of Dylan Thomas settings, pre-
mièred in its entirety in Washington Cathedral in April, 1976.
The author had the pleasure of helping to prepare two other
Corigliano choral works--"L'invitation au Voyage" and "Psalm
No. 8"--while employed as the San Antonio Symphony Chorus
pianist in 1976-1977. This chorus, also known as the Master-
singers, made a recording in May, 1977, under the direction
of Roger Melone, which included Corigliano's Psalm No. 8.
Since it is scored for organ accompaniment, the recording
took place in San Antonio's Beth El temple which had a suit-
able organ and acoustical environment.

The author's interview with John Corigliano was held
in the anteroom behind the temple sanctuary during intermis-
sions in the recording process which the composer had come
to San Antonio to supervise. Despite the unavoidable ten-
sions of this project, Corigliano was able to relax and divert
the intense focus of his energy to questions about his song
writing. Asked why he has written relatively few solo songs,

the composer replied that he has found "very few texts which he feels comfortable in setting."[37] Part of the reason for this is that he stays "very busy promoting [himself] as a composer," and therefore "has little time to read." The texts which he has chosen for solo or choral setting are either psalms or twentieth century poetry, both of which present the loosely structured meters with which he feels stylistically compatible.

In commenting on the position of the song medium in American music, Corigliano developed an interesting line of thought. "Twentieth-century American music," he said, "has a bare, uncluttered quality of simplicity in contrast to European music which equates complexity with progress. It follows that American composers would be drawn to songs, because you can't throw the voice around. A song is a di-rect, relatively simple statement of the vocal line and piano--not a big, complex, political decision like programming a symphony."

Corigliano's overall description of his personal approach to text setting is that "the structure of the piece comes out of the structure of the poem." He likes not to repeat words if possible, and before setting a text, types out the poem in double or triple spacing leaving room to plan the "emotional shape" of the piece. This includes "dynamics, interludes, words that reappear--always trying to follow the poet's in-tentions." In two of his vocal works, Corigliano was able to maximize the interrelationship of text and music by actual collaboration with the poet. One was the choral work "What I Expected Was" to a text by the British poet, Stephen Spender. The other was Corigliano's only major setting of American poetry, the cycle called The Cloisters,[38] in which three of the four component songs (all except "The Unicorn") were a collaborative effort with William M. Hoffman.

Hoffman was also born in New York City, a little more than a year after John Corigliano. He distinguished himself as an undergraduate at the City University of New York, and in 1960 earned a B.A. cum laude in Latin, as well as election to Phi Beta Kappa. Hoffman then began a seven-year stint as Assistant Editor and later Drama Editor at Hill and Wang publishers in New York. In this capacity, he edited three volumes of New American Plays (published be-tween 1968 and 1971) and also began his own creative work as playwright and poet.

William M. Hoffman
(Photo: Jerry Vezzuso)

During the past twenty years, Hoffman has written
twenty plays, of which all have been produced, and eight
published. He, himself, served as director in five of these
productions, and he has also appeared as an actor in four
plays by other authors, as well as in one film. Poetry is a
congenial but less prolific medium for Hoffman and he writes

that his poetry has been "published in magazines, set to music, and read in public."[39] A representative sampling, including three of the four Cloisters texts appears in the 1969 collection called 31 New American Poets.

In the seventies, Hoffman held positions as Literary Adviser to Scripts magazine, and as Playwright-in-Residence for the Lincoln Center Student Programs, the Changing Scene Theater in Denver, and La Mama in New York. He has also served as Visiting Lecturer at the University of Massachusetts (1973) and as Star Professor at Hofstra University during the early eighties. His many awards have included Mac-Dowell Colony and Guggenheim Fellowships and grants from the Colorado Council on the Arts and Humanities, P.E.N., and National Endowment for the Arts.

Besides his important collaborations with John Corigliano, of which the latest is an opera commissioned by the Metropolitan and based on Beaumarchais' third Figaro play, Hoffman has a number of other ties to the world of music. With song-writer John Braden he has written two musicals, Gulliver's Travels and A Book of Etiquette (both produced in 1978) and two of his three television plays have dramatized the lives of composers. These were Notes from the New World: Louis Moreau Gottschalk (1976) and The Last Days of Stephen Foster (1977). A poem of Hoffman's called "Screw Spring," which was also published in 31 New American Poets has been set by Richard Hundley, and a 1969 letter from Hundley to James Purdy indicates that Hoffman, even at that time, was an accepted member of the New York musico/literary scene. "Bill Hoffman," says Hundley, "has just called to tell me his new play is on for four days at the same theater where we saw Up Tight. Maybe Virgil will like it, too."[40]

The Cloisters is a relatively early, but artistically mature work of remarkable intensity and power, written when both composer and poet were several years under thirty. Their overall plan for the cycle was that each song would treat a different season and a different aspect of love, all to be unified by the geographical setting of the medieval Cloisters which the Metropolitan Museum maintains and opens to the public in an upper Manhattan park area bordering the Hudson River.

The first text of the cycle, "Fort Tryon Park: September," brings us to the Cloisters as autumn begins. Falling leaves and berries, a waning sun, and a scarcity of visitors menace the lovers who "flee into dreams of permanence." Hoffman has written two stanzas of varyingly accented seven lines each, and Corigliano employs a metre-less rhythmic structure, with three to five eighth notes to a measure, that enhances the free flow of the poetry. In combination with this, the composer gives us a tightly worked, modified strophic form with two recurrent melodic phrases announced by the upper piano line and voice part as the song opens:

Example 6.27, measures 1-6. Copyright © 1967, G. Schirmer, Inc.; used by permission.

The mingling of old and new stylistic elements continues as the "early-music" sounds of the spare counterpoint and modal melodic constructions are blended with later techniques of motivic development, and the idiomatic "Romantic" piano writing of the interlude between the verses:

Example 6.28, measures 19-24. Copyright © 1967, G. Schirmer, Inc.; used by permission.

The result of this skillful mixing provides a sense of contemporary alienation cast in a medieval setting.

As Corigliano had pointed out in the 1977 interview, the creators of this song collaborated in a major poetic change which the composer felt necessary to the musical form and "emotional shape" of the piece. They decided together that the song should end on the wistfully haunting line "Homeless, we seek the cobbled court," and that the poem's ironic addition, "where our laughter rises like pigeons" should be omitted.

The seasons of this cycle do not all seem to follow in their natural order, and it appears likely that the songs have been arranged from the point of view of expressive contrast. The text of number two, "Song to the Witch of the Cloisters," suggests high summer, when the park is full of lovers who "wake ... [and] sigh and fold." The poet, now alone, conjures an imaginary witch who has overpowered "Christ, [lying] unresurrected" and encouraged these lusty rites, and he begs her to "make the lovers be still." In a dramatic setting, Corigliano expands his use of melismatic vocal writing barely hinted at in the previous song. Writing many notes to one syllable, in the ancient fashion of Gregorian Chant, he not only makes the medieval reference but uses the extended phrase to build powerful emotional crescendos.

Example 6.29, measures 42-52. Copyright © 1967, G. Schirmer, Inc.; used by permission.

Chant-like repetition is another feature of this vocal line, and when this is used in the opening in conjunction with snickering grace notes and scampering staccato octaves in the accompaniment, the musical materials serve to give us a portrait of the very speech and movement of the wily witch.

Example 6.30, measures 1-10. Copyright © 1967, G. Schirmer, Inc.; used by permission.

Number three is "Christmas at the Cloisters," a text which uses many short phrases to celebrate the Christ child's birthday and invoke His praise. The flexibility of this verbal structure allows Corigliano to weave a brilliant, rhythmically accented, jazzy accompaniment around a vocal line which alternately maintains repetitions of the G major dominant (D) or joins the churning syncopations.

Example 6.31, measures 11-20. Copyright © 1967, G. Schirmer, Inc.; used by permission.

An exciting climax to this "joyful noise unto the Lord" is set up by a wild melisma structured in melodic thirds on the word "God." The tension of the two fermatas is then released in a crescendo of "Hallejujahs" which begins softly, rises to frenzied heights, and ends in a whispered "Amen." (See Ex. 6.32, page 289.)

The last poem of the set, "The Unicorn," was actually the first to be written, and the one which had inspired planning for the cycle. It is spring now, and the poet sees himself in the guise of the unicorn, the mythical medieval beast whose savage behavior was purported to be soothed

Example 6.32, measures 75-84. Copyright © 1967, G. Schirmer, Inc.; used by permission.

to gentleness by the sight of a virgin at mating time. The poetry is a seductive invitation to his virginal object not to let Spring's return to the Cloisters catch either of them unfulfilled and "three nights sad." Corigliano bases his setting on a poignant melodic phrase announced in the first four vocal measures, whose chromatic intervals (three minor seconds and an augmented fourth) are filled with the unease of longing.

Example 6.33, measures 1-4. Copyright © 1967, G. Schirmer, Inc.; used by permission.

This phrase returns many times in the voice part and accompaniment and is transposed to a number of different pitch levels. In an extensive piano interlude, it flowers to an imitative climax following the textual imagining of sensual fulfillment.

Example 6.34, measures 18-27. Copyright © 1967, G. Schirmer, Inc.; used by permission.

The unicorn now intensifies his seductive plea, which emerges as the climax of the song. It is a ravishingly lyrical, dolcissimo passage in D major, replete with a bel canto vocal curve and a warmly supportive sequence of thirds in the pianistic harmony. (See Ex. 6.35, page 291.)

In the penultimate phrase, a long, widely ranging vocal melisma on the first syllable of "unicorn" has a dual purpose. Stylistically, it relates "The Unicorn" to numbers two and three of the cycle where the device is heavily employed, and dramatically it suggests the barely controllable transports of desire.

Example 6.35, measures 38-46. Copyright © 1967, G. Schirmer, Inc.; used by permission.

NOTES

1. Author's interview with Richard Hundley: New York City, December 2, 1982.

2. Unless otherwise indicated, all the ensuing Richard Hundley quotations are from the December 2, 1982, interview.

3. For further information on these Metropolitan Opera Studio concerts, see: a. "Names, Dates, and Places," Opera News, XXXVIII:6-7 (Jan. 6, 1973). b. "Debuts and Reappearances," High Fidelity/Musical America, XXII:MA 18 (June 1972).

4. Robert Finn, "Richard Hundley, non-conformist," The (Cleveland) Plain Dealer (June 3, 1983), p. 4.

5. Ibid.

6. Richard Hundley, "Softly the Summer" (New York: General Music Publishing, 1963). High voice.

7. James Schevill, "The Search for Wonder and Joy," Kenneth Patchen: A Collection of Essays, Richard G. Morgan, ed. (New York: AMS Press, 1977), p. 110.

8. Holly Beye and William McCleery, "The Most Mysterious People in the Village," Morgan, p. 49.

9. Ibid., p. 50.

10. For example, see: David Diamond, "Be Music, Night" (New York: Carl Fischer, 1948). High voice.

11. Richard Hundley, "Maiden Snow" (New York: General Music, 1961).

12. Letter dated January 16, 1965 from Ned Rorem to James Purdy. Held in collection of Humanities Research Center, University of Texas at Austin.

13. Letter dated June 25, 1967 from Rorem to Purdy. Also in HRC Collection, Austin.

14. Quoted in: James Vinson, ed., Contemporary Novelists, second edition (New York: St. Martin's Press, 1976), p. 1130.

15. Ibid.

16. Tony Tanner, "Birdsong," Partisan Review, XXXIX (Fall 1972), p. 610.

17. James Vinson, ed., Great Writers of the English Language: Novelists (New York: St. Martin's, 1979), p. 995.

18. Letter dated December 7, 1967 from Richard Hundley to James Purdy. HRC-Austin Collection.

19. Richard Hundley, Eight Songs (New York: Boosey & Hawkes, 1981). Medium high.

20. Letter dated August 3, 1969. Hundley to Purdy. HRC-Austin Collection.

21. Letter dated August 6, 1969. Hundley to Purdy. HRC-Austin Collection.

22. Letter dated August 12, 1969. Hundley to Purdy. HRC-Austin Collection.

23. Tanner, "Birdsong," p. 618.

24. Robert Finn, "Season Finale," The (Cleveland) Plain Dealer (May 16, 1985).

25. Author's interview with Robert Baksa: New York City, December 2, 1982.

26. Unless otherwise indicated, all the ensuing Robert Baksa quotations are from the December 2, 1982, interview.

27. Carolyn Heafner has recorded Hugo Weisgall's Four Songs on Poems by Adelaide Crapsey (see Chapter I) for Composers' Recordings, Inc. (CRI SD 462).

28. Letter of June 6, 1985, from Robert Baksa to the author.

29. Thomas H. Johnson, ed., "Introduction," Complete Poems of Emily Dickinson (Boston: Little, Brown, 1960), p. VIII.

30. Robert Baksa, Seven Songs to Poems of Emily Dickinson (New York: Composers Library Editions, 1977). Medium voice.

31. Robert Baksa, "Man as Music Listener," Music Journal, XXXIII:12 (February 1975), p. 38.

32. Ibid.

33. Robert Baksa, More Songs to Poems of Emily Dickinson (New York: Composers Library Editions, 1978). Medium voice.

34. William Hoffman, "John Corigliano on Cracking the Establishment," The Village Voice (February 21, 1977), p. 69.

35. David Ewen, Composers Since 1900, First Supplement (New York: H.W. Wilson, 1981), p. 77.

36. Hoffman, p. 68.

37. Unless otherwise indicated, all ensuing John Corigliano quotations are from the May, 1977, interview.

38. John Corigliano, The Cloisters (New York: G. Schirmer, 1967). Mezzo-soprano. The four songs of this cycle are published separately.

39. Ron Schrieber, ed., "Autobiographical Notes," 31 New American Poets (New York: Hill and Wang, 1969), p. 255.

40. Letter dated August 7, 1969, from Hundley to Purdy. HRC Collection, Austin.

EPILOGUE

"The American experience" says Wallace Stegner, "has been the confrontation by old peoples and cultures of a world as new as if it had just risen from the sea."[1] The wonder of this newness was indeed proclaimed by America's nineteenth-century writers[2]--Emerson, Melville, Whitman, and their confrères--but the ties to older musical cultures lingered, and, as we have seen, the American art song began as an offshoot of the European Romantic tradition.

In the course of these volumes, we have watched it strive self-consciously for the sound and feel of America and then, having achieved this goal, come in full maturity to the realization that (paraphrasing Virgil Thomson) "American art song is art song written by Americans." What this means, of course, is that twentieth-century American composers setting American poetry have been subject to all the musical and literary influences of neo-Romanticism versus the avant-garde, and all the psychological influences of post-war despair (twice) and intermittent idealism that have produced the infinite variety of their work.

Yet the author would be remiss if she failed to share with the reader a conviction that three general trends do seem to emerge from the wealth of material that has formed the basis of this study. The first of these has to do with the underlying rhythmic frame of reference in the American art song, which brings us back to Ned Rorem's idea of instrumental as well as vocal music deriving from national speech patterns.[3] Ruth Schonthal develops this suggestion, and with the keen ear of one who is not native-born points out to us the open, deliberate middle-tempo cadences of American, as opposed to European, language.[4] Some of our poets, such as James Purdy, consciously pursue "the American soul [through] the rhythms and accents of American speech,"[5] and others do it unconsciously. It remains for the composers to translate this, as they do, into an amalgam which draws from the crisp authority of New England and its village bandmasters, the gentle flow of the speech and ballads of the South and the West, and the energizingly heavy accent with a syncopated overlay of the African culture and its descendants (spirituals, ragtime, jazz, and Broadway).

The rhythmic schemes which result tend to have a direct, forceful, uncluttered quality which ties in with the second observable trend, i.e., simplicity.[6] Dickinson's and Wylie's bare-bones poetry, Thomson's naked, diatonic chords, Weisgall's breath-takingly brief settings of Crapsey's laments, Baksa's tiny motifs which contain the seed of a song--all these are representative of what seems to be a national artistic urge to cut away the dead wood, as it were, and get to the heart of the matter. Not surprisingly, it is this very quest that brings us to the third characteristic.

Americans, in our origins, are the sons and daughters of rebels, pioneers, and adventurers. With the crossing of the seas, the old order has been abandoned and the struggle becomes a search toward a new order. Although he virtually exterminates the native American, the new immigrant absorbs his intoxication with the land and the spirit indwelling in the land, and it could almost be said that Transcendentalism is the Indian heritage passed through the New England intellectual tradition.

The new order, then, towards which America's artists are groping in the nineteenth and twentieth centuries is an inward construct of the mind and spirit. Cut off from the geographical mother country, the American must find his roots in a spiritual grasp of the universal order, and must find a framework that can support the successive horrors of the Civil War and the more recent global catastrophes.

The search for this spiritual order runs through the American artsong like a silver thread. Bowles and Tennessee Williams give us a simple, folk-like solution in "Heavenly

Grass"; Rorem and Roethke portray the Oriental path of mystic union with the Absolute in "Memory"; and in "Sure On This Shining Night," Barber and Agee define the quest in terms of the Romantic, "wandering far alone" and weeping for wonder at a Beauty which he cannot name. The poetic tradition of pre-occupation with the spiritual order derives from Emerson and is upheld by Whitman, Dickinson, Frost, Stevens, and Roethke, to name only the major protagonists. An impressive number of the composers of this study have been inspired by poetic accounts of this journey, and have added their individual musical perceptions to the lining out of its tortuous but luminous path.

*   *   *

America has come of age in the art song, it has produced a veritable chorus of voices in its maturity, and the century continues to advance. We contemplate with gratitude the riches of the past, and eagerly await the future.

NOTES

1. Wallace Stegner quoted in: Pete Hamil, "All Need What's Left," San Antonio Express, October 14, 1981.

2. See: Irving Howe, "The American Voice--It Begins on a Note of Wonder," The New York Times Book Review, July 4, 1976.

3. See Volume I, p. 14.

4. See Chapter IV, p. 182, of this volume.

5. See Chapter VI, p. 257, of this volume.

6. See remarks by John Corigliano, Chapter VI, p. 282.

BIBLIOGRAPHY

A. Bibliographical Tools

Anderson, Elliott and Kinzie, Mary. The Little Maga-
    zine in America: A Modern Documentary History.
    Yonkers, N.Y.: Pushcart Press, 1978.

Carman, Judith, et al. Art Song in the United States:
    An Annotated Bibliography. University of Iowa:
    National Association of Teachers of Singing, 1976.

_____. Art Song in the United States: An Annota-
    tated Bibliography, First Supplement. University of
    Iowa: National Association of Teachers of Singing,
    1978.

Dissertation Abstracts International. Ann Arbor, MI:
    University Microfilms, 1938 --.

Granger, Edith, ed. Index to Poetry and Recitations.
    Chicago: A.C. McClurg, 1918 (and supplements).

Jackson, Richard. United States Music, Sources of
    Bibliography and Collective Bibliography. Brooklyn,
    New York: Institute for Studies in American Music,
    1976.

Mead, Rita. Doctoral Dissertations in American Music,
    A Classified Bibliography. Brooklyn, N.Y.: Insti-
    tute for Studies in American Music, 1974.

Music Index. Annual index to articles on music in
various periodicals, 1949 --.

Nicely, Tom. Adam and his Work, a Paul Goodman
Bibliography. Metuchen, N.J.: Scarecrow Press,
1979.

Oja, Carol J., ed. American Music Recordings: A
Discography of 20th-Century U.S. Composers.
Brooklyn, New York: Institute for Studies in
American Music, 1982.

Sadie, Stanley, ed. The New Grove Dictionary of Mu-
sic and Musicians. London: Macmillan, 1980.

Slonimsky, Nicholas, ed. Baker's Biographical Diction-
ary of Musicians. New York: Schirmer Books, 1978.

B.   American Music

Anderson, E. Ruth. Contemporary American Compos-
ers. Boston: G.K. Holland, 1976.

Barber, Samuel. "On Waiting for a Libretto," Opera
News, XX:13 (January 27, 1958), pp. 4-6.

Beeson, Jack. "Grand and Not So Grand," Opera News,
XXVII:8-13 (January 5, 1963).

Dello Joio, Norman. "The Composer and the American
Scene," Music Journal, XXII:31-32 (March 1964).

_____. "The Quality of Music," Music Educators'
Journal. XLVIII:5 (1965), pp. 33-35.

_____. "The Contemporary Music Project for Creativ-
ity in Music Education," Music Educators' Journal,
LIV:4-72 (March 1968).

Ewen, David. American Composers. New York: G.P.
Putnam, 1982.

Flanagan, William. "The Riotous Garden of American
Opera," High Fidelity, VIII:42-44 (November 1958).

_____. "How to Succeed in Composing Without Really Succeeding," Bulletin of the American Composers' Alliance, XI:1 (1963), pp. 6-8.

Gruen, John. The Party's Over. New York: Viking, 1972.

Ivey, Jean Eichelberger. "The Contemporary Performing Ensemble," College Music Symposium, VIII:120-128 (Fall 1968).

_____. "Electronic Music Workshop for Teachers," Music Educators' Journal, LV:91-93 (November 1968).

_____. "The Composer as Teacher," Peabody Conservatory Alumni Bulletin, XIV:1 (Fall/Winter 1974).

Larsen, Dr. Arved M. "The Contemporary Woman Composer," Pan Pipes, LXVIII:1 (November 1975), p. 2.

Owen, Lynn. "Wife, Mother, Opera Singer," Music Journal, XXV:36 (April 1967).

Page, Tim. "Music-Debuts in Review," The New York Times, Sunday, April 8, 1984.

Persichetti, Vincent. Twentieth Century Harmony. New York: Norton, 1961.

Southgate, Harvey. "Rochester Report: Artistic Climate Revamped," High Fidelity/Musical America, XVI:133 (March 1966).

Thomson, Virgil. American Music Since 1910. New York: Holt, Rinehart and Winston, 1970.

Weisgall, Hugo. "The 201st Quarterly," Perspectives of New Music, III:2 (1965), pp. 133-136.

C. American Art Song

Ardoin, John. "Rorem-Flanagan Concert," Musical America, LXXXII:37 (May 1962).

Bloomquist, Marvin Robert. "The Songs of Ned Rorem." Kansas City: The University of Missouri Dissertation, 1970.

Flanagan, William. "American Songs: A Thin Crop," Musical America, LXXII:23 (February 1952).

Friedberg, Ruth C. American Art Song and American Poetry, Volume I. Metuchen, N.J.: Scarecrow Press, 1981.

_____. American Art Song and American Poetry, Volume II. Metuchen, N.J.: Scarecrow Press, 1984.

Middaugh, Bennie. "The Songs of Ned Rorem," The NATS Bulletin, XXIV:36-39 (May 1968).

Miller, Phillip L. "The Songs of Ned Rorem," Tempo, CXXVII:25-31 (December 1978).

Nathan, Hans. "The Modern Period-United States of America," in A History of Song, ed. Denis Stevens. New York: Norton, 1960.

Rorem, Ned. "Music for the Mouth," in Music from Inside Out. New York: George Braziller, 1967.

_____. "The American Art Song," in Setting the Tone. New York: Coward-McCann, 1983.

D. Composers

Albee, Edward. "William Flanagan," Bulletin of the American Composers' Alliance, IX:4 (1961), p. 12.

Baksa, Robert. "Man as Music Listener," Music Journal, XXXIII:12 (February 1975).

Beeson, Jack. "In Memoriam: Douglas Moore," Perspectives of New Music, VIII:158-160 (Fall/Winter 1960).

_____. "Virgil Thomson's Aeneid (The Operas)," Parnassus, V:2 (Spring/Summer 1977), pp. 457-478.

Bowles, Paul. Without Stopping. New York: Putnam, 1972.

Broder, Nathan. Samuel Barber. New York: G. Schirmer, 1954.

Diamond, David. "Integrity and Integration in Contemporary Music," The Alice and Frederick Slee Lectures. University of Buffalo, Spring, 1961.

_____. "From the Notebook of David Diamond," Music Journal, XXII:24-25 (April 1964).

Downes, Edward. "The Music of Norman Dello Joio," The Musical Quarterly, XLVIII:2 (April 1962), pp. 149-172.

Eaton, Quaintance. "Beeson on Camera," Opera News, XXIV:13 (May 21, 1970).

Evett, Robert. "The Music of Vincent Persichetti," The Juilliard Review, II:2 (Spring 1955), pp. 15-20.

Ewen, David. Composers Since 1900. New York: H.W. Wilson, 1969.

_____. Composers Since 1900, First Supplement. New York: H.W. Wilson, 1981.

Finn, Robert. "Richard Hundley, non-conformist," The (Cleveland) Plain Dealer. June 3, 1983.

_____. "Season Finale," The (Cleveland) Plain Dealer. May 16, 1985.

Flanagan, William. "My Ten Favorite Composers," HiFi/Stereo Review, XIX:68-69 (September 1967).

_____. "Ten Composers I Hate," HiFi/Stereo Review, XIX:89 (October 1967).

Garland, Peter. "Paul Bowles and the Baptism of Solitude," in Americas: Essays on American Music and Culture (1973-80). Santa Fe: Soundings Press, 1982.

Glanville-Hicks, Peggy. "Paul Bowles-American Composer," Music and Letters, XXVI:2 (April 1945), pp. 88-96.

Goss, Madeleine. Modern Music-Makers. New York: Dutton, 1952.

Hoffman, William. "John Corigliano on Cracking the Establishment," The Village Voice. February 21, 1977, p. 68f.

Holms, James. "Ned Rorem" in The New Grove Dictionary of Music and Musicians. London: Macmillan, 1980. Vol. XVI, pp. 190-191.

"Jean Eichelberger Ivey--a Retrospective," Peabody News (July 1983).

Kolodin, Irvin. "Farewell to Capricorn," Saturday Review/World, I:44-45 (June 1, 1974).

LePage, Jane Weiner. Women Composers, Conductors and Musicians of the Twentieth Century. Metuchen, N.J.: Scarecrow Press, 1980.

Owen, Richard. "Husband, Father, Attorney, Composer," Music Journal, XXV:37 (April 1967).

Page, Robert. "In Quest of Answers--an Interview with Vincent Persichetti," Choral Journal, XIV:3 (November 1973), pp. 5-7.

Reilly, Peter. "William Flanagan," Stereo Review, XXI:5 (November 1968), p. 134.

Rorem, Ned. "(William Flanagan) ... and his music," Bulletin of the American Composers' Alliance, IX:4 (1961), pp. 13-19.

_____. The Paris Diary. New York: George Braziller, 1966.

_____. The New York Diary. New York: George Braziller, 1967.

_____. Music From Inside Out. New York: George Braziller, 1967.

_____. Music and People. New York: George Braziller, 1968.

_____. Critical Affairs. New York: George Braziller, 1970.

_____. The Final Diary. New York: Holt, Rinehart and Winston, 1974. Reprinted by North Point Press as The Later Diaries.

_____. Pure Contraption. New York: Holt, Rinehart and Winston, 1974.

_____. An Absolute Gift. New York: Simon and Schuster, 1978.

_____. "Interview," The NATS Bulletin, XXIX:2 (1982), p. 5ff.

_____. Setting the Tone. New York: Coward-McCann, 1983.

Saylor, Bruce. "The Music of Hugo Weisgall," Musical Quarterly, LIX:2 (1973), pp. 239-262.

Schumann, William. "The Compleat Musician: Vincent Persichetti and Twentieth Century Harmony," Musical Quarterly, XLVII:3 (July 1961), pp. 379-385.

Trimble, Lester. "William Flanagan (1923-1969)," Stereo Review, XXIII:118 (November 1968).

E.   Poets and Poetry

Agee, James. Permit Me Voyage. New Haven: Yale University Press, 1934.

_____. Letters of James Agee to Father Flye. Boston: Houghton Mifflin, 1971.

Amacher, Richard E. Edward Albee. New York: Twayne, 1969.

Bassan, Maurice, ed. Stephen Crane, a Collection of Critical Essays. Englewood Cliffs, N.J.: Prentice-Hall, 1967.

Beckett, Lucy. Wallace Stevens. London: Cambridge University Press, 1974.

Berryman, John. Stephen Crane. New York: Octagon Books, 1975.

Bianchi, Martha Dickinson and Hampson, Alfred Leete, eds. The Complete Poems of Emily Dickinson. Boston: Little, Brown, 1937.

Blessing, Richard Allen. Wallace Stevens' "Whole Harmonium." Syracuse, N.Y.: Syracuse University Press, 1970.

Bowers, Neil. Theodore Roethke. Columbia, MO: University of Missouri Press, 1982.

Butscher, Edward. Adelaide Crapsey. Boston: Twayne, 1979.

Buttel, Robert. Wallace Stevens, The Making of Harmonium. Princeton, N.J.: Princeton University Press, 1967.

Cady, Edwin H. Stephen Crane. Boston: Twayne, 1962.

Capouya, Emile. "The Poet as Prophet," Parnassus, III:1 (1974), pp. 23-30.

Chase, Richard ed. Melville--A Collection of Critical Essays. Englewood Cliffs, N.J.: Prentice-Hall, 1963.

Cowley, Malcolm. "The Case Against Mr. Frost," in Robert Frost, ed. James M. Cox. Englewood Cliffs, N.J.: Prentice-Hall, 1962.

Crapsey, Adelaide. Verse. New York: Knopf, 1922.

Crawley, Thomas. The Structure of "Leaves of Grass." Austin: The University of Texas Press, 1970.

cummings, e.e. <u>Complete Poems</u>. New York: Harcourt, Brace, Jovanovich, 1972.

Deutsch, Babette. <u>Poetry in Our Time</u>. Garden City, N.Y.: Doubleday, 1963.

Doty, Mark A. <u>Tell Me Who I Am</u>. Baton Rouge: Louisiana State University Press, 1981.

Falk, Signi. <u>Tennessee Williams</u>. Boston: Twayne, 1978.

Fitzgerald, Robert, ed. <u>The Collected Short Prose of James Agee</u>. Boston: Houghton Mifflin, 1958.

Goodman, Paul. <u>Collected Poems</u>. New York: Random House, 1973.

Gould, Jean. <u>Amy--The World of Amy Lowell and the Imagist Movement</u>. New York: Dodd, Mead, 1975.

Gregory, Horace and Zaturenska, Marya. <u>A History of American Poetry, 1900-1940</u>. New York: Harcourt, Brace, 1946.

Hénault, Marie. <u>Peter Viereck</u>. New York: Twayne, 1969.

Heyen, William, comp. <u>Profile of Theodore Roethke</u>. Columbus, OH: Charles Merrill, 1971.

Hine, Daryl and Parisi, Joseph, eds. <u>The "Poetry" Anthology</u>. Boston: Houghton Mifflin, 1978.

Hoffman, Daniel. <u>The Poetry of Stephen Crane</u>. New York: Columbia University Press, 1956.

Johnson, Thomas H., ed. <u>The Poems of Emily Dickinson</u>. Cambridge, MA: The Belknap Press of Harvard University Press, 1958.

Johnson, Thomas H., ed. <u>Complete Poems of Emily Dickinson</u>. Boston: Little, Brown, 1960.

Kalem, T.E. "The Laureate of the Outcast," <u>Time</u>, March 7, 1983, p. 88.

Katz, Joseph, ed. The Poems of Stephen Crane. New York: Cooper Square Publishers, 1971.

Kennedy, Richard S. Dreams in the Mirror (A Biography of e.e. cummings). New York: Liveright, 1980.

Kunitz, Stanley J. and Haycraft, Howard. Twentieth Century Authors. New York: H.W. Wilson, 1942.

_____. Twentieth Century Authors, First Supplement. New York: H.W. Wilson, 1955.

Litz, A. Walton. Introspective Voyager. New York: Oxford University Press, 1972.

Londré, Felicia Hardison. Tennessee Williams. New York: Frederick Ungar, 1979.

Macdonald, Dwight. "Death of a Poet," New Yorker, XXXIII:38 (November 16, 1957).

Melville, Herman. Billy Budd, Benito Cereno and The Enchanted Isles, foreword by Carl Van Doren. New York: Readers' Club, 1942.

_____. Works (Volume 16, Poems). New York: Russell and Russell, 1963.

Meredith, Robert. "Everywhere a Single Voice," Poetry, CXXVIII:2 (1976), pp. 100-105.

Miller, Jr., James E. Walt Whitman. New York: Twayne, 1962.

Moreau, Genevieve. The Restless Journey of James Agee. New York: William Morrow, 1977.

Morgan, Richard G., ed. Kenneth Patchen: A Collection of Essays. New York: AMS Press, 1977.

Moss, Howard. Writing Against Time, Critical Essays and Reviews. New York: William Morrow, 1969.

Murphy, Frances and Parker, Hershel, eds. The Norton Anthology of American Literature, Volume I. New York: Norton, 1979.

Nasso, Christine, ed. Contemporary Authors. Detroit:
Gale, 1978.

Ohlin, Peter H. Agee. New York: Ivan Obolensky,
1966.

Ostriker, Alicia. "Paul Goodman," Partisan Review,
XLIII:2 (1976), p. 286ff.

Patchen, Kenneth. The Love Poems. San Francisco:
City Lights, 1966.

_____. Collected Poems. New York: New Direc-
tions, 1968.

Prokosch, Frederic. Chosen Poems. Garden City,
N.Y.: Doubleday, 1948.

Purdy, James. An Oyster is a Wealthy Beast. Los
Angeles: Black Sparrow Press, 1967.

_____. Mr. Evening and Nine Poems. Los Angeles:
Black Sparrow Press, 1968.

_____. The Running Sun. New York: Paul Waner
Press, 1971.

Riddel, Joseph N. The Clairvoyant Eye. Baton Rouge:
Louisiana State University Press, 1965.

Roethke, Theodore. Collected Poems. Garden City,
N.Y.: Doubleday, 1966.

Schreiber, Ron, ed. 31 New American Poets. New
York: Hill and Wang, 1969.

Seaver, Edwin, ed. Cross-Section, 1945-1948. Nendeln,
Liechtenstein: Kraus Reprint, 1969.

Sewall, Richard B. Life of Emily Dickinson, Volumes I
and II. New York: Farrar, Straus, and Giroux,
1974.

Spiller, Robert E.; Thorpe, Willard; Johnson, Thomas J.;
Canby, Henry Seidel; and Ludwig, Richard M., eds.

Literary History of the United States. New York: Macmillan, 1963.

Squires, Radcliffe. *Frederic Prokosch*. New York: Twayne, 1964.

Stein, William Bysshe. *The Poetry of Melville's Later Years*. Albany: State University of New York Press, 1970.

Stephenson, Nathaniel Wright, comp. *An Autobiography of Abraham Lincoln*. Indianapolis: Bobbs-Merrill, 1926.

Stevens, Wallace. *The Collected Poems*. New York: Knopf, 1955.

Stovall, Floyd, ed. *The Poems of Edgar Allan Poe*. Charlottesville: University Press of Virginia, 1965.

Tanner, Tony. "Bird song," *Partisan Review*, XXXIX (Fall 1972).

Teasdale, Sara. *Collected Poems*. New York: Macmillan, 1966

Viereck, Peter. *New and Selected Poems, 1932-1967*. New York: Bobbs-Merrill, 1967.

Vincent, Howard P. *Collected Poems of Herman Melville*. Chicago: Packard, 1947.

Vinson, James, ed. *Contemporary Novelists*, second edition. New York: St. Martin's, 1976.

————. *Great Writers of the English Language: Novelists*. New York: St. Martin's, 1979.

————. *Great Writers of the English Language: Poets*. New York: St. Martin's, 1979.

Wakeman, John. *World Authors, 1950-1970*. New York: H.W. Wilson, 1975.

Warren, Austin. "Emily Dickinson," in *A Collection of Critical Essays*, ed. Richard B. Sewall. Englewood Cliffs, N.J.: Prentice-Hall, 1963.

Whitman, Walt. Complete Poetry and Selected Prose and Letters. London: Nonesuch Press, 1967.

Widmer, Kingsley. Paul Goodman. Boston: Twayne, 1980.

Williams, Tennessee. In the Winter of Cities. Norfolk, Conn.: New Directions Books, 1956.

_____. Androgyne, Mon Amour. New York: New Directions, 1977.

_____. Letters to Donald Windham, 1940-1965, ed. Donald Windham. New York: Holt, Rinehart and Winston, 1977.

Young, Stark. The Pavilion. New York: Scribner, 1951.

F. Poetry and Song

Friedberg, Ruth C. American Art Song and American Poetry, Volume I. Metuchen, N.J.: Scarecrow Press, 1981.

_____. American Art Song and American Poetry, Volume II. Metuchen, N.J.: Scarecrow Press, 1984.

APPENDIX I: INDEX OF SONGS CITED

APPENDIX II: INDEX OF SONGS BY COMPOSER

318

GENERAL INDEX

Accent 169
Adelphi University 179
After Dinner Opera Company 139
Agee, James 10-17, 29, 297
    Collected Poems 13-14
    Collected Short Prose 13
    A Death in the Family 13
    Knoxville, Summer of 1915 11, 14
    Let Us Now Praise Famous Men 12-13
    Permit Me Voyage 12, 14
    "Sure on this shining night" 14-17, 297
    "They that Sow in Sorrow Shall Reap" 17
Aiken, Conrad 153
    "'Morning Song' from Senlin" 153
Alan Neil Quartet 253
Albee, Edward 5, 163, 164, 165-168, 209, 257
    Bartleby 163
    The Ice Age 163
    "The Lady of Tearful Regret" 165
    Malcolm 163, 257
    The Sand Box 163, 178
    "Song for a Winter Child" 165, 167-169
Alice Tully Hall 258
Alley Theatre 194
American Academy (Italy) 73
American Academy of Dramatic Art 194
American Music Center 153, 181
American poetry movements 4, 5, 253
    "Beat" movement 4, 253
    Concrete poetry 4, 253
    Poetic renaissance 4, 5
    Poetry/jazz movement 4, 253
American Symphony 281
"Americanism" 122
Amherst College 66, 107

326

James, William 213
Jeffers, Robinson 213
Jewish Theological Seminary 43
Johnson, Thomas H. 105, 107, 108, 110, 270
Johnson, Thor 246
Joyce, James 10
Juilliard School 43, 64, 73, 84, 138, 207
   Juilliard Opera Theater 121
Junior Bazaar 171

Kagen, Sergius 41, 179
Kansas City Lyric Theater 122
Kennedy Center--Friedheim Award 181
Kenyon Review 212
Kizer, Carolyn 153
Koch, Kenneth 211
Kodály, Zoltán 266
Kopleff, Florence 192
Kraus, Lili 191
Kunitz, Stanley 226

Lafayette College 139
Lake George Opera Festival 268
Lanier, Sidney 27
Lawrence College 256
Leach, Richard P. 192
Lederman, Minna 3
Lehman College 279
Lemercier, Eugène Emmanuel 93, 95
   Lettres d'un Soldat 93, 95
Leschetizsky, Theodor 7, 8, 118
Library of Congress 240
Lincoln, Abraham 125-128
   "Bear Hunt" 127
   "Indiana Homecoming" 125-128
Lincoln Center 268
   Lincoln Center Student Program 284
Literary World 78
"Little magazines" 3, 5
Little Review 147
Loeffler, Charles 179
Lowell, Amy 44, 141, 147-149, 269
   Men Women and Ghosts 147
     "Patterns" 147-149
Lucarelli, Bert 281
Luening, Otto 279
Lunt, Alfred 66

McBride, Robert 266